Kompromat

Giorgi Rtskhiladze

Kompromat

My Story from Trump to Mueller and USSR to USA

Rare Bird Books
Los Angeles, Calif.

This is a Genuine Rare Bird Book

Rare Bird Books
453 South Spring Street, Suite 302
Los Angeles, CA 90013
rarebirdbooks.com

For more information, address:
Rare Bird Books Subsidiary Rights Department
453 South Spring Street, Suite 302
Los Angeles, CA 90013

Set in Minion
Printed in the United States

10 9 8 7 6 5 4 3 2 1

Publisher's Cataloging-in-Publication Data

Names: Rtskhiladze, Giorgi, author.
Title: Kompromat: My Story from Trump to Mueller and USSR to USA /
Giorgi Rtskhiladze.
Description: First Hardcover Edition | A Genuine Rare Bird Book | New York, NY;
Los Angeles, CA: Rare Bird Books, 2020.
Identifiers: ISBN 9781644281031
Subjects: LCSH Rtskhiladze, Giorgi. | Businessmen—Russia (Federation)—Biog-
raphy. | Businessmen—Georgia (Republic)—Biography. | Governmental investiga-
tions—United States. | Presidents—United States—Election, 2016. | Propaganda,
Russian—United States. | Elections—Corrupt practices—United States. | United
States—Foreign relations—Russia (Federation) | Russia (Federation)—Foreign rela-
tions—United States. | BISAC BIOGRAPHY & AUTOBIOGRAPHY /
Personal Memoirs | HISTORY / United States / 21st Century.
Classification: LCC DK678.3 .R77 2020 | DDC 914.758/092—dc23

For my wife, Ayanat, and for my children

In memory of my late mother, Giuli

"There is nothing so powerful as truth—and often nothing so strange."

—Daniel Webster

Contents

Donald J. Trump Verified Account @realDonaldTrump

Who's going to give back the young and beautiful lives (and others) that have been devastated and destroyed by the phony Russia Collusion Witch Hunt? They journeyed down to Washington, D.C., with stars in their eyes and wanting to help our nation…They went back home in tatters!

5:41 a.m.—27 May 2018

Introduction

IN May 2018, I sat inside a black SUV with tinted windows speeding toward the Department of Justice building in Washington, DC, where I was about to be questioned by FBI agents and senior prosecutors from the team of Special Prosecutor Robert Mueller in what was surely the most talked-about investigation since Watergate.

I was worried that the minute I stepped outside the car, I'd be harassed by the media, filming me or snapping their cameras while a crowd of journalists shouted outrageous questions. I could see the cable news headlines flashing in my face and blaring my name to the world as one of the suspects in the Mueller investigation, falsely tarring me as Michael Cohen's and Donald Trump's Russian connection (which was exactly what later happened).

You may be wondering, as my wife and I have done so many times in the last two years, *Why me?*

Perhaps the reason is that my love for my native country, the Republic of Georgia, is too great. Or, more simply, because in 2009 I had a big idea: I wanted to bring the Trump brand to the former Soviet region, specifically to the Russia and the Republics of Georgia and Kazakhstan. In the process, I became directly associated with the Trump Organization, Michael Cohen, and Donald J. Trump himself. Perhaps that was my crime.

Even so, as I sat in the SUV on that spring morning, I wondered to myself, *How did I get here? What brought me to this rendezvous with history?*

—

IN MARCH 1991, I came to this country on a one-way ticket from the former Soviet Empire, just prior to its collapse. With just fifty dollars in my pocket and giant dreams, I was just another immigrant—in my case from the Republic of Georgia. At the time, I was overjoyed to leave behind the ever-present feeling of being watched, the lack of privacy, and the intrusiveness of the Communist State. In time, I was fortunate to achieve the "American Dream" both professionally and personally, and today, I am proud to say that I am an American citizen of Georgian descent.

However, about three years ago, right after Mr. Trump went from real estate mogul to forty-fifth president of the United States, I once again found every aspect of my life under intense scrutiny and subject to mischaracterization and misrepresentation. My character, even my name, was assailed. Only this time it wasn't the Soviet State doing so, but the US Justice Department, the FBI, and the Robert Mueller probe.

As anyone who has not been living on the moon knows, Attorney General Jeff Sessions appointed Robert Mueller as a special prosecutor to lead the "Russia Probe" to determine if the sitting US president had colluded with the Kremlin and President Putin himself to win the presidency and/or continued to do so once in office.

As a witness called before the grand jury in the Mueller investigation, and later before the House Intelligence Committee and the Senate, thousands upon thousands of my texts, emails, and phone calls, as well as thousands of business and private documents, were subject to Department of Justice and Congressional Review. It was a nightmare.

To defend myself, I felt it necessary to hire high-priced white-collar criminal defense lawyers, spending an enormous amount of money on legal fees. At the same time, as a businessman I became radioactive. Even my friends and closest associates kept their distance, not wanting to be tainted by the Mueller probe. My business dried up. And for what? To what end?

Even now, I am still trying to make sense of it.

When I left the USSR and came to the "land of the free" in New York City, on March 20, 1991, never in my wildest dreams could I have imagined that twenty-eight years later, my name would appear in one of the most consequential documents in the history of the United States, the Mueller Report. Robert Mueller, whom I held in the greatest respect, nevertheless devoted an entire footnote (#112) to me and my connection to the controversial Steele dossier and its claim of Russian *kompromat*, salacious videotapes of Donald Trump in Moscow.

There was no real connection between me and the Steele dossier, but the footnote made it seem as if there was. The Mueller Report accused me, an American citizen, of being a Russian businessman who was working with the president's personal lawyer, Michael Cohen, to destroy the release of compromising video—or kompromat, as it's called in Russia—about then-candidate Donald J. Trump,.

The Mueller Report's false, inaccurate, and highly selective version of events had the effect of being nothing more or less than character assassination. Thanks to my unnecessary and inaccurate appearance in the Mueller Report, media outlets believed I was a primary link in the story of a potential Russian kompromat on the sitting president of the United States.

Print and TV media picked up the story, amplified it, and spread the false characterizations of me, my nationality, and my actions. Online trolls cast me as an agent of the Kremlin and called for my imprisonment. People obsessed with removing Trump from the White House didn't care if I was guilty or not. It was accepted gospel that anyone in Trump or Michael Cohen's orbit was guilty, and any foreign deal—even one which was never fully consummated—was proof of corruption and a vehicle for Russian influence or blackmail.

You might think that an average American citizen is not going to have his life overwhelmed by the government for some business deals that were never completed. I certainly thought so. I thought, *This can't happen in the USA—not in 2019*. However, in the blink of an eye, my family and I went from living the American Dream to having to fight our way out of a nightmare.

Rachel Maddow, the highly sarcastic TV talk news personality from MSNBC, spent twenty minutes ranting about me. Maddow went so far as to call me Trump's "Soviet buddy," letting her listeners believe that somehow I was the one who had access to the kompromat against Trump and that I made sure that the salacious and compromising tapes stayed in Russia and never made it to the United States. As if that were not enough, Maddow mocked my last name and my heritage, and made me out to be a traitor.

While writing this book, I realized that " kompromat"—the word that had haunted my family and my existence in the former Soviet Union— had come back to haunt me and try to ruin all that I had worked so hard for in the United Stated for myself, my wife, and our children.

Improbable as it sounds, suddenly the forty-fifth president of the United States and I shared the same challenge: to prove our innocence in the alleged case of "Russian Collusion."

—

IN THIS BOOK, I have shared the details of my life, both before I came to the United States, in Georgia and Russia; and once I arrived in New York. I also describe my business dealings in the United States, Georgia, and Russia, and go into great detail about my dealings with Michael Cohen and Donald Trump as well as my own experience with Mueller's Team and before the grand jury. I do this so you can form your own opinion about my character and my dealings with Donald Trump, the Trump Organization, and Michael Cohen rather than rely on the Mueller Report or what you might hear from less-than-responsible media outlets.

My story will give you a real sense of what it was like to grow up under those Communist and Socialist regimes—what little joy we experienced as well as the tragedies we witnessed as part of a lost generation yearning for freedom and independence. I also aim to explain how business was done in Russia as the Soviet Empire breathed its last gasps, and how my partners and I navigated the disarray and the absolute chaos from which Vladimir Putin emerged. I hope this book also gives you a greater understanding of Putin's agenda—why we, as Americans, should be wary; but why I always believed Trump colluding with Russia was unlikely, if not impossible.

Above all, my story should be a warning to every American that with a knock on the door, your life can be hijacked and changed forever. What happened to me can happen to you! It really can.

When it does, or if it does, you need to know that the only person you can rely on is yourself, and if your conscience is clear, you must tell the truth and nothing but the truth and hope that God will help you when you are under oath and everything you say can and will be used against you. Still, you can never let any person or any government suppress your right to dream big.

—

So let us return to May 2018:

We arrived at the DOJ. As my mind flooded with worry, I barely registered that we had passed the DOJ building's main entrance unnoticed. Instead we entered through a loading dock where security guards waved us into a very dark underground parking lot before they closed the garage door behind us.

Everything was superbly organized, planned, and orchestrated. One of the agents was already waiting for the car. I became extremely nervous—I could hear my own rapid breaths. To calm myself, I thought of my mother smiling at me, a memory that always brings me confidence and peace of mind.

The FBI agent walked up to open my car door. I was ready to go.

The agent led me through the various security checks and metal detectors. She walked me right into the building, which has no windows and whose walls are a drab, institutional off-white. The door locked behind me.

I was then instructed to place my cell phone in what looked like a gym locker.

Then a different door opened and they walked me into a very plain, simple room with very dark brown furniture. If you have seen any police programs—ever—you understand that this is the room in which you'll be interrogated.

They made me wait for a while. Again, this was no surprise—it's a common enough interrogation technique. But even if you are aware of it, as I was, it still works. I was already somewhat on edge and, on top that, I was drained from being unable to sleep the night before.

My lawyer, leaning closer to my ear, reminded me that when asked questions, "Keep it short. Only yes or no answers. Don't go any further than that." My lawyer's concern was that as a businessman and a creative person, I would overthink my answers and overshare.

"This is the only place where you don't negotiate anything," he told me. "This is not a place where you make deals. This is the place to say yes or no."

Easier said than done, as I would soon learn.

I felt relieved that my wife, children, and the rest of the world wouldn't be seeing me on the evening news and that perhaps people would still want to do business with me after I was done here so I could continue to feed my family.

My biggest concern was the interview. Would Robert Mueller himself be present? Would his prosecutors be doing the questioning?

I knew that I was innocent, but that didn't make me any less anxious. Was Mueller's team determined to nail me? If they had brought me to DC and spent time, energy, and money to interview me, I must be of value to their investigation—which is, in and of itself, a scary thought.

Who wants to be used against a sitting president of the United States or his personal lawyer? It's one thing to be making a licensing deal with a New York luxury high-rise developer; it's a whole other thing to have that deal scrutinized by the Department of Justice with a presidency in the balance.

As I waited in the depressing room with no windows for my DOJ inquisitors, my mind began to question itself, to ask those questions I expected would be forthcoming about my background, my business dealings, my business partners, my family and friends, and certainly my interactions with Donald Trump, the Trump Organization, and Michael Cohen.

I was very aware that Mueller & Co. had deep pockets and great resources to drill down to a very granular level. I wondered if, in fact, they knew something I didn't—or had forgotten. What did I know of the intricacies of American law? Perhaps something I had done in my past was of concern to Mueller's team. My mind kept racing, going over details of my recent past, and plunging further and further back in time, in case there was an important detail—a person, a place, or even a transaction that took place in the former USSR...

It was like waiting for the most important exam of your life to start while you refresh your knowledge one last time—except in this case a failure could put you behind bars, and you are only innocent before you open your mouth and speak. I kept thinking, *What brought me here?*

1

Back in the USSR

Beginnings

I WAS BORN IN Tbilisi, the capital of Georgia, in the former Soviet Union to a prominent Georgian family. Vasili Rtskhiladze, my father, a congenitally honest man, is a world-renowned scientist, a graduate of one of the most prestigious academies for scientists in the Soviet Union, the Institute of Gold, Ferrous, and Non-Ferrous Metallurgy.

My mother, Giuli Oziashvili-Rtskhiladze, was an accomplished chemist and, most importantly, an incredibly gentle and loving mother who was a kind and giving person. She was born on July 4 in Soviet Georgia and died as an American citizen in Litchfield, Connecticut, in 2002. God bless her soul.

My sister, Lilly Rtskhiladze, is an accomplished musician and a graduate of the Georgian Theatrical University. She has lived in the United States since 1996 with her daughter Natasha Misabishvili (my niece), who is a top executive at the famous Neue Galerie museum in New York.

My grandfather, Giorgi (Gulo) Rtskhiladze, was one of the most important athletes in Stalin's time. As a young man, he was a gymnast who was the absolute champion of the Soviet Union three times in a row.

Due to his success, he was invited in 1936 to the Kremlin in Moscow. At that time, the head of the KGB was Lavrentiy Beria, a fellow Georgian. Beria had been chief of the Communist Party in Georgia before joining the Central Committee and being appointed to run the KGB.

In Georgia, they were so concerned about my grandfather that they gave him an apartment across the street from Beria's office, so he could be closely watched. Over time, they became friends, and Beria would often go across the street to my grandfather's for lunch. On occasion, Beria gave him gifts that, strangely enough, were all American-made, like a Jeep and a Harley-Davidson.

My grandfather was also a great pianist. He studied at the Moscow Conservatory with the famous Russian pianist Sviatoslav Richter.

One day Beria came over and told my grandfather he was going to have to quit his piano studies. "We have many great pianists in the Soviet Union, but not athletes like you."

The Soviet Union was preparing to participate in the first European Gymnastics Championships in Antwerp. They made my grandfather captain of the Soviet team. Stalin told them they had to win the championship. This was not a statement; it was a command. It was clear: if you don't win, don't bother returning. Failure could mean death.

The Soviet team travelled to Antwerp. My grandfather carried the flag in the opening ceremonies. The Soviet team won the championship for the first time ever and my grandfather was safe.

Upon their return to Moscow, most of the team was sent away to train in a remote location. My grandfather was invited to the Kremlin to meet Stalin, who was also from Georgia, and Voroshilov, a general of the Soviet Army at the time. Stalin gave my grandfather a golden watch with his signature and the next morning there was a photo of him and Stalin on the cover of *Pravda*, the national newspaper of the Soviet Union.

After that, he was appointed the minister of sport and culture in Georgia. Gymnastics would come to be an elite sport for the Soviet Union and a symbol of its dedication, discipline, and the healthy Soviet lifestyle, and my grandfather became its poster child. In 1957, he was given the Order of the Badge of Honor, one of the highest civilian honors in the USSR.

I was named for him. He died when I was only three, so I have no personal memories of him. But in Tbilisi, and whenever I went to Moscow and even among my family, I always heard many stories about him.

My grandfather's presence loomed large in my childhood. I didn't take up gymnastics, but from the age of five, I played tennis competitively. Every training day and/or competition I heard the same thing from my coach: "Go and make your grandfather's soul proud!"

The positions of respect held by my grandfather and parents in Georgia and the former Soviet Union meant a great deal to me and account for the many positive feelings I have for my homeland and my heritage.

Soviet Privilege

IN THE UNITED STATES, there is much discussion about income inequality, and about the 1 percent versus the 99 percent. In the Soviet Union, under the Communist regime, there was a comparable division among its citizens, but it was a "privilege" inequality that separated the top 1 percent from average citizens.

If you were a privileged member of the Soviet State, either by being a high-ranking Communist Party Member, part of the *Nomenklatura*, or someone valuable to the State such as a dancer, artist, athlete, filmmaker, or even a prized scientist, you lived better than 99 percent of the people. Today you would call them "the elites."

My grandfather, Giorgi, was an important figure in the Soviet Union. He was granted all the benefits and privileges of his position—better living conditions, access to superior goods and services, and a thousand perks large and small.

However, my family did not benefit from any of that—directly. My grandfather had divorced my grandmother when my father was quite young. My grandfather remarried a much younger woman and had a second family with her. In time, my grandmother remarried as well. As a consequence, my grandfather's new family got all the privileges and my father none. My father was, in fact, prohibited from visiting his father. My grandmother (my father's mother) died at a very young age, forty-two.

According to family lore, my grandfather's last word was to call out my grandmother's name, "Nanu." In the end, she was his one and only true love. However, having betrayed her, he could never be with her again—a sad but powerful love story that strengthens my commitment to love and marriage every time I think about it.

Nonetheless, my father became an important scientist and we were considered part of Georgia's elite.

My father was forced to join the Communist party—otherwise he would have no job and we would have no apartment. He was no ideologue, and neither was anyone in the family. My father, like many of his generation, had respect for what Stalin accomplished both before, during, and after the Second World War, but had also heard firsthand many horrific stories about Stalin's gulags.

My father's eyes light up every time he tells me the story of how he attended Stalin's burial in Moscow. He nearly got crushed by the mass of people desperate to get a glimpse of the iconic Soviet Monarch, "Uncle Joseph," as he was called, or the *Vozhd* ("the chief").

My mother was a free soul, very giving, always looking to do things for everyone around us. Although private business was prohibited in the Soviet Union, my mother had a knack for business, and when she could, she would trade goods available in Georgia with friends in other Soviet bloc countries to their mutual profit.

When my sister Lilly and I recall the complex trades and transactions our mother engineered with her friends in other Communist bloc countries like Hungary or Yugoslavia, we are fascinated because her success at doing so seems so impossible or improbable. Hungarian and Yugoslavian goods were going in and out of our house like hot potatoes and somehow she still managed to hang out with her friends in our kitchen with the coffee, reading while getting the latest update on the hottest gossips in Tbilisi, and making it to work at the academy of science on time and keeping us fed. Amazing…When I hear moms complaining about nannies or mates doing a lousy job while they are watching them from the sidelines, I think of my mother and shake my head.

Like all Soviet children, my sister and I were made to join the Pioneer Youth movement, which was sort of like the Boy Scouts. Not only did I resist joining, I was actually expelled from the Pioneers because I refused to wear the red handkerchief around my neck.

However, as a teenager, I was made to join the Komsomol, the Soviet Youth Brigade. The Komsomol was a robust organization pushing you to love, respect, and promote Lenin and the Communist Party. The Komsomol would have you believe that Lenin was your father and that all the Communist Party wanted to do was to foster world peace, despite the aggressions and animosities of Imperialist America. America was, our Soviet leaders told us, a country where the rich were treating the poor like dirt, and that there were more homeless people in America than we could count.

The Komsomol's problem was that not many in Georgia believed them. My family and friends knew that the Soviet apparatus was telling massive lies. As young people in Georgia we knew that rock 'n' roll, Coca-Cola, and Levi's jeans weren't made by the devil; and that the devil did not live, as we were often told, in the White House.

Let's Get a Car!

My family lived in a large, beautiful three-bedroom apartment right in the center of Tbilisi on Rustaveli, its most elegant avenue, where all the massive Soviet parades were held. All my best friends like Vato and Zizi Tokhadze, a beautiful family, lived in very close proximity to us, so I was happy. We were able to hold on to another apartment as well as a private house that was left to my father, which we were allowed to rent out.

My father's job and his membership in the Communist party allowed him access to two different *dachas* (country houses), one in the mountains and one by the sea, each of which was beautiful. We definitely lived a privileged life.

Back then, you couldn't just go and buy a car. You needed connections to be even allowed to have a car. Besides, there were not enough cars being made, so getting one was all the more difficult. And very few people could afford them.

Remember that during the Soviet Union, everyone was being watched. If anyone were to suddenly have a car, people would ask, *How can that person afford a car?* And that could be followed by a knock on the door from the Security Services.

In order for you to get a car, your boss or your organization had to fill out an application saying that you wanted a car. And it was your boss and the company you worked for that received the allocation of cars and distributed them to the best workers.

This system was totally entangled in corruption. However, as crazy as it was, we understood the system—and the system worked and made perfect sense to all of us. Certainly we knew no other way to get things done. As a result, everyone lied; everyone was corrupt or accepted corruption as a way of life. This is probably the greatest difference between being Soviet and being American. In the Soviet Union there was no point, and no advantage, to being honest, fair, and transparent—in fact, doing so could mean failure at your job. Unless you participated in the corrupt system, you couldn't even buy bread and butter. Corruption was a lifestyle, not a crime.

If you wanted a car or you wanted a better car, you had to bribe someone to get it and bribe someone else to let you have it. And that was how the system worked for anything and everything you really wanted. Or you needed to know someone who had those privileges and who was also corrupt at a higher level.

My father's best friend was the famous Georgian actor Ramaz Chkhikvadze, who always called himself my godfather. Ramaz was one of the most celebrated stage actors in the world and he was funny as hell; every word coming out of his mouth was filled with humor. In 1979, he appeared in Shakespeare's *Richard III* on the stage of the Edinburgh Festival in a production by the Rustaveli Theater of Tbilisi, Georgia. Legend has it that Sir Laurence Olivier saw the performance and proclaimed Ramaz to be the greatest Richard III he had ever seen.

Ramaz toured England, Ireland, and Australia and received rave reviews wherever he performed. He was like a second father to me. In 1980, Ramaz convinced my father to drive from Georgia to Latvia, over three thousand kilometers away, in a Soviet-made car. He was shooting a film in Latvia and he wanted me to play a small role. It was the trip of a lifetime. We were smart to bring some food with us, as the drive through Russia, Belarus, and Ukraine before we got to Latvia was rough; often when we stopped to eat, the menu was limited to boiled eggs and potatoes. We even managed to stop in Moscow where the infamous 1980 Soviet Olympics were going on. I would need to write a separate book to describe the incredible adventure I experienced with Ramaz and my father traveling through the final decade of the Soviet Empire.

Ramaz was part of the elite. Ramaz was so famous that, on occasion, he would show up at our apartment saying, "Let's go get you a new car." The next day we had a brand-new car.

Ramaz was not my father's only powerful friend. Georgia is a small country. My father was part of a generation, and a group of friends, who came to run the country. Among his former classmates were the head of internal forces and the minister of aviation, among others.

Knowing the minister of aviation came in handy when I wanted to go to Moscow because he could get me on an empty plane that was flying there. I don't want to say I took advantage of this privilege, but there was an ice hockey championship match in Moscow that I was desperate to get to, and the minister was all too happy to accommodate me. I flew to Moscow to the big hockey game where I met the legendary Soviet goalie, Vladislav Tretiak. I traveled in the equivalent of first class with vodka and caviar in what was essentially a private plane there and back.

In the Soviet Union, our votes didn't matter; there was no free press and no freedom of speech. Still, I led a privileged life there.

Growing up in the Soviet Union, we had our good times. We enjoyed, we loved, we laughed, and we created art and entertainment. Although the Communist and Socialist system was like this dark cloud constantly hanging over us, watching our every move and listening to our every thought, there were times when the sun broke through the clouds and we felt the warmth of freedom inside of us. It was a rare feeling, and I loved experiencing it. It stayed with me because the most powerful things in life are love and freedom. In fact, for Georgians, freedom has always been our love and love has always been our freedom.

This was especially true because our centuries of traditions imbue us with a culture that has a love for wine, food, song, and hospitality. No amount of Soviet pressure could alter our Geogrgian identity. The Soviet Union would have liked to erase our nationality, our language, our religions, our culture, our very identity as Georgians. But it could not. Let's not forget: Georgian traditions have survived for thousands of years, while the Soviet Union lasted only seventy-five years—I rest my case!

I remember vividly how our family and friends lived a double life— as most Georgians did. One was the life of the Soviet Georgians, loyal citizens of Lenin's ideals, a lifestyle that was imposed by Moscow and would please Moscow. The other was a life of resistance in which we kept our Georgian traditions alive. In private we spoke Georgian and taught Georgian to our children, we made and drank Georgian wine, we continued to eat Georgian food, we continued to observe Georgian customs and traditions, and we continued to practice our faith—a rock-solid belief in God and a tolerance for every religion.

Art, music, and films expressed our resistance, created even though for some the result was persecution and imprisonment.

Georgians of my generation always believed Georgia belonged to us, not to the Soviet State. We pretended that our fate was in our hands although it was being manipulated and controlled from Moscow. We were in a state of denial and a state of resistance, both powerful tools in achieving our dreams and our freedom.

At dinners there were toasts to life before the Communists, and to a life after…when Georgia would once again be an independent republic. It was a dream. But a dream that came true in my lifetime.

Dissidents

FOR AS LONG AS I can remember, I was aware that my family in Georgia was being watched. My father was very important to the Soviet State. He had developed five different technologies for extracting arsenic from ore without polluting the environment. The Soviets had brought this technology to projects around the world, including in India and even the United States.

Although my father's technology was being sold around world by the Soviet Government, we never saw a penny from it.

There were times when some of the foreign business leaders demanded a meeting with the person who developed the technology. Our foreign visitor would always arrive in the company of a group of Russian scientists who we could easily tell were undercover KGB operatives.

My mother used to cook incredible Georgian dinners and our relatives from Kakheti (a wine region in Georgia) would bring great red and white wines. Although my sister and I knew what was going on, we still loved those dinners. It was beyond intriguing to watch the KGB operatives in action. They listened to my father's every word carefully, they watched our every move, and they always kept their eye on the foreign guest. The other remarkable thing was that they never got drunk—no matter how many wine glasses they emptied as my parents made toast after toast.

We were also watched for another reason: my uncle Victor was one of the most famous dissidents in the USSR.

Victor was my favorite uncle. He brought me vinyl records of Elvis Presley and Louis Armstrong that he somehow managed to get from American or European sources on the black market.

However, when I was just eight years old, in 1975, the KGB arrested Victor and several of his fellow dissidents, including Zviad Gamsakhurdia (who would later become the first democratically elected president of the newly independent Georgia). Victor was a great communicator and he had managed to persuade a growing number of people to support a coup to secede from the Soviet Union.

The night he was arrested, we were watching the main television channel, *Vremya* (meaning "time"), a propaganda channel of the Soviet State, when on the nightly news program we saw footage of Uncle Victor.

He was sitting at a table and seemed totally out of it, sedated or on drugs. He was talking but it was clear he had no idea what he was saying. He was probably reading from a prepared statement. He admitted his guilt and stated that the Soviet system was the best in the world.

After that, we learned he'd been sentenced to fourteen years in the Gulag in Kazakhstan.

Victor's arrest and conviction put our family under a lot of pressure. Our neighbors began to avoid us. We were too closely related to a convicted enemy of the State.

Several days later, two Soviet agents showed up at our door. They spoke to my parents and then took them away, leaving me in the care of my sister who was only thirteen, some five years older than me. They didn't tell us where they were taking our parents or if they would return. We were paralyzed with fear and could not leave home.

Our parents returned, but our family was blacklisted by the Soviet State. My father, who had received an offer to teach in Canada and who had worked in England, was no longer permitted to go there. A five-year travel ban was imposed on our family (most likely to discourage my father from considering defecting to the West).

For me, the worst part was that, as an avid tennis player, I had hoped to compete in European tournaments—which I was no longer allowed to do.

A few years later, in November of 1983, Gega Kobakhidze, a close family friend of ours who was an older brother figure to me, became a figure of much controversy. He was a very serious and talented actor. His father, Mikheil, was a genius film director who made masterful silent films that were studied and beloved by film historians and film fanatics. However, these same films often contained sly anti-Soviet messages, for which Mikheil was, at one time, jailed. So Gega grew up with strong anti-Soviet sentiments that we all shared, but he was way more outspoken about it.

Gega got married to a lovely young woman, a talented artist, Tinatin Petviashvili. I was only fourteen at the time, but I remember it was an unusually solemn wedding, especially for a Georgian wedding, which are known to be loud, happy, and bright celebrations.

At the party afterward, at my friend Dato Evgenidze's apartment, Gega threw a pack of American cigarettes, Camels, on the table, and said, "Turkish blend," which was what it said on the pack of Camels—and laughed. I had no idea what he meant by it but, sadly, we were about to find out.

After the party we all went to the airport to see Gega, his wife, and his wedding party off on their honeymoon. Gega, his bride, and five of their friends all boarded a flight in Tbilisi to the Georgian seaside resort of Batumi. Among them were Gia Tabidze, a painter and actor; Tinatin Petviashvili, Gega's wife; the painters Davit Mikaberidze and Soso Tsereteli; and two doctors, Paata and Kaki Iverieli.

There were fifty-seven passengers and seven crew members aboard when Gega and his friends announced that they were hijacking the plane to Turkey—to escape to the West to "have a better life and live in a free society."

The pilots, however, had their own plans. They tricked Gega by executing a series of sharp turns that directed the plane to land not in Turkey, but back in Tbilisi.

Once on the ground, the Soviet authorities began hostage negotiations.

We were sitting at home, watching the evening news, when *Vremya* came on to announce that for the first time ever, a Soviet airliner had been hijacked by terrorists. It was frightening news, but we still had no idea who the terrorists were.

Eduard Shevardnadze (the future Russian Foreign Minister and eventual second president of the Georgian Republic) was then head of the Georgian Communist Party and in charge of Soviet Georgia. Shevardnadze, while pretending to have a dialogue with the hijackers, authorized the deployment of Russian Special Forces.

The Special Forces, called Alpha Group, arrived on the scene. They launched an attack that recaptured the plane and arrested Gega and his friends, one of whom, Davit, was my brother's best friend.

We rushed to the airport and watched as Gega and his friends started to emerge from the plane—with the Russian Special Forces surrounding them. Suddenly, Davit grabbed a gun from one of the Special Forces and shot himself in the head. It was a gruesome and frightening moment.

Not only had the hijacking been a fiasco, but now this traumatic suicide had occurred while all of Georgia was watching. In many ways, this dark but very powerful moment changed me—and Georgia—forever. We were now witness to the cruelty of Soviet oppression and what happens to anyone who dares voice their opposition or attempt to leave. This made leaving all the more desirable to young people all over Georgia, including me.

We were standing right there. We watched as all of them were taken away.

The KGB searched my best friend Vazha Mikaberidze's apartment, turning it upside down for clues as to why his older brother, Dato (one of the hijackers on the plane), would commit such a crime.

Gega and the four other men who were captured were all sentenced to death and executed. We never saw them again. Their parents never saw them again. The only thing their families received were the clothes they were wearing—some of which had blood stains and bullet holes. That was it.

Gega's wife, Tinatin Petviashvili, was the only one spared, sentenced to fourteen years in jail as a coconspirator.

I was very upset. I was Georgian. Yes, maybe my friends made a mistake. They wanted to escape the Soviet Union. But was there really any reason to bring in the Special Forces and murder them? Why not just exile them? But the Soviets wanted to show their strength and bully all Georgians. That was what the Soviet system was like.

Music to my Ears

MUSIC HAS ALWAYS BEEN important to me. Since childhood, I've always been able to close my eyes and think of music—I hear it inside my head and then I dream big—way beyond whatever is going on in our daily lives. I followed in my grandfather's footsteps in terms of musical ability, but as a child my instrument was the violin.

Among my childhood friends, violin wasn't exactly an instrument you wanted to be seen with—it could be cause for some serious bullying. So, in order to keep my street credibility and reputation intact, I devised a plan. I would have my eighty-five-year-old great-grandmother, Ariadna (my daughter is named after her), deliver the violin to my class in advance, before I arrived. My ruse worked: by age twelve, I was performing in classical concerts at the Georgian Conservatory of Music.

A few years later, I was taking classes at Moscow's famous Gnessin Specialized Musical School for Gifted Children (Evgeny Kissin is one of the more famous graduates). Living in Moscow in the mid-1980s was both fun and downright dangerous. Although I was only a teenager of fifteen or sixteen, my life was very different than that of most American teenagers.

There was no way for teenagers in Russia to have a part-time job and make money. But the black market trade, which was pervasive in Russia, always needed extra hands, and teenagers were not obvious couriers. Also, there was no drinking age in Russia, so my friends and I often went to a local bar after music lessons.

During one of those outings with my buddies at a popular bar restaurant, Nikitskie Varota, a middle-aged guy came over to our table. He pulled a pile of cash out of his pockets and flashed it in my face, saying, "You wanna make some dough or you wanna die poor?"

I laughed and said, "Sure, I want to make money."

He leaned closer and said, "You Georgians are smart and clever." Then he spoke very low. "I have an easy job for you, but it pays well." The job was simple: I had to pick up a gym bag at his house and deliver it to someone else at their house. The bag had a lock on it—and I could never, ever look inside. If I did that, he would pay me a hundred rubles (which was a lot to me).

It was risky, and if my parents ever found out they would've killed me, but a hundred rubles made it seem worthwhile. And, as advertised, it was simple. No one thought twice about a kid carrying a gym bag. I went wherever I was told to, and I made good pocket change.

However, my adventures as a courier ended one day after my violin lesson when I went to my boss's apartment to pick up the latest delivery. As I arrived, I saw a bunch of giant tough guys dragging him out of the building. He was beaten badly and his entire face was bloody. They shoved him into one of those Soviet SUVs and off they went.

I saw him looking at me, but his face was so messed up he couldn't speak. I slowly retreated to hide behind a tree. Luckily, the tough guys never noticed me.

I never saw the man again in my life. To this day, I have no idea what was in that gym bag. I was curious, but I didn't want to mess with the lock. I can tell you it wasn't all that heavy. But that's all I know. It wasn't long after that that my music lessons ended in Moscow and I went back to Tbilisi.

Upon my return later, I was admitted to the Georgian Conservatory and started composing as well. I was fortunate to have Andrei Balanchivadze, George Balanchine's brother, as one of my composition professors.

By eighteen, I was a singer-songwriter. My music videos were among the first performed on Georgian TV. My songs were also performed by some of Georgia's biggest stars such as Eka Kvaliashvili, Maya Dzabua, and others. It was rewarding and exciting to bring a brand-new sound to the Georgian music scene, and even to write and perform songs in English. But, frankly, I didn't see having a long career in Georgia as a singer-songwriter. Perhaps it's just in my nature: I am always looking for the next challenge, and once I achieve it, I am on to the next challenge.

I had always dreamt of performing my music in America, in New York City. I used to stay up all night and listen to American rock and pop music on the radio. Although the sound was horrible because the Soviets were jamming and distorting any Western transmission, I didn't mind. Hearing even a little piece of American music, like the sounds of Frank Zappa, Miles Davis, Stevie Wonder, or Michael Jackson, was enough for me to stay inspired during the grim Brezhnev era.

In 1987, when I turned eighteen, I was drafted into the Soviet Army for a two-year term. As I mentioned earlier, my father had powerful connections in Moscow and Tbilisi. My parents could have kept me out of the Soviet Army, or kept me out of harm's way, but I told my parents that I wanted no special favors or special treatment. I wanted to serve with my fellow Georgians doing our national obligation of military service. But what I saw, what I experienced, would forever change me and lead to my leaving the Soviet Union.

A Toast to America

IN THE USSR, MILITARY service was compulsory. Whether you were from Russia or, as in my case, Georgia, didn't matter. Whether you lived in Tbilisi or Kiev, Minsk or Kerch, as a Soviet subject, you were required to enter the military for two years (three for certain Navy conscripts). This usually happened at eighteen (though occasionally individuals sought and received deferments to complete their education).

Soviet military service was a rite of passage, part of becoming an adult. You usually had to serve far away from home, with people from all over the Soviet Union and occasionally with soldiers from Soviet satellite states such as Poland, Hungary, and East Germany.

If you were a boy, this was part of your becoming a man. Accordingly, much like Americans do for turning twenty-one, you gathered your wolf pack for one evening of serious drinking and partying before leaving for military service. As a young Georgian and Soviet citizen in 1987, the place for your "going-away party" was Moscow.

Our party was to gather at the Hotel-Tower International, at that time Moscow's poshest hotel and one of the tallest in all of Russia—located just 220 yards from Red Square.

Just to set the scene a little: Moscow in 1987 was pretty grim—years of economic ravages perpetrated by Soviet State had taken their toll. The streets of Moscow were calm, but there were plenty of whispers that Gorbachev's "Perestroika," the loosening of the State's iron grip on its citizens, could spell the beginning of the end of the Communist State.

That our country's future as well as our own was uncertain only made the celebration seem more urgent. In times of trouble and imminent change, when corruption is widespread, there is often opportunity, as well as an increasing stream of opportunists.

The Hotel-Tower was officially designated for *Inastrantsi*, foreign guests. However, my friends and I knew that a bribe to the doorman with a very good bottle of Georgian wine could open doors for us—literally and figuratively.

We had booked a table at the fancy high-end restaurant on the hotel's second floor. There was a Russian band playing bad covers of Stevie Wonder and tables full of Moscow's elite who had similarly disregarded the "for foreigners only" designation.

We were drinking with abandon as Russians and Georgians are known to do. We were raising our glasses and toasting each other.

As we waited for our feast to arrive, I noticed the arrival of a tall, blond man, surrounded by Russians dressed in black suits, white shirts, and black ties that signaled they were private security.

One of my friends, the son of a prominent and powerful Russian official, said, "Do you know who that is?"

The face was vaguely familiar but I couldn't put a name to it.

"Who is it?" I asked.

"That's Donald Trump. The American business tycoon," my friend said. "He has more money than the president of the United States!"

We all laughed because to us, the president of the United States, Ronald Reagan, was the most powerful person on Earth. We could not believe that an ordinary citizen could be wealthier than the leader of the most powerful capitalist country.

My friend continued, "No, really, guys, in America, businessmen have more money than the politicians."

We laughed again. That seemed absurd.

"This guy Trump can make you rich and change your life in a snap!" my friend said, snapping his fingers.

We all looked at Donald Trump engaged in a dialogue with his Russian hosts. It was hard to tell what they were saying, but Trump was nodding along.

"If he's so rich," another friend asked, "what is he doing here in the poor Soviet Union?"

That provoked even more peals of laughter.

"Rumor is…" my friend said, "Trump wants to build a *nebaskreb* here, just like he has in New York."

At this time, there were no skyscrapers in Georgia and very few in Russia that were not state-owned office buildings. The only time we saw skyscrapers was in Hollywood movies. There were certainly no branded American businesses. It would still be several years before American businesses such as McDonald's and Estée Lauder opened stores in Russia.

I stood up and proposed a toast to the United States of America. Our entire table of twelve stood up, raised our glasses in salute to Donald Trump's table, and looked his way. Trump noticed us and glanced at our table. We took that as a sign of approval and downed our vodka, and then sat down for more caviar before our meal arrived.

Special Forces

IN THE SOVIET MILITARY, I received basic training in a boot camp situation, followed by substantial one-on-one training in hand-to-hand combat. Then we were trained for security operations such as the guarding of dangerous prisoners as well as prison security. Let me be clear: at no time during my military service was I trained or taught any spy or intel strategies or tactics. I was never exposed to any KGB training. I wouldn't have done it even if I were forced into it.

Although I was away from home, my mother's spirit was never far away. My mother always worried about me and my time in the Army was no different. She talked my father into taking monthly trips to visit me at my battalion, bringing food and even warm clothes for me.

My mother even arranged for me to have a few days' leave. This was the Soviet era, when corruption was commonplace and a well-placed bribe of Georgian wines and spirits or cold hard cash could accomplish almost anything. My mother would get me back home and feed me warm meals. My friends would come over. I would get a night or two of good sleep, and then I was back to the military barracks.

At one point, my mother even managed to have me assigned to the military chamber orchestra. They didn't have violins in the marching band, so I picked up a kick drum—not realizing that meant I would have to wake at 5:00 a.m. to beat the drum as a wake-up call for our whole Soviet Army unit.

For the first year or so, all our postings and assignments were for internal security, watching over serious criminals serving their time under brutal conditions. From a humane point of view, I felt so bad for some of the prisoners that I used to smuggle tea and cigarettes for them, and I would listen to their painful life stories. Doing so made me feel like my Red Army service was a walk in the park.

One thing I noticed was that, for the most part, these prisoners showed no remorse. To the contrary, they were proud to be outlaws of the Communist system. Some even considered themselves political prisoners. To that point, one of the prisoners I got to know was arrested for selling banned Western literature. The prisoners warned me that if I remained a Communist, the United States would never let me visit, and that once the USSR was vanquished they would be welcomed there as heroes.

The opposite was also true. As long as I was in the Red Army, I learned to never say anything positive or admiring about the United States. One could only enjoy those American performers whom the Soviets had approved, like Harry Belafonte and Dean Reed (the so-called Red Elvis).

During one of our shooting exercises, one of our captains put President Ronald Reagan's face on a target and told us to shoot at it. One of my army buddies and I refused. Although the US and Soviet Union had been engaged in a cold war for many decades, it did not feel right to promote the assassination of an American president. But that was not how the

Soviet Army looked at it. For refusing my captain's order, I was sentenced to three days in an army jail, the *Gaodbakht*, as we used to call it.

As soon as we arrived at the prison, my army buddy and I were set upon by about seven military personnel. They beat us—not only for refusing an order but also for being Georgians who dared to refuse a Russian captain's orders. They beat us until we were near death. I was bruised and bloody, had broken ribs, could barely see out of one eye, my jaw was broken, and I had received dangerous blows to my kidneys.

It took me weeks in prison to recover. I was glad to have the time—my friend and I used it to plot our revenge against those military officers who nearly killed us for the crime of being Georgian. I won't say how we exacted revenge but suffice it to say we made sure they suddenly became so violently ill that they understood Georgians would not back down and would always deliver retribution for Soviet punishment. I returned to my unit.

Officially, no alcohol was allowed in the Soviet Army, but without vodka no Russian can live. Some of the Russian soldiers went to extremes to satisfy their craving for alcohol.

One frightening experience that I will never forget occurred one night when one of the Russian soldiers, named Gorbachev (of all names; no relation), a giant (*Bagatir* in Russian), was so desperate in his alcohol withdrawal (in Russian we would say he was feeling *Lomka*) that he drank a couple of bottles of cheap Russian cologne, which made him stark raving mad.

Gorbachev burst into our bunks wielding an AK-47. He had one of those spooky smiles that you never want to see. He mumbled something about his wife, his screwed-up life, and how he wanted to end it all and take everyone with him.

I was petrified. The other soldiers there, more senior than I, paid him no attention. So Gorbachev ran outside.

We then heard the sounds of shots being fired. We all rushed to see what was going on: Gorbachev was shooting at cars passing by on the highway. Thank goodness, he was too crazed and drunk to hit anyone.

Eventually, he grew tired and passed out. No one ever said anything about it.

In early 1988, one morning we were woken up at 4:00 a.m. and told to prepare for mobilization. We were herded into a set of military trucks. We didn't know where we were headed. There was a rumor that we were being sent to Afghanistan.

Suddenly, in the middle of nowhere, they stopped our convoy. For reasons we were never told, the deployment was halted.

Instead, because war had broken out between Armenians and Azerbaijanis in Karabakh, we were sent there. Despite having shared the same land for decades (if not centuries), the ethnic violence was ferocious and we saw a great number of atrocities, which we were powerless to stop or prevent.

At the end of our tour of duty there, a Russian officer appeared at our barracks. He took me aside and ordered me to walk with him. I expected the worst. This usually meant some awful assignment. Instead, he was offering me two weeks' break and the opportunity to go home to Tbilisi. There was one condition: he was, personally, going to deliver me home. I assumed he had a girlfriend in Tbilisi or some other personal reason for wanting to be there.

My journey with the Red Army officer was certainly no fun, but we arrived at my parents' home, much to my family's surprise.

It was a Saturday night, and my mother being a gracious host, treated the Russian officer to a delicious Georgian meal and wine. By the time the officer left our home, he was pleasantly buzzed, in love with Georgia, and ready to fight for Georgia's independence. That was my family: we treated guests like one of our own, regardless of their nationality or status. That is the essence of Georgian hospitality.

I never learned why he needed to go to Tbilisi. Perhaps he forgot himself. Because that night was April 8, 1989, and the next morning everything would change for Georgia. The next morning remains in my memory as one of the worst dreams ever. One that I would forget if I could.

The April 9 Tragedy

TODAY IN GEORGIA, APRIL 9 is celebrated as the "Day of National Unity." However, it also commemorates the tragedy that took place in Tbilisi on April 9, 1989. That's when the Georgian people stood up to a massive Communist machine and, in the end, won the battle. It's important to point out that the April 9 massacre in Tbilisi happened two months before the brutal Tiananmen Square events in China.

In the late 1980s, Georgia was still part of the Soviet Union, Gorbachev was still in power, and Shevardnadze, a Georgian whom my father knew, was the Soviet foreign minister. These two Soviet leaders were often praised by the Western media for their progressive policies and openness toward the West, but inside the crumbling USSR it was a very different story.

The Soviet people were at the end of their rope: basic needs for survival, such as food, clothing, and electricity, were largely unavailable. In such an environment of uncertainty, Russia's economy was in free fall. Soviet satellite countries were jostling to become free—and the Soviet leadership was desperately trying to maintain their hold on those countries, which they needed for natural resources. They seemed to have no plan in place for a satellite-free future.

Putin once said that the collapse of the Soviet Union was the biggest tragedy of the twentieth century, but the real tragedy was what the innocent people of the former Soviet Union were forced to endure—the poverty, despair, armed conflicts, and death toll caused by the death rattle of the Soviet Empire.

Not much of this was reported by the media in the West, as Gorbachev was seen as a hero for dismantling the evil empire. For me, on the one hand, I loved what Gorbachev and Shevardnadze were doing, but on the other I saw the total devastation that unfolded in front of my very eyes.

For much of the previous year, many Georgians had been demonstrating to become an independent republic as Georgia had been briefly between 1918 and 1921. At the same time, several thousand Soviet and Russian supporters in the Abkhaz region (sovereign Georgian territory), who were opposed to Georgian independence, declared their intention to secede from any Georgian Republic and join the Soviet Union as an autonomous Soviet Republic.

In response to the secession movement, those Georgians in favor of independence started to organize protest rallies in Tbilisi, gathering before the House of Government on Tbilisi's central thoroughfare, Rustaveli Avenue, where our family home stood. By early April, tens of thousands of protesters were demonstrating and holding hunger strikes for Georgian independence.

Georgia's Communist Party leader, Jumber Patiashvili, anxious to restore order, asked the Soviet leadership for help, a decision that I can only hope he regretted deeply for the rest of his life. Georgia's own militia was ordered to disarm as Soviet troops, the Vnutrenie Voiska (the Internal Forces, the same Soviet security forces that I served in), entered Tbilisi and surrounded the protesters massed on Rustaveli Avenue. The protesters, estimated as some one hundred thousand, intended to stay there, night and day, until Georgia was free.

I will never forget the morning of Sunday, April 9, 1989. My entire family, including my parents, my older sister Lilly, and my five-year-old niece Natasha, and I were awoken by an ungodly commotion coming from the street.

At 3:45 a.m., Soviet forces acting on an order to clear the avenue of demonstrators by any means necessary, advanced on demonstrators using batons and, in some cases, shovels.

From our windows, we saw a sight so horrifying that I could barely believe my eyes.

The security forces plowed right through the crowd. They stopped for nothing in their mission to clear the square—not for women or children, not for the injured or the murdered. The street became a battlefield between innocent, unarmed people and the monsters from internal forces.

During the confrontation, a sixteen-year-old was chased down and beaten to death (a video of the attack exists). A stampede occurred as protesters tried to escape the Soviet forces attacking them. Gas was used against the demonstrators causing the asphyxiation of some, as well as vomiting and respiratory problems. Video shows that Soviet forces did not allow emergency responders to help the injured.

I was determined to help. I put on my Soviet internal forces uniform, went downstairs, opened the door to our building, and started helping people to get inside. I knew that the Soviet forces wouldn't touch me because I was one of them.

The horrific images we saw that night will never be erased from our memories. It remains a national trauma, a collective wound that emotionally scarred my family and friends and all who saw it.

In the end, twenty-one deaths and more than a hundred injuries were reported by the Soviets, but there were many, many more. Russian officials blamed the deaths on the demonstrators and on agitators looking to take advantage of Russia's progress in democratization. No one believed that.

My friends and I were outraged, angry, and extremely disheartened by the actions of the Soviet forces. The next day, I burned my uniform and left the Army. I had a little more than a month remaining in my service but the Army, knowing full well what had transpired in Tbilisi, discharged me with honor.

The Soviet Forces imposed martial law in Tbilisi. No citizen could be on the streets past 11:00 p.m. One night, Gia Karseladze, who was one of our friends and was only twenty-five years old, was rushing to get home by curfew. He was found the next morning shot dead, sitting in the passenger's seat of a friend's car. The Soviets left that as a warning: defying the Soviets would only bring more bloodshed to Georgia.

However, if outwardly the Soviets had reimposed order and asserted control of Tbilisi, inwardly they had lost the hearts and souls of the Georgian people forever. The April 9 tragedy was a wound that would not heal until the Soviets left Tbilisi permanently and Georgia was once again an independent Republic.

From that moment on, I, along with millions of other Georgians, broke from the Soviet Russia, morally, spiritually, and in my heart. Over the next several years as the Soviet Union collapsed, and republic after republic declared independence, we understood that our union forged by force and fear had finally rotted from within. We were always Georgians first, but from then on we all worked toward an independent Georgia.

After witnessing the April 9 tragedy, my mind was clear, and my resolve was firm that I had to find a way to leave the USSR and make it to America. The feeling was so strong that I knew nothing could stop me, not even an Iron Curtain.

2

Person of Interest

A Knock at the Door

IT WAS ON A spring evening in April 2018 that the FBI first came into my life—and they did so by knocking on my door and ringing my doorbell.

I was at home in Connecticut, sitting in our living room, putting our four-month-old baby girl, Ariadna, to sleep.

It was the first week of April and I had just spoken to my father on the phone. We recalled Georgia's April 9 tragedy and the brutality of the Soviet forces, and all the innocent lives they had ruined.

The TV was on and one of the news outlets was droning on about the Mueller investigation. Everyone was talking about Michael Cohen, and what the recent FBI raid on Michael's hotel room and office might turn up that would prove fatal to the Trump presidency.

Ayanat, my wife, lowered the volume and spoke to me quietly. "It's so surreal to see Michael on every news channel," she said. "You did so much business with Trump and Michael. Are we going to be okay?"

"We are going to be okay," I told her. "Doing business isn't a crime."

I put our son to bed. It was about 8:00 p.m. Our daughter is a bad sleeper, so my wife was about to take her outside in the stroller to try to calm her to sleep that way. I intended to do a few more hours of work once the kids were asleep. I had big business plans on the horizon.

Suddenly, I saw a gray American-made car pull up in our driveway at the front of the house. I turned the TV off and watched as two men walked up to the front door.

They flashed their IDs and identified themselves as FBI agents. Politely, they said, "Can we come in and talk to you briefly?"

The sight of federal agents at our door shocked my wife. She, too, had been raised in the former Soviet Union—in Kazakhstan, where police agents at the door was never a good thing. She looked at me, worried. She grabbed our little girl, pushed past the agents, and left the scene. This was exactly what she was worried about.

I was hesitant to let the agents come in. However, my Georgian heritage has taught me to treat any visitor as a guest sent from God and to welcome them accordingly.

Given that since 2010 I had worked closely with Michael Cohen, the Trump Organization, and Donald Trump himself (whom I even managed to get to travel to Georgia), I wasn't surprised that the FBI wanted to interview me. I was surprised, however, that they would come to my home, at night.

It would have been wiser to say "I'd rather not talk without my lawyer," but I knew I had done nothing wrong and had nothing to hide. I invited them inside.

What was supposed to be a brief chat with the agents turned out to be a detailed interrogation for which I certainly wasn't prepared. The agents were clearly very experienced professionals. They were reserved, kept their cool, and were very methodical in their questioning. At the same time, I sensed they had an urgency to get the most out of me while I still had no lawyer present. They knew what they were doing.

It was amazing how much they knew about me, my business dealings, and especially about my relationship with the Trump Organization in general and with Michael Cohen, in whom they seemed particularly interested. The agents did not record the interview but were taking everything down by hand, scribbling notes furiously. Actually, one was asking the questions, and the other taking notes.

They asked a series of wide-ranging questions about my Soviet Georgian heritage, my connections to Russia, my connections to Trump, and my connections to Michael Cohen. Everything was on the table.

I answered each question honestly to the best of my knowledge. They asked no question that I felt I couldn't handle.

However, when one of the agents placed a piece of paper before me and pointed to a printout of one of my text messages to Michael Cohen, at that moment I realized for the first time how extensive their investigation was, and how intrusive. I had no idea that they were monitoring my texts, emails and phone calls—and no idea that they could do such a thing. No corner of my life appeared beyond their reach. I was troubled that the FBI would do such a deep dive on me, who was only connected to Cohen and Trump through potential business deals that were never consummated.

Finally, when the agents stood to leave, they handed me a subpoena to appear before Mueller's grand jury two weeks later. The letter said that when before the grand jury, I did not have to answer any question if doing so truthfully would incriminate me; at the same time, anything I said could be used against me in a subsequent legal proceeding.

This meant that their questioning was not as innocent as they made it out to be; if I knew I was being subpoenaed from the outset I would have certainly considered having a lawyer present. The subpoena signed by Robert Mueller personally did not give me long to prepare before I was in DC, in the hot seat, and under oath.

A second letter asked me to preserve all documents, communications, and materials related to their investigation, and was signed by a Jeannie S. Rhee, the Senior Assistant Special Prosecutor. They asked for any and all materials related to Donald Trump, the Trump Campaign, the Trump Inaugural Committee, the Trump Victory Fund, the Republican National Committee, and the Trump Presidential Administration; related to Michael Cohen, Essential Consultants, LLC, and Michael Cohen & Associates; and related to the Crocus Group and Aras Alagarov and Emin Alagarov.

As I watched the two agents walk down my driveway to their modest parked car, my wife was heading back up the driveway pushing our baby in her stroller. As she passed by them, they stopped her to look at the baby.

This may have been a normal, very human impulse, but given the situation, it unnerved me and my wife. Government agents being kind to your child was a signal understood by anyone who grew up in the former Soviet Union: we know your family and they, too, will be at risk if you do not cooperate. Right or wrong, true or false, that's how our experience made us react.

Once I rushed my wife and baby back inside the house, I hugged her tight, telling her, "Don't worry, I am innocent, and we are in America, not the USSR."

Afterward, my wife went upstairs to put our baby in her crib. I stayed in the living room, sitting in the dark.

I felt this massive weight on my shoulders. My mind was racing. I kept thinking about how this might impact my family, my business partners, my friends—and my ability to make a living.

Was this investigation going to imperil my good name, not only in the United States but also in my native Georgia? Could this even impact relations between the US and Georgia? I was a wreck thinking that, in some way, I had let everyone down.

Suddenly, I heard a notification sound on my phone. Weirdly enough, it was President Trump's new tweet saying in capital letters, "NO COLLUSION! A WITCH HUNT!"

Although there would be many times that I disagreed with Donald Trump, in this case I was reassured because I knew he was 100 percent correct.

However, I realized my fate was not in Trump's hands, but in those of Mueller, his team, and the grand jury he'd convened.

A Bad Dream in DC

I HAD ARRIVED IN DC feeling well prepared and confident for my meeting with Mueller's team. Two of my lawyers would accompany me: one from the New York office, who was the partner I first contacted, a tall, skinny man with reddish hair, about thirty-seven years old; the other from their DC office, a young woman associate who was about twenty-eight years old.

That afternoon, after checking into my hotel, the Fairmont, I went straight to my attorneys' DC office. The younger associate was waiting for me in a conference room where we sat for several hours as we reviewed emails, texts, and documents I had sent over the last decade concerning Trump-related matters.

It was a little creepy, sitting there with someone reviewing my private texts and messages. Still, over about seven hours we reviewed some 5,400 documents, texts, and emails. We worked until 11:00 p.m. and then I headed back to the hotel to get a good night's sleep before the interview the next day.

By midnight, I found my confidence evaporating. I was anxious, on edge. I put my head on the pillow but couldn't force myself to sleep or keep my mind from racing. I tossed and turned like never before, sleeping not more than forty-five minutes the whole night—all of which probably contributed to a very strange dream I had.

In the dream, my lawyer and I were walking. We were going to a meeting with the FBI and the DOJ. However, even though I knew we were late for our meeting, I suddenly realized that I was dressed down. So I ran into a store to buy something appropriate for the occasion. The store, for some reason, would not let me buy anything and my lawyer was not understanding that my not being able to purchase what I needed in this store was delaying our arrival to the FBI meeting. I felt like the store was playing with me and doing so on purpose. I knew I was late, and, at the same time, I knew that if I was late, I could be arrested and taken into custody.

Then, suddenly, I saw my mother waving at me, standing on the stairs of the DOJ building. I waved back, puzzled. She suddenly rushed into the building. I felt better knowing that my mother was there, protecting me. I then walked into a room where I was surprised to find my mother at the meeting, speaking on my behalf.

My lawyer was there and she and my mother and the government lawyers were all looking through my papers. But they were not looking at any papers that concerned my partners in Georgia or the Trump licensing deal. No—they were looking instead for something else in a pile of documents that we never went over.

My lawyers told me, "You have nothing to worry about. You're making this much bigger than it is," to which I replied, "This is very big. Bigger than big." And then I woke up. I had the nagging feeling that there was something that my attorneys and I had overlooked.

Georgians believe our dreams tell us truths we need to be aware of. After this nightmare, I couldn't go back to sleep.

For me, one of the most difficult aspects of this experience was that I couldn't talk about it with the people I cared about most. I couldn't call my father and speak to him (although if I had, my father would have freaked out). And I couldn't call my wife because there was probably someone listening in on the line.

Being subpoenaed means you lose control over your privacy. You're not allowed to delete your emails, calls, or text messages. In fact, you are required to visit a special tech office where their specialists get into your email server and your phone data and retrieve anything and everything that may interest the grand jury. They change your passwords and passcodes. They basically control your phone and any other device you have.

So, who can you talk about this with?

Since there was no one alive to talk to, I spoke to my mother's spirit out loud—as I've done many times in the past. I voiced my worries and concerns that night. Afterward, I felt slightly better knowing that she was listening and protecting me.

The Nice Agent with the Gun

THE NEXT MORNING, WHEN the FBI car arrived to pick me up and bring me to the interrogation room at the DOJ building, I offered the blonde agent who was driving a coffee. She said she couldn't accept that.

The agent had a large purse, large enough that she couldn't both hold the bag and drive. My lawyers offered to hold her bag.

"Better not," she said. "I have a piece in there." She flashed a big smile in the rearview mirror at me.

I smiled too—it was all pretty crazy: the nice agent with the gun in her bag; driving me to the DOJ building so Mueller's team could question me as part of the possible Trump-Russia collusion case that the whole world was talking about night and day.

Whenever I turned on CNN, I would see Robert Mueller's image and the chyron saying, "Breaking News." The news was spending its day-long, nonstop coverage speculating whether Michael Cohen was likely to flip on the president while everyone who was ever in business with or had any ties with Cohen was now a suspect in the case. Including me.

Once inside the DOJ, my thoughts about my past were interrupted as two FBI agents and the female agent who had accompanied us to the DOJ finally walked into the interrogation room and took seats across from me and my lawyers.

They were courteous and noticeably polite. They began by talking about the agents who had come to my home and interviewed me, saying that they were sorry they couldn't be here today. They had wanted to continue the conversation, they said, but the agents in the room would do so.

I said, "Sure, no problem."

They told us that we would be joined shortly by another more senior attorney. They explained that the questions they were going to ask me were so I could be prepared for the sort of questions I might be asked in front of the grand jury.

I imagined that they would be asking me about the Trump Tower Batumi and about Michael Cohen. I was relaxed and felt I had nothing to worry about. My lawyers, who were smiling at the agents, kept on whispering to me, "Keep your answers short."

The agents began with very basic questions in a very relaxed and friendly manner. As if what they were doing was of no major importance but rather a formality. This went on for about a half hour. I had been drinking a lot of water that morning, and I asked to be excused for a second to take a bathroom break. They said, "Of course." They opened the door and pointed me in the direction of the restroom.

As I was walking down the hall, who did I see coming the other way? It was the agent who had come to my home. I just gave him a curt nod—but in my head what I was thinking was, *He's here!* And that the other two agents had lied.

He walked by me fast, smiled, and, pronouncing my difficult name perfectly, said, "Giorgi, how are you? How is your family, kids?"

"Good, thanks," I said. Before I could remember his name, he was gone.

That was the moment I realized that no matter their posture, this was a serious interview for which Mueller's team had planned every detail to their tactical advantage.

It was no mistake, I thought, that I was no longer being questioned by the agent who'd been to my house and met my wife and children. He was one of the few people I've ever met in the United States who wasn't Georgian but still knew how to pronounce my last name correctly.

Maybe that wasn't a coincidence either.

I returned to the room with new focus and attention to what I was being asked.

The Interrogation

SUDDENLY, THE DOOR OF the interrogation room opened and we were joined by another prosecutor from Mueller's team, Jeannie Rhee. This was the person they had mentioned at first who, I was made to believe, was more senior than the other interrogators. The minute she looked at me eye to eye, I knew the honeymoon was over.

She was older than the others, in her late forties, dressed very well wearing quite expensive jewelry. She was also, clearly, a killer—a very experienced prosecutor. Everything about her—her tone of voice, the way she asked questions—was sharper and much more blunt. She never smiled and was stingy with compliments. She got right to the point, no soft start, no icebreakers. She started driving the conversation. I really started to feel...not questioned, but interrogated.

I later learned that Jeannie Rhee was one of the top prosecutors on Mueller's team and an exceptionally skilled and talented attorney.

Rhee was the child of Korean immigrants (and I believe an immigrant herself). She had been high school valedictorian and attended both Yale University and Yale Law School. She had been an assistant US attorney in DC and served as deputy assistant attorney general and had provided counsel to the former Attorney General Eric Holder during the Obama administration. She had been a partner at Wilmer Cutler Pickering Hale and Dorr, where Robert Mueller also practiced.

Rhee handled the case against George Papadopoulos and against Michael Cohen. Previously, Rhee represented Hillary Clinton during the 2015 lawsuit regarding her private emails and the Clinton Foundation in a 2015 racketeering case. I admit that it still strikes me as very odd that someone who worked for the Clinton Foundation and defended Hillary Clinton in an extremely high-profile case regarding her private emails— all matters that Trump was relentlessly critical of during the campaign and since the election—was chosen as one of the chief prosecutors in the Russia Probe of Trump and his associates.

Rhee was there to ratchet up the tension and to delve more deeply into my life and what I knew. It was unsettling. It was as if I knew I was about to have a root canal, but I wasn't told which tooth. Rhee was the sound of the drill turning on... From that moment I knew that this wasn't just about the Trump licensing deal; everything from my past and the past of my parents and grandparents was on the table. I knew I had to dial back deeper.

The Baddest Cop

MUELLER'S TEAM MADE A big show of the many thick binders they had assembled that they placed on the table before me. The amount of information they had amassed about me was impressive—and intimidating. But I knew better than to show fear.

Looking back, I now realized they were masterful at playing "good cop, bad cop" with me—and Jeannie Rhee was, unquestionably, the baddest cop in the room.

Rhee continued to probe my Russian contacts and connections. I began to realize that perhaps they saw me as the perfect conduit between Trump and Russia and as a potential link in a chain that would prove Russian collusion. They clearly had already written their script and what part they wanted me to play. In me, they clearly thought that they had caught some kind of "big fish" in their net.

I understood that I needed to make clear immediately that they had the wrong person.

When Rhee stated that I came from a well-connected Russian family, I was at pains to explain to her again that we were Georgians, not Russians.

I tried my best to make clear that Georgia was an independent democratic republic that was an ally of the US and the natural foe of Russia, who had invaded Georgia in 2008. I realized I was becoming defensive—and I was no longer keeping my answers short—but what could I do? I had to stand up for myself and my native country.

Despite being of Georgian heritage, I am a lawful American citizen. Rhee must have known that, but perhaps calling me a Russian made me look like a potential suspect.

My Georgian heritage and my attempts to draw a clear distinction between being Georgian and being Russian didn't move the needle with Ms. Rhee at all. There were no cordialities, no forced smiles.

Rhee just pushed on, asking the same question a different way, exploring a different tack before circling back and then forward about my relationship with Michael Cohen.

Much to my surprise, she wasn't interested at all in the Batumi Trump Tower, just in Michael Cohen and Russia. I kept asking myself, *Am I being used to strenghten the collusion argument? Am I part of her hidden agenda?*

This, more than any of her other questions, worried me.

With my attorneys, we had gone over thousands of documents, texts, and emails, most concerning different licensing deals I worked on with the Trump Organization and Michael Cohen. But there were another at least three thousand documents we did not go through.

This was my nightmare coming true: they were looking for something for which I was unprepared.

I wondered if I should confer with my lawyers but decided that would only prolong this ordeal (one that my attorneys were billing me dearly for). I decided that my best course of action was to be myself and tell my truth.

At the same time, I was adamant that how I knew Michael Cohen had nothing to do with Russia.

However, as the interrogation progressed, Rhee continued to raise questions about Russia, or possible deals in Russia and about certain Russian individuals.

For example, the Trump Organization had been interested in doing a Trump Tower Moscow deal for many years leading up to and continuing during the campaign.

Trump's presidential campaign did not stop the Trump Organization from looking for new deals and new ideas for deals. For a businessman and a business organization, that is normal.

Now, it is true that there may be special rules about what a presidential candidate, or a president-elect, or even an elected president can or can't do in terms of their private business interests, but I was never made aware of any restrictions like that. Michael was always chasing deals. And I was, too. That is what you do in New York: chase and close deals.

I was one of the business individuals who proposed how a Trump Tower Moscow could happen. My proposal was never taken up. Nonetheless, it was clear that Mueller's team had retrieved my emails on the subject, including a letter to the then mayor of Moscow.

To Mueller's team, that made me a possible agent of Russia. Nothing could be further from the truth. What I wanted to make clear to the investigators was that for the last twenty-five years, my sole political agenda had been strengthening US–Georgia relations, which was contrary to what Russia wanted.

Still, the investigators had retrieved emails and texts, some of which I had made in jest, or were jokes—the kind of comment you might send a friend to tease them—but that I now realized were being taken dead seriously by Mueller's staff.

Rhee forced me to recollect and answer whether Cohen or Trump ever gave an indication that he was, in any way, influenced by the Russian government or Russian businesspeople connected to Putin. And let's face it: if you are succeeding in big business in Russia, it is because you are on Putin's good side.

Then there's was the matter of Dmitry Peskov, Putin's spokesperson.

During one of our meetings, Michael told me he was anxious because he was getting nowhere on a deal for a Moscow Tower and that he was just going to reach out to the Kremlin, to Peskov, for help. I told him that was stupid and that writing to Peskov directly was never going to help build a Trump Tower.

I told him, "Don't do it."

Cohen's response was, "Whatever." After that, I used to tease him about his good friend Peskov. And I did so in an email. Later I would read in the Mueller Report that Cohen did, in fact, attempt to email Peskov directly, and then, finally, was able to reach him through one of Peskov's assistants.

Now, as I sat in a windowless room with three agents from Muller's team questioning me, it no longer seemed so funny. I realized that everything I said, even in jest, was under intense scrutiny. And for any person, that is a scary thought.

Could There Be Kompromat?

BACK IN THE INTERROGATION room, I tried to explain to Mueller's team the importance I attached to Michael having a Georgian nanny. Rhee's response? "It's of no importance to us." But I told her that she was wrong. Georgian nannies know everything about everything. And when you know a Georgian nanny, you know everything you need to know about Georgia.

Mueller's teams started to dwell on my interactions with Michael Cohen. They were very interested about the period of time surrounding the release of the *Access Hollywood* tapes. At the time, it seemed like that tape, and others, if they existed, could sink Trump's presidential bid.

At the time I was only a green card holder, so I couldn't vote, but I admit I supported Trump. He had visited Georgia with me, which meant a lot to me. I felt he would be good for Georgia. And Michael had become my friend, and I imagined Trump becoming president would be a dream come true for him. I suppose I was wrong about that.

Around the time of the *Access Hollywood* tapes, I heard a rumor about tapes of Trump in Moscow. In a casual phone conversation with a friend of mine from Moscow, he mentioned he was at a party or dinner where some random person was "bragging about some tapes" of Trump in Moscow.

In Russia, when people talk about "tapes" existing, they are usually referring to kompromat—compromising tapes of misconduct, often of a sexual nature, that could possibly be used for leverage or blackmail. The KGB has a long history of using "sparrows," or what we call "honeypots"— that is, agents who lure foreigners into sexual entanglements. Over the years, corrupt Russian businessmen were also known to adopt these practices.

Trump had visited Moscow on several occasions beginning in 1987 when I first saw him there, and more recently in 2013 when the Miss Universe pageant was held there.

However, in this case, I didn't believe for a second that the bragging should be taken seriously, or even that there were any tapes—because honestly, it was hard for me to imagine Trump putting himself in such a position in a foreign land. But given that the *Access Hollywood* tapes had just been released, the rumor of such a tape concerned me. Even an unproven rumor can be a dangerous thing.

I was concerned about Trump's business reputation, which would directly impact the business dealings in which my partners and I had already invested substantial resources and funds.

I decided to text Michael about the rumor, assuming he already knew about it, basically conveying that there's nothing to the rumor, and it was just a stupid gossip. Our text exchange read as follows:

Rtskhiladze: Stopped flow of some tapes from Russia but not sure if there's anything else. Just so u know.

Cohen: Tapes of what? [I was surprised that based on his reply Michael wasn't aware of any rumors]

Rtskhiladze: Not sure of the content but person in Moscow was bragging [that he] had tapes from Russia trip. Will try to dial you tomorrow but wanted to be aware. I'm sure it's not a big deal but there are lots of stupid people.

Cohen: You have no idea.

Rtskhiladze: I do trust me!

And that, I thought, was that. I was badly mistaken.

—

MUELLER'S TEAM HAD RETRIEVED those texts between me and Michael and confronted me with them. To them, it seemed like I had a connection to the Moscow tapes—which I did not.

I gave Mueller's team a very logical, honest explanation of those conversations. Nonetheless, the questioning on the subject went on for some thirty-five minutes. Their questions went back and forth, repeating points and questions. It was confusing, and I don't get confused easily.

My lawyers kept giving me the message: "Short answer, short answer!" But I had to keep reiterating the truth. That was all I knew how to do.

At a certain point, Mueller's team said, "Okay, let's move on."

They still wanted to know who the friend in Moscow who first called me was (I eventually told them). They wanted to know about the person who claimed to have the tape. I told them that I didn't know, and as far as I knew, my friend didn't know that person. I also said that I had never followed up with my friend, and we didn't discuss it again.

Still, this one incident led to the Mueller team grilling me about all of my contacts in Russia.

I never imagined I would be called to account for every connection my father and grandfather had in Russia. I explained that this was not as extraordinary as it sounds. Back in the days of the Soviet Union, anyone who rose to prominence in any field had to be party members and would have to live in Moscow at some point. But Mueller's team went over this for what felt like four hundred hours.

And this wasn't even the grand jury. I began to understand how difficult that would be.

Our session ended shortly after. I had not realized how much pressure I was under. I was drained and went back to my hotel.

However, what I learned from the day's questioning was that Mueller and his investigators and his grand jury were not interested that much in the Trump Tower Batumi deal.

What they cared about were my Russian connections (and anything involving other Russians or Moscow), Michael Cohen, and Donald Trump. And any time any of those intersected.

My dream from the night before had come true. I should have listened to my dream, as Georgian tradition tells us to do.

I met again with my lawyers, telling them, "You guys missed the mark. The Special Counsel's office, which you said you were in regular contact with, was not interested in the Trump licensing deal for the tower in Georgia. It was all about making me into Michael Cohen's and Trump's Russian connection, the Moscow Tower, and tying me to the tape in the Steele Dossier. You did not adequately prepare me for that."

Lawyers being lawyers, they argued the merits of their position. They needed to prepare me for any eventuality, they said. As they explained to me, I was at great risk: I could start by being questioned by Mueller's staff and the grand jury as a person with information and leave as a target of the investigation.

Mueller's team could confront me with any of my past statements, emails, or texts. If I made statements in the room that conflicted with other information they had, I could be indicted for perjury or for making false statements. Those were the concerns for which they were protecting me by urging me to only give short answers.

When the FBI agents first visited me, I should have never agreed to talk to them without a lawyer present (and should the FBI visit you, you should learn from my mistake and not invite them into your home). Being honest and open is the best policy—except on those occasions when you should have a lawyer present.

3

My American Dream

Leaving Georgia

THE TBILISI TRAGEDY WAS a traumatic event that left all the Georgians of my generation anxious and uncertain about the future, resistant to authoritarian undemocratic government but also patriotic and resilient. I now realize that this experience made me and my friends, like George Ramishvili, absolutely determined to do everything in our power for the well-being of our homeland, Georgia.

After witnessing the Tbilisi massacre, I realized that as much as I loved Georgia, I was going to have to leave. If I wanted to be an artist, if I wanted to create, if I wanted to have freedom, that would not be possible as long as Georgia remained under Soviet rule. At that time, we weren't allowed to go to church (although we often did). You could get in trouble just for wishing someone a "Happy Easter," particularly if you were a Communist party member (which my dad was but not by choice). Nonetheless, we celebrated Easter every year.

I had many Jewish friends in Tbilisi who were not only prohibited to practice their religion, but were also discriminated against under Soviet rule, so my family and I celebrated the holidays together with our Jewish friends. Georgia has an eight-thousand-year history of friendship with the Jewish people (we believe our Kings were descended from King David) and that was not going to change no matter what the Soviet leadership wanted.

This is what being Georgian was. This is what being a Georgian still is. Georgians are democratic, humane, and free people at our core. It is in our DNA to be multinational, tolerant, and accepting of anyone and everyone regardless of their background, religion, or race. We love wine, songs, and dance. Our credo is freedom. However, once our freedom is suppressed, we fight back. For us it's all or nothing when it comes to freedom. These values are shared by Georgians and Americans.

America may be distant geographically from Georgia, but Georgia is more aligned with the United States than it is with our direct neighbors, Russia and Turkey. That is why I feel at home in America and why I feel such loyalty to the United States.

—

Soon after my discharge from the Soviet Army, my sister through her job invited me to play violin at a cultural event for about twenty American tourists who were ballet fans and had come to Georgia to see the land of the famous ballet master, George Balanchine, and of Vakhtang Chabukiani, one of the most influential male dancers whom some even credit with reinventing the male's role in ballet.

At the after-party, I met a very nice American woman, Adrian, from Cold Springs, New York, and another from Louisiana. I had no idea where those places were or what they looked like but I filed away the information in my head. They loved the way I played and encouraged me to continue my music education in the United States. I smiled but I was thinking that these nice women had no idea how difficult it was for a young Soviet to travel to the States.

Imagine my surprise when my newfound American friends sent me an invitation to visit them in the United States. Through my family contacts in Moscow, I submitted the invitation to the US Embassy to get permission, and a visa, to travel to the United States. I never imagined it would be approved.

Why I Will Never Be a Criminal

IN THE EARLY 1990S, most Americans assumed that to have a successful business in Russia, you needed to work with the Russian criminal world. I don't blame them because it is not easy to understand how the criminal underworld operates in Moscow.

However, I want to make it clear that I have made a point in all my business dealings and in all my adult life not to have anything to do with the criminal underworld in Russia or elsewhere.

The reason for this is not just the way I was brought up with my parents wanting me to be a concert violinist and a professional tennis player, for heaven's sake—my parents' influence is certainly the greatest reason—but it is also because of a specific experience I had, and a lesson I received, when I was little more than sixteen.

I was a student living in Moscow then. One of my newfound friends invited me and my friends from Moscow to a restaurant called Rus (Russia). It was on the outskirts of Moscow in a wooded area. He thought I would be impressed because it was a place that you had to know about and that not everyone had access to, so we arranged to go there.

We arrived at the restaurant and were having a drink there. As we waited, these tough-looking local guys dressed in tracksuits arrived at the restaurant. They looked out of place, more like small-time criminals looking for trouble.

They walked by our table. They overheard us speaking Georgian and stared at us and at the two women who were at the table with us, who were family friends. It was annoying.

One of them passed by and shoved my shoulder. I told him that we were there to have dinner with our friends and to leave us alone.

Of course, he took this as a provocation, and said, "Or what?"

"Or you will get hurt," I replied.

He laughed and said we can go outside now and see who kicks whose ass.

I told him I was going to have dinner with my friends but after I'd eaten I would meet him outside, if he was still there.

He told me he'd be waiting outside with his pals (his pals looked pretty big and ready to help him).

That did not make for a relaxed, fun dinner. The whole time I was thinking about what to do. And as we were sitting there, we kept hearing more and more motorcycles arriving.

It was becoming increasingly clear that once I went outside, I was done for. I didn't see a way out.

However, as we were sitting there, we suddenly heard a big commotion. The restaurant manager started chasing after the waiters, shouting at them to hurry up and clear the way to the table in the back. It was late and a lot of people had already left, but the ones who were still there, like us, were puzzled about what was happening. I overheard one of the waiters telling another in panic, "Puso is here, PUSO!"

Suddenly, the door opened and in came several big security guards surrounding a short, very skinny man with a dark complexion and a receding hairline. Although I'd never seen him before in person, I'd heard his name my whole life: Puso was the one-name nickname for Valeryan Diomidovich Kuchuloria, a much-feared man who was at that time the "supreme" Thief-in-Law, the boss of bosses in the criminal world. The Don of Dons, the Godfather, if you will.

I had heard about him from my dad. He had grown up in Tbilisi and was my father's next-door neighbor. He was just a year younger than my father but, at that young age, one year makes a big difference.

Back then, Puso was no criminal, and he was still pretty small. His father worked for the government and his family was well off. As my father told me many times, Puso's parents always dressed him like a prince: he had curly hair and a clean, pale face and would wear ruffled shirts and nice clothes. As you can well imagine, Puso was often the target of older, stronger bullies. My father was the one who stood up for him and defended him. Again and again. Something Puso never forgot.

Puso was not destined to be a criminal. The story is that he killed a man while defending a woman's honor. They sent him to prison and it was there that he began to climb the criminal ladder. He was not a typical one, but once he was on the path of criminals, his intelligence, strategic abilities, and ruthlessness insured his domination and rise until he was the head of the Thieves-in-Law. He had been in prison twice, about thirty years in total, but had been recently released (it was said thanks to a corrupt politician). As the chief of the Thieves-in-Law, he had absolute power among criminals to settle their disputes.

I decided the only way I was going to survive the night was if I appealed directly to him. But would he know who I was? And would he care?

He was sitting in a booth that was closed off and protected by several security guards.

I walked straight up to them. They looked at me like I was an insect they were about to swat away.

"I'd like to talk to Mr. Kuchuloria," I said. They first laughed and pushed me away. But they saw I wasn't going to quit. I took a big chance and said, "I'm like his godson, tell him I am Dato Rtskhiladze's son Giorgi."

One of the skinny guys went up to Puso and whispered to him. Shortly after, the corridor opened up and it was my turn to save my life and that of my friends.

I walked up to his table and he invited me to sit down facing him.

Puso had a great deal of charisma. He had a hardened face, a prominent Roman nose, and a bulging forehead. His face was creased and tough like leather. He was small but had the coiled intensity of a cobra about to strike. He was wearing an expensive outfit but had a number of tattoos on his hands.

"How is your father?" he asked in what was a surprisingly gentle tone for such a rough person.

"My father is well. Still working for the Institute."

"He was always very nice to me. I would like to see him once more, if I can. I would like to visit him when I'm in Tbilisi," he said.

I said nothing.

"So, now tell me," Puso said, "what brought you here, to my table, and what the hell are you doing out this late at a young age?!" He had this subtle but challenging tone in everything he said. He spoke in a very low voice but articulated every word, making it absolutely clear that every one of his words had meaning and weight.

As I mentioned, part of the role of the boss of the Thieves-in-Law was to mediate and settle disputes.

So, with enormous caution and respect, I explained to him what had occurred and that I was concerned that if I went outside the men there would probably beat me to death.

Puso didn't say anything. He called to his security guard and told him to bring the criminal in question before him.

The guy was brought in, and he was certainly surprised and scared to see me sitting there.

Puso asked him to tell his side of the story. The man laid out his version and said he had done nothing wrong. It was his right to take what he wanted. And those that did not show him the proper respect needed to pay the price.

When he finished, Puso send him back outside to wait, telling him he would render his decision shortly.

Once we were alone again, Puso turned to me and said, "I know he lied. He's a fucking cheap criminal and a bastard to boot and he will have to be punished for lying. If he had told me the truth I would've spared him from harm, but he lied and that's too bad for him."

There is no small irony that truth mattered among thieves, as it would matter throughout my life, as it would matter when speaking before the grand jury, under oath.

"Look at me, look me in the eye," Puso said. I saw a sudden shift in the tone that he so masterfully controlled. He had immense power, and when he spoke that way to you, it went straight to your depths.

"You will never again have anything to do with any criminal," Puso said to me. "Ever. If you see one, you will cross the street, leave the room, or get out of the restaurant. Even if you are in a situation where you need help, you will never ask for it from a criminal. Because once you do, your life is over. Once they have even the slightest piece of you, they will not think twice to take the whole and there will be nothing you can do about it.

"Remember what I just told you," Puso said, "because you'll never hear this again: never, ever cross the line, because there's no going back. Understood?"

I said I understood.

"Now, get the hell out. My guys will escort you and your friends to your car. And give my regards to your father. And tell him if I am ever in Tbilisi, I'd like to see him once more."

My new friends and I were escorted outside and went home safely.

I never saw him again, nor did my father. Puso died in 1988. And I have never, ever had any business dealing with any criminal. I have kept my word to Puso.

Our Generation

THE IMPACT OF STREET violence, crime, lawlessness, and drugs on our generation and our group of friends was extensive. Add in those who died during Soviet military service and the numbers climb even higher. I estimate I lost fifteen or so friends who never made it to adulthood.

In the 1990s, Georgia was living on a prayer, teetering on the brink of imminent collapse.

Things were so bad in Tbilisi that people were leaving their apartments to warm themselves at large communal bonfires that they fed with their belongings. There was no water or power for days, weeks, months.

Some of the greatest minds in Georgia, university professors, were out on the streets living like homeless people because they couldn't even afford a piece of sugar.

I had so few friends left that I occasionally went to the cemeteries just to talk to them. My father had no job. Nobody had jobs.

And we had criminal elements always looking to profit from our misfortunes. There were also bad actors from Chechnya and the Abkhaz region who infiltrated Georgia to do harm for their own criminal or national purposes.

During this period of lawlessness and danger, one could not rely on the security forces or even the police. Russia hoped Georgia would be brought to its knees and beg to return to be part of a new federation of Soviet States. However, every day Georgians resisted. Some even fought back.

Individual citizens created their own safety associations to protect their homes and those of their families and friends. To defend their homes, to prevent their friends loved ones from being robbed, or worse, being raped, they organized their own protective force. The purpose was to defend Tbilisi and Georgia, at least until such time as an independent and free Georgia returned to normalcy. Some of my close friends were part of this effort to protect Tbilisi and defend Georgia, and I was very proud of them for doing so.

Georgians saw this happen to our country and understood that it was not just our generation being destroyed but the generations to come. If we had been engaged in childish or meaningless pursuits before, we knew we had to grow up fast. We vowed to do whatever we could for Georgia. To protect and strengthen our homeland, a victim of the collapsed Soviet Empire. Georgia had never wanted to be part of the Soviet Union to begin with; we were forced into it by Lenin and our fellow Georgian, Stalin.

The Night That Changed My Life

MY MOTHER HAD BEEN working on getting my visa for my improbable trip to the United States. As she could get the approval at any moment, I was in Moscow with friends celebrating what was either a night out or a farewell party.

—

WITH ME WERE TWO of my best friends: George Kharabadze, a son of one of the elite Georgian actors, the great Gogi Kharabadze, and Gia "Chubik" Chubinishvili.

Chubik's grandmother was a remarkable woman whom I respected very much. Whispers had it that when she was eighteen years old she was recruited by Lavrentiy Beria, the founder of the KGB, to work for him. The stories she used to tell us were mind-blowing! Once Beria was arrested and killed, she, too, was arrested by the Khrushchev's gang and was sent to the Gulag for a decade.

After she returned, she was so resilient that she finished medical school and became a doctor. She was a very tough woman, God bless her soul. She used to make me breakfast when I stayed at Chubik's place. If I was lying I couldn't look her in the eyes. When she asked where Chubik and I were going out at night, I would crack under her questioning every time.

That night Chubik and I were having a feast of vodka and caviar. It was normal to have vodka in Moscow. It was cold there and the city was pretty grim, but I didn't mind; Moscow was at that time one of my favorite cities in the world (it still is).

While my friends and I were toasting to my possible departure, my mother, the creative and capable person that she was, had arranged everything. She called me on the phone, and I still remember her gentle voice like it was yesterday as she told me, "It's done, Gio. I got you a ticket and you're going to America tonight! I'm not letting you stay in Russia because Moscow is becoming too wild and dangerous."

I knew what my mother was saying was true. The Soviet Union was collapsing, and crime was rising like crazy. There was tremendous corruption. In everyday life, people smuggled to get goods. At the same time, the whole of Russia was being privatized and taken over by the early oligarchs who were equally ruthless in their acquisition of wealth and power. My mother's fear was that I would either be shot dead or forced to join the Russian criminal world that was on the rise in Moscow at the time.

I understood that if my mother, who loved me more than life itself, and whom I loved dearly, wanted me to leave the country so badly, it was for the best.

Who knew if I would ever get this opportunity again? And so that March night in 1991, I cast my fate to the wind and flew to the United States, slightly buzzed on Russian vodka and giant American dreams.

That night, March 19, 1991, was the night that changed my life forever, the night I left the USSR thinking I might never return. It was the last time I saw the Moscow that I knew and had grown to love—a Moscow that would disappear before I ever returned and be so transformed as to be barely recognizable.

I had no real destination. I didn't know one city from another. I was only twenty-one and had already downed a bottle of vodka with some of the same friends with whom I'd celebrated just a few years earlier.

—

At Moscow's Sheremetyevo International Airport, as I was about to pass by customs and security, I looked back to take one last look at my mother. I could see that she was trying to hold back tears.

The Russian customs official, a woman, asked how much American currency I had on me. I told her I had $1,000 (which was not easy to come by back then). She asked me to present the official document confirming that the money indeed belonged to me. I didn't have anything like that. I told her I wasn't aware I needed such a document.

"Either you show me the document or I'll have to confiscate the money," she said, "or you can keep the money and stay in the Soviet Union."

For a moment I hesitated, looking back at my mother one more time. I had to make a very quick decision. "How much am I allowed to take if I can't show you the document?" I asked.

Smirking, she said, "Fifty dollars."

How was I supposed to live in New York with fifty dollars? But I knew there was no going back. I handed $950 to the customs agent who then promptly waved me through. I imagine the $950 never made it to an official accounting and ended up instead in the lady's pocket.

Now, twenty-seven years later, as I look back, the only thing I can say is thank you, Mom, for your courage and bravery in sending your only son to a foreign land. The $1,000 she sent me off to NYC with (even if I only arrived with fifty) was a good investment for our future, mine and hers. Her American dream lives on in her US-born grandchildren.

4

The Questions Begin

Back in the Hotel Room

A s I sat in the DOJ's windowless room being grilled about the Trump Organization, the questions intensified. I was also keenly aware as the questioning dragged on of how much this was costing me in legal fees, to defend myself for having done no wrong.

Mueller's team was very interested in Felix Sater. What do I know about him? Where had I met him? How often had I met with him?

I told the investigators about the first and last time I saw Felix Sater, at my initial meeting with Michael Cohen. There wasn't much to tell. But I could tell they didn't believe me. Which made me wonder: Was I forgetting something? But I knew I would have remembered if I'd seen Felix Sater again.

—

WHAT I WANTED MUELLER'S team to understand was that all I ever wanted was to do great things for Georgia. I had proposed a series of business opportunities to Donald Trump, Michael, and the Trump Organization—and not only had nothing come of them, but my partners and I went to great expense and suffered great losses because these deals were scuttled. I had become friendly with Michael Cohen and we had exchanged text messages, had rare dinners.

On occasion, as is often the case between friends, he'd asked me for help with innocuous things, like when his daughter wanted to get into a party thrown by Russian oligarch Roman Abramovich. Even though I was unable to help. Yet, here I was, having to defend myself about what, exactly? About "doing favors for Michael Cohen"?

Finally, after nearly four hours of interrogation, it was over and I was a free man again. I felt relieved that at least that part was behind me, although I had no idea what the prosecutors' impression of me was. Were they persuaded, or had I left them even more suspicious?

I decided to go back to the hotel and dive even deeper into my past and present on the wake of my grand jury appearance where I was going to be placed in the hot seat and under oath. Not an easy task, I assumed. The most worrisome thing about the grand jury is the severe consequences it could have if you wobble or blink. You could lose your freedom even if you're innocent, and I admit that was pretty scary to me.

Beyond the Small Door

WHEN I GOT TO my hotel room I started pacing back and forth. The idea of being under oath and interrogated by the Mueller team in front of the grand jury made me restless.

I obsessed about remembering nearly every event that transpired in my past, in Georgia, Russia. I was ready to scrutinize my family connections, business associations, and business partners. I had a lot of homework to do before the next morning.

The next morning, I was drained from examining my past and present, playing devil's advocate to find the potential traps Mueller's team could have set. I put my suit and tie on and, after having a gallon of coffee to stay awake, I went downstairs to face my next and biggest challenge: the grand jury proceedings.

I was waiting outside my hotel when a government car came for me. An SUV. This time the driver, the agent, was a man. He was cold, steely. No chitchat. He opened the door. I got in. And then he locked the doors.

We drove in silence, and I was brought in through the tunnel again. I was slated as first to appear before the grand jury that day (others—I didn't know who—were going to appear later that day).

This time everyone seemed more serious. They looked at me like someone who had done something wrong. Or at least that's the way it felt to me.

Other witnesses may have been seated elsewhere in the building. All I know is that I was taken directly to the grand jury room on a path where we encountered no one else.

They led us to a room, but it wasn't the grand jury room. It was a small waiting room. I sat there with my lawyers, also in silence. There was nothing more to say. And there was the not-so-paranoid concern that we were being listened to and watched. Nonetheless, my attorneys reminded me that they would be outside the grand jury room if I had any questions or needed a break. They were not allowed inside.

An agent appeared for me and then led me down a long corridor. We were walking and walking until we came to a secure mirrored little door that I thought would lead to another corridor.

Instead I opened the door and suddenly found myself in front of some twenty-five people in a somewhat shabby, rundown auditorium (that strangely enough reminded me of the former Soviet Union).

Nervous, Not Intimidated

PASSING THROUGH THE DOOR that the FBI agent opened for me, I found myself suddenly in the grand jury room. There was no common denominator to the jurors: they were old and youngish, well dressed and not, of a variety of races and ethnicities—a collection of reasonably average United States citizens.

I was led to a seat and before I really got my bearings, I was asked to raise my hand and was sworn in to tell the truth.

And then the questioning began…

Standing before me was Jeannie Rhee, the same prosecutor from the day before. Her questions were numerous and they came at me rapidly.

There were way more questions than I expected. And her questions seemed trying to make a point for which I was not prepared: the possibility that I was a conduit between Russia and Trump.

The prosecutors were aggressive, at one minute telling me, "You understand you're under oath here, to tell the truth and only the truth and everything you say will be recorded." They told me that "anything you say you can't recollect or that's not accurate can be used against you," and that "perjury is a serious crime for which you can be charged and prosecuted, and for which there is sure to be jail time."

I am not someone who is intimidated easily. However, I have to confess that just hearing that made me understandably anxious. I knew I had done nothing wrong. And I fully intended to tell the truth.

So, you may wonder, what was I worried about? Unless you've had the experience, it's hard to understand. But realizing that you are talking about events and conversations that took place over more than a decade, and that you could have forgotten something or recalled something inaccurately—all completely human foibles and faults—for which you might be charged with a crime and go to prison, seemed, at that moment, an imminent danger.

I don't falter under pressure. But I was definitely sitting in the hot seat. The full weight and importance of the Mueller hearings hit me. It wasn't just that US officials were investigating me, it was that they were doing so in a probe about the president of the United States.

As I was questioned before the grand jury, I was conscious that the assembled grand jury members had been listening to many people testify—people who were, at least in my opinion, far more connected to the probe than I. The fear crept in that every word I said was being compared with those of all the other witnesses, and that any discrepancy or misimpression I gave, or any fact I offered up that contradicted someone else's testimony—even if just my impression or recollection—could be reason to charge me with perjury. That was a scary thought.

The pressure was such that a little voice in my head started saying, "Maybe the jurors and the government attorneys know something I don't."

Otherwise, why are they all sitting here, and why are they spending the time to question me?

All this nervousness, doubt, concern, and anxiety took hold. At that point, I suddenly found myself stuttering. I was thinking over—really overthinking—each question.

When you are in the grand jury room and look out at all the persons gathered there, it no longer matters if the investigation is, as President Trump called it, "a witch hunt," or a legitimate inquiry into the wrongdoings of a president or his associates. It is suddenly very real. And very serious. All I could think about was that I was going to be questioned by a highly experienced investigative and prosecutorial team.

Depending on what they asked and what I answered, I was at risk of going from a peripheral figure to a target of the investigation. In that way, my fate was in their hands.

5

My America

Next Stop, New York

THE FLIGHT TO NEW York was very long and did little to improve my hangover. The plane made long stops in Ireland and Canada before arriving at New York's John F. Kennedy International Airport.

After deplaning, I followed my fellow passengers down the long corridors and stairs to the luggage carousel. And then I waited. And waited. And waited until I was the only person left. I approached a luggage handler working there, and in a slightly panicked voice said my luggage had not appeared. He directed me to what can only be described as a scene out of Kafka, the lost luggage room.

The person there did not seem to really care about my not having any of my belongings, or about my luggage or anything much at all. He told me to fill out several forms—which was no easy task as a non-native with limited skills in speaking English and even fewer in writing English.

The lost luggage clerk said my bags might be on the next flight, which arrived the next day. He suggested I check back then. I decided I wasn't going to leave the airport until I had my luggage.

I had only fifty dollars in my pocket and wasn't even sure where to go. I had a small gym bag as my carry-on that had very little in it that was of use. So, for the next several hours, I walked around the airport.

Although this was a decade before 9/11, it was around the time of the Gulf War, and Americans looked suspiciously at swarthy men with beard stubble carrying a black gym bag.

I purchased a pack of cigarettes and went and sat at a nearby bar where I ordered a beer and a hamburger. That cost me twenty dollars—and with only thirty dollars left, I began to freak out.

I left the bar and was wandering around trying to pick a place to sit and wait until the next flight arrived from Moscow. I must have looked suspicious because two NYC policemen started following me.

When I sat down in a metal chair near the exit, the officers came over and stood before me, saying, "ID, please."

I had no idea what ID meant. I just shrugged.

"Sir, do you have ID?"

Again, I shrugged and smiled like an idiot.

The second officer now asserted himself:

"Hey, do you have a passport?"

Passport was a word I understood so I showed them mine. The officers then asked to look inside my bag. Some people had gathered to watch. I could tell they were nervous as if there might be a bomb inside my bag.

When I pulled out my T-shirt and underwear, everyone started laughing, relieved. The officers ended up being nice people. When they heard my story about leaving Russia and losing my luggage, they actually bought me coffee and a piece of coffee cake. Thanks to those two officers, I've always had warm feelings for the NYPD.

They then showed me how to use a pay phone (I had never seen an American one before) and waited as I used it, in case I had any problem.

I knew only one person in the United States: Adrian, whom I had met in Georgia, and who had said in the way Americans do, "If you are ever in the United States, give me a call and come stay with me." I'm sure she never imagined that I would be calling.

I dialed her number as I'd been shown. When I heard Adrian's voice I started talking—I was so excited that I was shouting. I said I was at the airport with no money, no return ticket, hungry, and that she was the only person I knew in America.

I had not realized that I was talking to her answering machine.

The answering machine recorded my chaotic rant. When I didn't get a response, I looked at the officers.

I explained what had occurred and they then told me what had really happened. They advised me to call back and leave the phone number of the pay phone on her machine so she could call me back. They also told me that once I did that, I should never leave the site of that pay phone and not let anyone near it.

I still remember that desperate feeling I had hoping to hear back from Adrian. But I sat and waited. What choice did I have?

America Was Crazy

I HAD BEEN WAITING for several hours for Adrian's call. When the pay phone started ringing, I was so excited I barely knew what to do. I picked up—and it was her!

She sounded very concerned after hearing my message. She promised she'd send someone to pick me up, but I would have to wait another three hours before her friend could get to JFK from Cold Spring, New York. I had no idea where Cold Spring was.

She then said she could send me money in the meantime by Western Union.

I had no idea what Western Union was. I didn't know if it was a city or a place in New York City. But she explained that it was a store that was like a bank and that I could go there and show my passport and there would be money there for me.

I left the terminal and found a taxi driver. I explained that I had almost no money on me but that we were going to a Western Union and if he waited for me, and brought me back to JFK, I would be able to pay him then.

"I'll share the profits with you," I said.

He said, "You pay me two hundred dollars and we're good." I knew he was taking advantage of me but I felt that I had no choice, so I got in.

It's hard to describe what it felt like seeing Manhattan for the first time. As you arrive from Queens, the highway and the streets are unremarkable. The certainly do not look particularly rich or distinguished. It could be a number of places. But then suddenly you see that skyline, that famous array of high-rises and it's breathtaking. It's the New York of the countless movies I watched as a kid.

Once in Manhattan, I felt as though I knew every street—it all looked so familiar. We pulled up to a Western Union, I went inside, and they gave me $500. It was amazing! I'd never seen anything like that. America was a crazy, incredible country.

—

WHEN WE GOT BACK to the airport, I still had time to kill, so I went back to the eatery where the TV was on.

Suddenly I saw a familiar face on TV, the same American man I saw at the Moscow restaurant, Donald Trump. He was being interviewed by one of the news outlets in front of his Fifth Avenue Tower.

I smiled. Seeing Trump on TV in front of the massive skyscraper, as I sat there, without my luggage and with fewer than $300 in my pocket, gave me a strange boost of confidence. I was at the start of my American journey, in a city and a country where, if you looked at Donald Trump, anything seemed possible.

My Inspiration

SOON AFTER MY ARRIVAL to Adrian's house in Cold Spring, I took a train back to the city and got off at the stunning Grand Central Station that I only had seen in movies.

All I wanted to do was walk the streets of New York (which is still my favorite thing to do). It was mesmerizing to walk outside Grand Central and see the PanAm building straddling Park Avenue, and the Chrysler Building and the Empire State Building all close by. But as imposing as all of that was, as I started to walk downtown, the magic of the Twin Towers of the World Trade Center held me rapt.

So, I walked from Grand Central to the Twin Towers. It was a long but very educational walk. All my dreams and fears, worries and excitement, were on display. I was an emigrant with no right to work in a city where everyone looked beyond busy at work. I never before felt the way I felt that night; on one hand I thought I was walking in a dream and didn't want to wake up. New York City already felt like home although this was really the first time I had ever walked its streets.

At the same time, I was dumbfounded by all the stores and all the goods, consumer electronics, and clothing stores that were filled with merchandise, in an abundance I had not thought possible. Contrary to Soviet propaganda, the United States was indeed the land of plenty, and it made a good argument for the success of capitalism.

On the other hand, I was quickly aware that not everything we had been told in the Soviet Union about America was false. The number of homeless, many of whom were people of color, was very present on the streets of New York. One African American homeless man berated me at length, and when a woman walked by with her small white dog, he said, "You see that?! Even fucking white dogs are treated better than we are!"

I never forgot that.

—

I WALKED ALL THE way down to the Twin Towers, mesmerized. By the time I got up close to the buildings, it was nighttime—the streets surrounding the World Trade Center were silent and lonely.

I felt so small but so lucky. I suddenly wanted to share this incredible experience with my family and all my friends. (Unfortunately FaceTime wouldn't happen for another twenty years!)

Staring up at the Twin Towers, the mecca of money and power, gave me this electrifying energy of capitalism, which inspired me. The towers had captured my imagination, and I believed that I could do great things in business.

As I walked away, I looked back at them and I said to myself, this is where I'll return to inhale the power to act. And that is why almost a decade later on August 11, 2001, I took an office just six blocks away, on Hudson Street, that looked out on the Twin Towers.

Making Music

ADRIAN AND HER FRIENDS in Cold Spring Harbor loved my music. She had a friend, Michael Danieli, who lived in Millbrook, New York, a beautiful small town in Upstate New York. Michael had a first-class recording studio, Millbrook Sound Studios. One of Adrian's friends, Lynette, took me to meet Michael and visit his studio.

Michael's studio was a dream for any musician. Eddie Kramer, the legendary engineer who had worked with Jimi Hendrix, Kiss, and others, often worked there. Ace Freely, Eric Carr of Kiss, Tears for Fears, and other famous musicians did also.

I played some of my music for Michael. He loved it. In fact, he loved it so much that he let me stay in a hotel room he had built as part of the studio for bands recording there. And he let me record a whole album of my music with his amazing sound engineer Paul Orofino. Paul became a true friend—and I think sound engineers like Paul are definitely missing from today's music scene. Paul had the best drum room ever.

I was not getting paid at this point. On the other hand, I wasn't paying for anything either. But the truth was, even if I could have afforded it, not just anyone was given studio time at Millbrook. I was a nobody from Soviet Georgia recording there!

It was also through the Millbrook Studio that I met a New York City music promoter, Pat Reali. Pat, in turn, introduced me to another legendary record producer, Tony Visconti, and his wife, May Pang.

If that name sounds familiar, it should. May Pang was working as an assistant to John Lennon and Yoko Ono when Yoko ordered John, who had been unfaithful to her, to leave their house and for May to accompany him. So began John Lennon's "Lost Weekend," which lasted about eighteen months before John and May returned to New York and set up housekeeping there, only to have Yoko take John back and leave May out in the cold.

Since then, May had become a successful music manager. She had married musician and producer Tony Visconti (most famous for his work with David Bowie, T. Rex, the Moody Blues, and others). They had two beautiful children together and had lived in London before returning to the United States.

May and Tony invited me to stay at their house. I was fortunate to work with such a legendary record producer as Tony. He genuinely liked my music. We worked on my record in the basement of his house in New City, New York, and at his home studio at his Manhattan apartment. It was one of the most amazing experiences of my music career.

Tony and May even invited my parents to their house. My mother cooked a fantastic Georgian feast for Tony, May, and Tony's father, who loved the food. I have very warm, fond memories of that time and when I think of Tony.

Tony and I finished our album in 1996. In time, the album was released. *Billboard* gave it a rave review. The album was released overseas and did well enough that I was offered some paying gigs.

My great friend, Michael, unfortunately suffered from juvenile diabetes. He was a truly amazing human being. His diabetes had made him color-blind and sick as hell, and although he was doing dialysis every four hours, he never missed a beat.

There was no nightclub or great restaurant that didn't know Michael. Michael and Paul jumpstarted the careers of so many great musicians. Michael was generous beyond belief. He often let young talent record for free until they made enough money to repay him—and in many cases they never did. He didn't care. He was funny and always ready to help musicians in need, even when he was the one who needed help the most.

Unfortunately, Michael died from complications of a kidney transplant. He was a true American spirit and lives on through his son, who was only three months old when Michael died.

After his death, I helped organize a charity benefit in Michael's honor for the Juvenile Diabetes Foundation to raise money to find a cure.

At that time, Mary Tyler Moore, who also suffered from Type 1 Diabetes, had a horse farm in Millbrook. Moore was diagnosed in 1970 at age thirty-three and had been International Chairwoman of Juvenile Diabetes Research since 1984. I approached her to ask if she would chair our benefit. To my surprise and delight, she agreed.

It was an amazing evening. We raised a lot of money for Juvenile Diabetes. And I even got to perform with my band as the headliner, which was a thrill because I knew Michael's spirit was there, enjoying the music.

However, when Michael died, all the plans I had with him, whatever investments or projects we contemplated, died with him. I was, in many ways, back to zero.

The America I Fell in Love with

I WAS ONLY TWENTY-TWO years old when the Socialist paradise that was the Soviet Union collapsed. I had to grow up fast and face complex, adult decisions. Although I was thousands of miles away from home, I was blessed to experience real American compassion and generosity that exists even in small suburban communities such as Millbrook, New York, and Brookfield, Connecticut, where some of my new friends lived. Mark Tylor, Dr. Richard Bailly, Owen Robertson, and the late Hall Meeker showed me the true American spirit—they were humane and kind to me when they certainly didn't need to be.

In typical American fashion, they didn't do this to get praise from anyone, or for the media, or to make themselves feel better or bigger. In fact, they acted like it was a natural thing to do, no big deal. They used to tease me endlessly, calling me "a Goddamn Red Commie Bastard," which I laughed at along with them. They were conservatives, and they were liberals, and there was even Mark, whom they called a "hippy."

Mark was a plumber by profession who, when out of a job, worked his butt off at the Mobil gas station on Route 44 during the day. At night

Mark liked to go clubbing in Poughkeepsie (it took me four years to learn to spell the name of the town right), and he often brought me along. No big deal. But it meant a lot to me.

It was with this new group of friends that I first experienced something very American, and sincere. These were hardworking Americans who loved their country dearly, no party lines, no complaints, just hard work and rock 'n' roll.

The sense of freedom and pride in being American was evident in everything they said and did. It was so amazing for me to see that because in Georgia I grew up being forced to love the Soviet Union—which was a union in name only. These young Americans of my generation were so different from me. I was only in my early twenties, but I felt much, much older, drained from seeing so much pain, fear, and suffering, and from years of being unable to express my views and opinions, or practice my religion openly.

I was continuously dumbstruck that my newfound American friends in Upstate New York and Connecticut embraced me, a young guy with a strange first and last name, from the communist USSR, who had a thick accent, whose English was less than perfect, and who came from a place, Georgia, and a city, Tbilisi, that they never heard of, and had a heritage they knew nothing about.

I was accepted like an equal. I was welcomed like their best friend and treated like any other American, or better. And I have to add, only because other people always ask, I never heard a racist word from anyone. In fact, among our extended circle was an African American State Trooper who is the only person I ever heard telling jokes about black people. They were funny and we all laughed.

This is the America I came to know; this is the America I fell in love with, of which I am proud to have become a citizen.

However, the America I see now is so very different that it is painful to watch. The real question is what happened in the last twenty-seven years. How can Americans hate each other so much?

It can't all be blamed on Trump.

The Great Motivator

WHEN MICHAEL DIED, I had been living in the United States for three years. I was making a good living for someone my age, an immigrant no less. But I had no regular paycheck, no health care. I wasn't an American citizen.

I was young, and while what I was attempting to do always seemed fun to me, it was definitely stressful. But I ignored those aspects and accepted them as coming with the territory. Since coming to the US, I had also changed my diet drastically, from home-cooked, organic food in Georgia to fast food and processed food in the US and saw no harm in that.

When I started having digestive issues and pains in my stomach, I attributed it to stress and didn't think much more of it. However, the pain got worse to the point that I had no choice but to go see a doctor.

I didn't want to go to a doctor. That was not what I wanted to spend my money on. But I really had no choice. I had no health insurance nor did I even understand what that really meant. Remember, I came from the Soviet Union where everything was free, from health care to education (it wasn't always good but the price was right). Besides, many of my parents' best friends were doctors, so we never had to worry about medical care.

When I say everything was free in the Soviet Union, that's not really true because corruption was so pervasive that to get anything, even a good doctor's appointment, you needed to pass cash under the table. And if you were wondering how those doctors got their degrees, some bribed their way into medical school—so you never knew what you were getting.

Back to my pain. It was so constant that I assumed I had a badly inflamed ulcer and that the doctor would prescribe some medication and a different diet and I would be on my way.

That is not what the doctor did. Instead he said, "We need to do a few more tests."

I was sent to a specialist, who made me have several more tests, before I found myself sitting in a small office with an elderly man who took off his glasses and told me, "You have cancer."

If you have never had that experience, I certainly don't wish it on you. Once those words are said, it is very hard to hear anything else. You suddenly see your whole life in front of you, you feel the urgency of needing to reach out to your family and friends to say goodbye, but I was a million miles away from home in a foreign country all alone.

At twenty-four, I thought that God was treating me unfairly. I was too young to go. I suddenly felt like someone underwater who is quickly losing breath.

The doctor told me there was a grapefruit-sized tumor in my stomach that was probably the reason I was experiencing such pain.

Then the news got worse. The cancer had already spread. It was in my stomach, in my lungs and lymph nodes. It had even gone to my testicles.

—

I DON'T KNOW IF my Soviet Army training made a difference. Or whether the Georgian spirit of positivity and celebrating life helped. Or if my Georgian Orthodox Faith was what actually sustained me.

All I can say is what every person knows: cancer is a beast and you do whatever you can to get through the treatments. If and/or when you do, you come out of it more resilient and determined to live a better and more meaningful life.

I spent a year getting round after round of chemotherapy. My hair fell out. There was some doubt that I would ever be able to have children. And the treatments cost many thousands of dollars which, given that I had no insurance, I had to pay.

Aside from the treatment, I was determined to figure out my own winning strategy against cancer. My strategy became living in denial. I refused to accept that there was anything wrong with me. I was determined not to give in one inch. I tried never to change my routine, and I worked even harder during this time. I continued recording and never quit going out. I continued to play tennis (with the exception of when I was injected with a Platinum-based agent after which I had to remain in bed for days).

On one occasion, my being overactive almost cost me my life. My white blood cell count was so dangerously low that I fainted in front of a supermarket just before I got into my car. I'm not sure how, but after about thirty minutes, I gathered my strength and drove myself to the hospital emergency room. What happened next is very foggy in my memory, but I only woke up three days later. The sun was shining in my eyes, and it felt so amazing to be alive again.

My recovery continued from there, but it certainly made me more grateful to be alive and more conscious of what I wanted to accomplish.

I suppose that cancer was, in my case, a great motivator. I needed to make money and I did. I didn't waste a lot of time on small opportunities. Instead I thought big and planned how to execute those big ideas. With big ideas came big returns. And sometimes big problems.

My First Deal

WHEN THE SOVIETS LEFT Georgia, there was a vacuum for goods that had been denied the people, and a tremendous opportunity for American brands. As was the case with other former Soviet satellites, the first companies and industries competing for a toehold were hard goods, and often those fundamental necessities and vices which people could not live without: liquor, tobacco, cosmetics, household products, and the like.

American brands flooded Georgia, but they were still black market goods. No major American corporation trusted the Republic of Georgia or its economy enough at this point to open their own distribution centers.

This created a tremendous opportunity for those willing to take the risk of distributing American products in Georgia. I was determined to ride this wave.

Which is why, one day, I traveled to Rye Brook, New York, home to the corporate headquarters of Philip Morris.

Mind you, I had no appointment. I knew no one at Philip Morris. But I had a plan.

I made sure to be in Rye Brook just around lunch time, and I seated myself in a little deli across the street from Philip Morris. In no time, a gentleman asked to share my table as we both ate our lunches.

This fellow, who worked closely with Philip Morris exploring international markets—I believe his name was Norman Braverman from Upstate New York—and I got to talking. I told him about my loyalty to and passion for my homeland Georgia and how important it would be to bring Philip Morris there, officially, rather than on the black market.

He introduced me to someone who introduced me to someone who introduced me to someone and, in good time, my Georgian partners and I had secured the rights to distribute Philip Morris in the Georgian Republic.

We had promised we could deliver the product to Georgia and that we could sell it and pay Philip Morris. Philip Morris was skeptical—and for good reason. Georgia was still recovering from sixty years of Communism.

Not an Easy Business

WHAT WAS THE ONE thing that all people in Georgia, and other former Soviet countries, do that they can't live without—and for which they would pay to have an American brand? The answer that came to me was smoking.

Keep in mind that at this time Russia and the former Soviet satellites were all dead broke. This was not an easy business to be in, and there was great financial risk. If it was easy, others would have been doing it. The business was also an easy target for corruption of one kind or another.

My partners always took the high road and, as a result, left a lot of money on the table. We did not do so because we were saints or better than others, but because as businessmen we were taking the long view. We wanted to have legitimate businesses and business relations with major brands for the long haul.

I never forgot what my parents told me as a child: "In the end all you have is your good name." It is truer now than ever before.

Once we had established business relationships and had proven we could be trusted, our operations became more opportunistic and expanded into lucrative fields such as oil, gas, and sugar. However, due to government regulations, taxes and duties, and a host of many other reasons, profits tended to shrink if they left the countries where they were made.

So we began to invest in local businesses. As concerns Georgia, we did so out of love for our homeland and wanting to strengthen the infrastructure and grow the Georgian economy.

This was a business dream, and I took it one step at a time. And each step along the way seemed incredible to me and not possible.

Frankly, I couldn't believe that I was sitting in a room with Philip Morris executives talking about a potential agreement with such an iconic American brand. It was surreal. And it was scary.

I was thinking; success making this deal may be my worst nightmare. How will we compete with the massive shadow of the black market and with organized crime backing the counterfeit and smuggled cigarettes? Smugglers and criminals didn't have to follow any of the regulations, customs requirements, foreign taxes, or import rules that a legitimate American brand would have to.

My friends Michael Daniele and Kevin Brenner (the man who taught me how to read American contracts) helped me structure a business deal that Philip Morris found attractive. Six months after I sat in the coffee shop across the street from Philip Morris headquarters, I had a deal that said my partners and I were official distributors of a giant US corporation.

While having the deal was great, the reality was that the infrastructure, logistics, sales, and marketing for the business had to be built from scratch. This was at a time of flourishing organized crime, government corruption, and crooked customs at the borders. Still, I knew that demand for the genuine American product would be high if only we could put the infrastructure in place to distribute our product. This was a very tall order.

Even the banking was a problem. The unreliability of the banking system in Georgia and the former Soviet satellite nations meant that we needed to keep large amounts of cash in guarded warehouses—although, in the end, not a dollar was lost or stolen. In time, we discovered that the most powerful strategy was to make partners and allies of our competition. We offered illegal smugglers and distributors the opportunity to become legitimate vendors. Sometimes that meant they earned less, but they did so to live longer and enjoy being able to tell their families what they actually did.

We were making up the business as we went along. My local partners like Mamuka Mikashavidze would have to fly the cigarettes to Amsterdam, and from there to Georgia.

This is not as easy as it sounds as the airport in Tbilisi occasionally had power failures that took out all the landing lights. But we found a way: whenever the plane was landing in Tbilisi at night, my partners had the runway lit with fire torches. Sounds insane—and it was. I wouldn't have believed it if I hadn't seen it with my own eyes.

—

THE EXPRESSION "DESPERATE TIMES call for desperate measures" was very true for our operation. However, we knew that with success in the Philip Morris deal, more would follow.

Still, it was a very challenging time: Michael Daniele died; I was battling cancer; and I was trying to make the Philip Morris deal work against all obstacles.

There were times when I thought, *What else can go wrong?*

The Missing Towers

THE TWIN TOWERS WERE the main reason I moved my business in 2001 to Tribeca in New York's financial district. I could see the towers right from my office window. Every evening, just before I left my office, I used to gaze at them. To me, there was something very soothing, familiar, powerful, and inspiring about looking at those buildings.

I signed the lease for the office on August 11, 2001, together with my good friend, Irakli Sanadze, and my dear friend and a fantastic lawyer,

George Nicholas. The office was new enough that I was still spellbound contemplating those towers every evening.

The night of September 10, I had been invited by friends to a Middle Eastern restaurant whose music was still playing in my head as I arrived at my office the morning of September 11. I had already developed a routine of walking to a neighborhood market on Hudson Street to have my morning coffee.

I was standing outside when the first plane struck the World Trade Center. As I try and recall those moments, it's as if all went silent. I stood there in disbelief as if my eyes were playing a trick on me. I was shocked and didn't know how to react. I was still standing there fifteen minutes later as we watched a second plane fly into the other tower.

As I started walking back to my office, a man ran out of the building saying, "It's terrorists. America is under attack."

Then the towers imploded, with the south tower collapsing, followed by the north tower some forty-five minutes later. My eyes were filled with tears and my heart with anger. I didn't know what to do to stop the madness unfolding in front of me. I had that same feeling I did on the April 9 Tragedy: helplessness and defeat.

Suddenly the streets were full of people rushing away from downtown, some of them dazed and covered in white dust looking like zombies from an apocalyptic movie. There was smoke and a terrible smell in the air. It sure looked like the end of the world.

I started walking slowly, then faster, and then much faster toward uptown. The smoke was chasing us. I made it to Fourteenth Street in the meatpacking district. I was absolutely shell-shocked, emotionally drained. I sat down in a chair outside a restaurant in the meatpacking district. All of downtown was engulfed in a massive cloud of smoke. I was literarily pinching myself trying to wake myself up from this epic nightmare. I was thinking that this just can't be happening in reality, the majestic towers I loved, the most stunning skyline of Manhattan, were gone. I was shocked and angry, and I couldn't comprehend what the hell had just happened.

That was the moment I became American. Although it would be another sixteen years before I was granted citizenship, that moment was when I pledged allegiance to the United States of America.

I sat there, sad, looking at my New York, suddenly very different, very vulnerable, a badly wounded giant. There was no question in my mind that the healing would take a long, long time, and that New York, the US, and the whole world would never be the same, ever!

At that moment, I looked to my right, and strange as this was, I saw Harrison Ford sitting not too far from me. No one paid him any mind. We all stayed there for a moment in silence.

For a moment, there was a genuine unity among everyone in New York City. We couldn't get out of New York so we camped out right above Canal Street (we weren't allowed to go below Canal). We were welcoming firefighters and volunteers as they arrived in rotating shifts to clear the massive amounts of debris at the site of the tragedy.

Suddenly, a very vulnerable and wounded New York became a symbol of World Unity. It was a beyond special feeling. Determination in the face of tragedy. Selflessness as we were surrounded by death and destruction.

We were together in the epicenter of the world. I remember sharing a meal with a homeless guy; we both had tears in our eyes. It really felt like the beginning of a very different America.

Today, almost twenty years later, I wonder what happened to that America.

Do we only unite if we are under threat? And if there's no external threat, do we have to create one internally?

I don't know the answer. But for those who blame our current divisions on Trump or on Russian meddling, I don't believe either could succeed if we were not already divided. There is no cure to be found in the Mueller Report or in impeachment, which will only create greater division among us.

In the days after 9/11, we saw the great love so many of us have for the United States—that is the feeling we need to return to if we are ever to heal as a nation.

6

The Wild, Wild, East

Subu

A T THE SAME TIME, in Tbilisi, my generation of Georgians were suffering. During the collapse of the Soviet Union, Georgia began to have a serious drug problem among Tbilisi's youth.

The failing Soviet system had bred economic and social stagnation in Georgia, but far worse was Georgia's deadly drug epidemic. This was a dark cloud that settled along with the uncertainty of the times.

To give a little context, Afghan's most profitable crops in those days were drugs: marijuana, hashish, and heroin. However, the Afghans, because of war and the country's extreme poverty (not to mention the rule of the Taliban), had trouble distributing their drugs. Instead they relied on their neighbors, the Azerbaijanis.

The Afghans sold their drugs to the Azerbaijanis and the Azerbaijanis sold it to Georgians, who drove trucks there, purchased the drugs, and then transported them to Georgia, to the Black Sea and from there to the Mediterranean for distribution to Europe and even the United States. Georgia, which had existed as a trafficking corridor on the Silk Road for centuries, became a player in the heroin trade. *Shavi* (black) was what they called the black tar heroin that poisoned our country.

After 2000, a new opiate arrived in Georgia called *Subu* (or *Subutex*) that spread so fast and so thoroughly that 5 percent of the population was thought to be addicted just to Subu. It was estimated at one point that there were a total of some 250,000 addicts in Georgia (out of a population of four million). Some lost their lives. Others had their lives ruined. It was a dark time for Georgia.

Eventually, doctors in Georgia figured out how to use Subutex like methadone to slowly wean addicts from heroin and subu. Today, Subutex is dispensed in very controlled situations like a medicine by a pharmacist. And since then, addiction and addicts have steadily decreased.

Georgia's Growing Pains

As TIME WENT ON, life in Georgia did not become less complicated.

In 1992, a year after declaring independence from the USSR, there was a coup against our first democratically elected president, Zviad Gamsakhurdia (the same Zviad who was arrested along with my uncle Victor for demanding Georgian independence).

What happened was that on September 2, 1991, there was a large protest against the government calling on it to rejoin a federation of nations as part of Russia. Whether the protesters were truly Georgians opposed to independence or were Russian agents, no one knows. However, in response to the protests, Gamsakhurdia had several opposition leaders arrested and their offices raided while pro-opposition newspapers were closed.

The National Guard of Georgia, in essence the country's militia, split into two camps: one pro-Gamsakhurdia, the other against. Other paramilitary organizations also took sides.

Protests intensified. On September 22, several protesters were killed. Two days later the government declared a state of emergency in Tbilisi. More clashes occurred between supporters and the opposition. By late October, most of the opposition had been arrested. However, opposition military forces, led by National Guard leader Tengiz Kitovani, withdrew to just outside Tbilisi and held their position there.

On December 20, 1991, Kitovani's forces returned to Tbilisi in a full-on assault against Gamsakhurdia. Barricades were mounted in Tbilisi. The Parliament Building where Gamsakhurdia and his supporters were headquartered came under attack. The opposition forces took control of much of Tbilisi and stamped out pro-Gamsakurdia supporters forcefully and violently, shooting into crowds and wounding several supporters.

On January 6, 1993, Gamsakhurdia and members of his government were forced to flee, first to Armenia, then to Chechnya, where he established a government-in-exile.

Rustaveli Avenue, the street where my home was, had been reduced to rubble. A total of some 110 people were murdered.

After the coup, the military established its own government led by Tengiz Kitovani, militia leader Jaba Ioseliani, and Tengiz Sigua, who had been a minister in Gamsakhuria's government but had split from him and joined the opposition. (Sigua was a close friend of my parents and had worked with them for over twenty years.)

This triumvirate ruled briefly before they ceded leadership to Eduard Schevardnadze, the Georgian-born former foreign minister of the Soviet Union and former chairman of Georgia's Communist Party who returned to Tbilisi in March 1992. Schevardnadze soon held elections at which he was elected chairman of the Parliament and head of state.

Gamsakhuria's supporters, called "Zviadists," continued to protest their leader's ouster. In the countryside outside Tbilisi, Zviadist followers grew. One of Georgia's southern autonomous regions, Adjara, closed itself off from both sides, establishing its own regime. At the same time, Russia, seeing that Georgia was weak and distracted, agitated to rouse pro-Russian militias in South Ossetia and Abkhaz, regions that Russia would soon invade and that Russia continues to control to this day, in violation of Georgian sovereignty and international law.

Gamsakhurdia allied himself with Loti Kobalia's militia forces, who were instrumental in taking control of Abkhaz. Gamsakhurdia traveled to the western city of Zugidi, where he held a large rally for his supporters. Gamsakhurdia extended his control in the region.

At the same time, popular support for Schevardnadze was falling. Schevardnadze asked Russia for help. Russian forces launched an attack on Kabalia's forces and sought to secure Georgia's railroads and ports. In return, Georgia had to agree to the establishment of Russian military installations within Georgia.

On November 4, as Russian forces entered Zugidi, Gamsakhurdia escaped with his supporters to the forests. At the end of December, it was reported that Gamsakhurdia had died. The official reports were that he had committed suicide rather than surrender. Whether this is true or not, the exact cause of his death has never been confirmed. Over time other Zviadist leaders were either captured or murdered.

This period of turmoil destabilized all of Georgia. It was only with the election of Mikheil Saakashvili in 2004 that stability returned to Georgia. Saakashvili rehabilitated Gamsakhurdia and granted pardons for several of his followers to put an end to "political disunity."

These were traumatic years for Georgia. It is no surprise that people retreated into drugs and alcohol and that depression was rampant. Every person sought their own way to cope.

I was fortunate that I had music to escape into. Making music, creating music, can be such a life-affirming, positive act. It saved me at the time.

I was also grateful that I had decided to leave Georgia for the United States. From the US, I could be productive, sending money and supplies back to Georgia and continuing to find ways to support Georgian culture, the Georgian economy, and Georgia as a nation.

Fighting Depression

BEING IN THE UNITED States and hearing about the ongoing tragedies occurring in Georgia, I was depressed—and I had never been depressed in my life.

Luckily, my friends Michael and Kevin as well as my good friend Karin Brown (daughter of the great Judge Brown, who was district attorney of Queens for three decades) recognized what I was going though and urgently took me to a psychotherapist in Brookfield, Connecticut, Dr. Borelli.

Dr. Borelli was a nice man who was calm and diligent. I didn't need to tell him the story of my life for him to see that I was in distress. He was experienced and expert enough in psychopharmacology to prescribe me medications which, at first, relieved some of my symptoms of anxiety.

Within ten days I couldn't recognize myself. While physically I was here, my head was deep in the clouds. I realized that, for me, pills were not going to help. I would have to do the hard work of digging deep within my mind and soul to accept myself and make peace with my worries.

I tossed the three pills in the garbage and didn't look back.

I made the effort to rediscover myself. To look back at my heritage, my family, and friends. What I loved about them and what they loved about me. What I liked about myself and what I didn't. To forgive myself and admit that I was just a human being doing the best he could. It was a difficult undertaking, but I started the healing process.

Facing your own demons is no walk in the park, but that is what it took for me to free myself from being prisoner to my fears and anxieties.

To this day, I consider what I did the most important win in my life: securing my peace of mind. Depression and anxiety are part of our human brains, and we just have to learn how to deal with them when we hit our lows. I even wrote a song in which one of the lines goes like this: "Can I be stronger than my fears to make them fear me instead?" That is what it took for me to overcome depression and anxiety and fear them no more.

The Good Guys

I HAVE NEVER WORKED for anyone in my life. It's probably what best suits my personality: I always wanted to be my own boss and have my time be my own. So, while I was lucky enough to work with Tony Visconti at his studio, I was also working on deals with my partners in Georgia and Russia. While fighting cancer I found strength within myself and we succeeded in making the Philip Morris deal a reality. After that, I was determined to go after other big American brands.

I made a cold call to Procter & Gamble's headquarters. I told the woman answering the phone to put me through to the international department because I was looking for distribution of P&G overseas in the former Soviet countries.

The operator hesitated. I felt she was about to put me off, so I added, "We currently are the distributors of Philip Morris products there."

It worked! Suddenly she sounded much more enthusiastic, saying, "Please hold while I try to find the right person."

She came back on in a few seconds, saying no one was presently available but that she would take my information and someone would get back to me.

I quickly asked her name, which was Heather.

"Heather," I said, "I really hate seeing P&G product sold all over there, illegally, and you guys don't see a penny from it."

"Really? There is P&G product over there?" she said

"Of course," I said. "They are bootleg, counterfeit products that only devalue your brand. They look awful."

"Hang on," Heather said. "I think I got someone for you." And then the hard part came: "And what is your name, sir, how should I introduce you?"

"Call me George, George Skiladze," I said, offering the most American pronounceable version of my name.

In a few seconds, she came back on, saying, "Here you go, George, I have Brian on the phone for you."

Brian was a very helpful fellow. He put me in touch with the P&G representative in Brussels who was in charge of all their Eastern European operations. He, in turn, connected me with their rep in Turkey, who held responsibility for all territories east of Turkey. Soon enough we were distributing P&G product in Georgia, and it was very lucrative.

Everything I had told Heather and every subsequent P&G rep was true: there were bad counterfeit and black market products in Georgia and people were eager for the real thing. This was good for us, but also good for P&G.

—

We were the good guys; we wanted to play by the rules. I was becoming Americanized and my partners in Georgia like Mamuka Mikashavidze and others were eager to bring real American products to Central Asia and Russia.

The big US brands needed guys like us. It was up to us to navigate the challenges the domestic market posed. To translate demanding legal language in the American licensing deals into the local language in simple terms that could be understood and didn't scare away local business enterprises. We had to educate our former Soviet partners about American brand awareness and why it was the top priority for American brands to protect their trademarks.

To be associated with American brands such as Philip Morris or P&G, you needed to first protect their brands. Only then could you reap the financial benefits of representing them. This ran contrary to the Soviet mentality of a short-term hit-and-run quick profit.

Potential partners in Georgia and Russia were forever wanting to bend the rules—and this we couldn't allow because it would mean sacrificing the brand. And so we lost a lot of potential business.

Over and over again, we were told by our Russian or Georgian counterparts, "Oh, that will never fly here in the former Soviet market," while our American partners said, "Can't do that no matter how much you guys are willing to pay." It was our job to reconcile these two over their objections.

Sometimes you had to really scrutinize a deal to understand what was at stake. On several occasions we received massive orders for Philip Morris or P&G products—orders that would have made us millions. But when we considered the size of those orders, we realized these were products the buyer intended to illegally divert to other markets such as China and back to Eastern Europe.

Sometimes, we learned, the best decision is not to take the bird in the hand, but to wait for the right opportunity. That was a lesson I would long remember.

A Surprise Reunion in Kazakhstan

TURNING DOWN OPPORTUNITIES TO make tremendous sums in the short term is never easy. But we had to do so, over and over again.

One such instance occurred in Almaty, Kazakhstan, in 2004, where I was reunited for the first time in many years with my good friend George Ramishvili, the chairman of Silk Road Group.

I was in Kazakhstan working closely on important deals with the head of the local oil distribution company, KazTransOil, Oskar Smankulov. Smankulov was a well-educated, stand-up guy who was determined to transform the Kazakh oil industry.

My American partners and I were looking at the possibility of acquiring a large Canadian oil company, Hurricane (then a publicly traded company on the NYSE), which was operating in Kazakhstan in the Kumkoil region.

The Kumkoil is one of the largest oil fields in Kazakhstan and is known as the best (white) oil. I had a dialogue with Bear Stearns's oil and gas division out of Houston, Texas, to secure cofinancing of the purchase; the other half we were prepared to deploy out of Russia.

The oil prices were low then, around twenty-one to twenty-two dollars a barrel. The Kazakh economy, heavily dependent on oil, was suffering, and Hurricane and its Kazakh partners weren't getting along. As a result, Hurricane was having difficulty getting access to the pipeline to export its oil, which was affecting the price of their stock. Hurricane's stock price was quickly dropping, which was working hugely in our favor.

Before leaving for Kazakhstan, we had a meeting at the New York offices of the law firm Jones Days Law to discuss whether we should attempt a hostile takeover of Hurricane or first make a tender offer. We discovered that not only was Hurricane not interested in selling but, as allowed by Canadian Law, they had a poison pill provision to block any hostile takeover.

Accordingly, our best option was just to watch the Kazakh-Hurricane dispute get worse and hope that Hurricane would sell before their business bottomed out. Once we acquired Hurricane, our plan was to use our local contacts to gain better access to the pipeline and bring the price of oil back up. There was a massive amount of money at stake. So I flew to Kazakhstan.

As I was waiting in the lobby of the Hyatt Hotel in Almaty (Kazakhstan's largest city), who do I see but George Ramishvili. We were delighted to see each other after nearly twelve years.

George had found success in building a rail-based logistics and transportation business that could transport oil and oil products from Kazakhstan and Central Asia and bring it to the Black Sea port for its Western clients. Basically, George's company (which would become Silk Road) was the only alternative to the oil pipeline, and one of his Western clients was Hurricane—the very same oil company I was pursuing.

In short order, George and I realized that we were on opposite sides of the deal. George and his company were solving Hurricane's pipeline access problem by bypassing it and moving the oil by rail to the ports on the Black Sea. His success at doing so would help Hurricane mitigate the price drop and bolster the company's stock price.

George, of all people, was standing in the way of our getting Hurricane cheap (if at all). We both laughed. It was an odd situation to be in.

George and I both were savvy enough businessmen to understand that many less scrupulous people in our position would come to an arrangement that served all our interests, and that would end with our both taking control of Hurricane, producing great wealth for us in the short and the long term.

But we were both not that sort of businessmen. Our loyalties were not to each other or to ourselves but to our companies and our partners. Doing the right thing was our only option.

I remember George saying, "I have to stand by my clients, I cannot let them down," to which I replied, "I totally understand." George stood by his client and his partners and I walked away from the deal.

This is as true for George as it is for me, and for our entire generation of Georgians who all are dedicated to doing the right thing in business and in our lives.

Russia's Missed Opportunity

MY PARTNERS AND FRIENDS in Georgia proved to be very resilient. Instead of bringing American products to Georgians, they focused on how their distribution network itself could provide value.

George Ramishvili's Silk Road Group eventually became the most important logistics and transportation company in the Central Asian region in the late nineties and early 2000s. With over seven offices in Central Asia and the Caucasus, Silk Road was guaranteeing the safe transport and delivery of products across the Central Asian and Caspian corridor. For example, they were instrumental in delivering necessary supplies to American and NATO forces in Afghanistan (including, on occasion, jet fuel).

During this same time, the Russian government decided to politically weaponize their oil, gas, and natural resources. Russia would threaten cutting off pipelines and supplies of oil and natural gas and other critical resources to countries that stood up to Russia—or became too aligned with the West. If a former Soviet Satellite such as Poland or Ukraine dared to discuss EU membership or hold joint military and security exercises with NATO forces, Russia treated this as an offense and acted as though it were an existential threat. Coupled with their aggressive political moves on foreign nations, Russia drove a wedge between itself and Western-leaning countries such as Georgia.

This was personally difficult for me. I had many close friends in Russia as well, business interests there, and, frankly, I loved my Russia, my Moscow—the Moscow of my youth, the Moscow of my parents who both studied there. (My mother used to joke that as she completed her graduate degree in Moscow when she was eight months pregnant with me, I should have also gotten a degree.)

It was tough to watch Putin close that chapter for me. This new Russia, spouting a message of isolation and Russia First, held little appeal for me and my fellow Georgians.

This was all the more disappointing because Georgia has played a large role in what is thought of as Russian culture and history—in art, film, music, dance, and literature. Georgian poets crowd the Russian poetry books. Many Georgians served Russia loyally, going back to the time of Napoleon's defeat where Georgian military commander Pyotr Bagration led the Russian Army to avert the French invasion; to Stalin, who was instrumental in Hitler's defeat. Georgians made the Russia we know today. But Russia today is no friend to Georgia.

7

Doing Business in Russia

Being Opportunistic in the New Russia

OVER THE LAST THIRTY years, doing business in Russia has been very confusing, even as it has changed and evolved. In the beginning, following the fall of Communism and the breakup of the Soviet Union, business in Russia was uncharted territory. No one in Russia knew exactly what commerce really was—the only thing we all knew about commerce was that it had been punishable during the Soviet era. No one knew what would or would not be punishable now.

By contrast, those people who were crafty enough to do commerce even during the years of the Communist regime, either because they found ways around the system or because they were deeply connected to the government, were the first to profit in the New Russia. They had a head start, well-trained instincts, and no fear to act.

I was fortunate in that I spoke Russian and still had a dozen or so friends in Moscow, each of whom was eager to expand their business and to find a way to do business with the West and with Western brands (there were no reliable brands in the USSR in terms of quality goods and services).

In 1992, I returned to Georgia, and once there, I flew from Tbilisi to Moscow. In Moscow, I met with George Inasaridze, the son of my father's best friend. We met at a hotel where he told me about his plans of building an export-import company. It was music to my ears as I was thinking about doing exactly that.

At this time, not only was it hard to make money in Russia, it was hard to get your money out of Russia and into a foreign currency as well. Import and export provided an opportunity to do just that.

As I was now living in the United States and he had no access to the American market, George suggested we team up. We were both very well connected in Moscow. His contacts could get us export licenses for any important commodity and could send me whatever Americans needed from Russia or Georgia, such as vodka and caviar. I would, in turn, send him goods that Russians wanted or needed. Most American brands were in desperate demand in Russia and in the former USSR.

He wasn't talking about toothpaste. What he had in mind was exporting oil, gas, lumber—large-ticket items—and importing computers, cigarettes, and home and consumer products. A wide range of goods and services. It was the opportunity of a lifetime after seventy-five years of the Iron Curtain.

I trusted him. I joined George in his and his partners' efforts to do global business through their Swiss company, *Torola*, which means "bird" in Georgian. The slogan of the company was "the Shortcut to the East."

Doing business was not easy. Corruption was prevalent. Everyone was stealing. We wanted a brand identity that said we were different—and our differentiator was that we would do everything on a legitimate basis. That was really important. The confidence that we could, in fact, deliver was the key to everything. There were dozens of scam artists selling anything and everything American. We were legit.

At that time in Moscow, "Park Place" was the only American-style office building. It was on the outskirts of Moscow on the Leninsky Prospect (on the way to Moscow from the airport). It had been built by Westerners and had a pool, tennis courts, luxury supermarket, and its own garage. Torola had its headquarters there.

They were beautiful offices. Lovely. To this day, I still feel that was the best office I ever saw in Moscow. It was also valuable to have offices there because it seemed as if every foreign company wanting to do business in Russia had its offices there.

In the meantime, David Antelidze and Mamuka Mikashavidze, who were both associates of Torola in Georgia, had opened a bank called Tbilkombank. As we brought American brands to Georgia and sold American goods there and in Russia, the bank was established as the reliable place for foreign companies and for companies who wanted to do business with foreign companies. The bank proved itself trustworthy, reliable, and without corruption, and soon other business accounts followed. Suddenly this small bank in Georgia was an international bank with respected foreign investors.

—

LET ME EXPLAIN HOW business was done in Russia in the 1990s and in the early 2000s. Everyone assumes that to be successful in business in Russia, you would either need government protection or to be in business with the government—which, in many cases, proved true.

If you were taking over or running a major government industry or facility, one that perhaps had been government-owned and government-run for decades, then yes, it was essential to have friends in government.

Those were large businesses that made a handful of people very, very wealthy. However, it was only a few businesses or industries—mostly oil, gas, metals, lumber, petrochemicals, heavy equipment, etc. The government no longer ran most businesses in Russia because it was simply incapable of doing so. Instead, the majority of business operated in the so-called "Gray Market." So much so that, in a sense, the government was working for the gray market, not the other way around.

A great deal of business at that time was done with the help of intermediaries called "*Krisha*" in slang (or "roof" in translation).

Krisha could be criminals but more often were persons with powerful government contacts. They were fixers who charged a fee to keep your business trouble-free or to find you profitable deals.

The Krisha came to do some of the jobs we associate in the United States with lobbyists, the major difference being that in the US there are laws and regulations governing lobbyists, while in Russia no one was certain what the rules were. Businesses followed *nevpisanie zakoni* (unwritten rules) that everyone in the business community was aware of but no one had written down.

Russia was a case of street-smart, savvy, and fierce people who were well-connected and opportunistic. People who had been in commerce illegally during the era of the Soviet Union were already skilled operators and enjoyed well-established networks. They had a tremendous advantage during that era. They were *Kommersants* or *Deltsi*, in slang—profiteers in close alliance with racketeers and smugglers.

These were the guys operating large industrial facilities with a special gift for cutting corners to deliver large profits. They lived like kings and flaunted their excessive wealth unafraid because of their Krishas or personal friends high up in the government, particularly in the Russian IRS (in Russia, the OBXSS).

There were also black market guys called "*Speculanti.*" These were the ones who could get you whatever you wanted: tickets to the Bolshoi Ballet or, for that matter, a Cadillac, a Jeep, or a helicopter—pretty much anything your imagination would desire. These fixers made money because they could deliver a unique, foreign product in high demand, a high-luxury product that would make one look cool and elevate your social status. And if to accomplish that they brought black market goods onto the gray market, they took that risk.

The black market was, at that time, as big as the Russian economy. It was very big and very powerful and quite sophisticated. To operate in the black market, you needed to pay off everyone in the chain, from the policeman to the customs officer to the local businesses to the top of the government, depending on how big your operation was.

The money always had to go to the persons in the top of the corruption chain. Otherwise, the next morning or soon after you failed to pay, the police would come and confiscate everything. If convicted, one could go to jail for twenty-five years.

The Kommersants, at that time, were often Jewish-Russian immigrants who'd been allowed to leave the country and had, for the most part, settled in Israel. They knew the system and seized opportunities for channeling goods and services from Europe, Israel, and the US.

Over time their businesses became legal. Some grew what they did into companies. Many did not because they had no understanding of running large companies. Others showed a great talent from the beginning for complex financial dealings and for running a business. They became very rich.

As these individuals accumulated enormous amounts of wealth, they made a smooth and legitimate transition into Western-style business operations with Western investors and partners. However, they never, ever abandoned the Soviet mentality of keeping the top contacts engaged and happy.

They earned their wealth. To operate a large-scale gray market business in Russia without hiccups, you needed to organize all aspects of the business from logistics to sales as well as securing the financial transactions and fees required. Doing so required very efficient strategies, tactics, and execution. And we are not talking about the strategies and tactics you learn at Harvard Business School. We are talking about the negotiating skills you develop on the streets and behind closed doors in Moscow; without them, having even the best contract is meaningless.

Gray market goods were those that found their way to consumers but were often neither authorized to be sold in Russia nor supplied directly from the manufacturer. Such items were often goods that had been diverted from European or even Asian markets.

The gray market was a very complex web of business predicated on the goods and services in deficit working for one goal and one goal only: to squeeze the most profits while the business lasted, while never failing to deliver and never losing trust from customers. This was sort of a hidden Amazon for the Russian (former Soviet) consumer.

The gray or black market was the underpinning for the establishment of Russian capitalism. Those that succeeded in these markets did so because they were very good at it. Were there criminal entities involved? They certainly attempted to be involved in whatever they could. It was a free-for-all, and lots of bad people were looking to make money however they could. And there was always a need for enforcers, people to provide protection and to collect payments.

If all of this sounds intriguing, shady, or fascinating, it was all of that and then some. It's not like America hadn't seen any of these elements, but it was different because this was the product of a collapsed Communist system; people were hungry, angry, and many of them desperate to strike and escape with whatever they were able to snatch.

My partners and I understood well how difficult it was to do business and how nimble you had to be to avoid getting entangled in the web of corruption—because once you got in, there was no way out of it. That's why we developed the strategy of applying logic to the madness by focusing on foreign goods and resources that Russians wanted domestically. We became the gateway to these brands and goods.

At the time, this was an entirely new way of doing business. If you did it right, you were absolutely invaluable to the local businesses dreaming to get their hands on authentic foreign goods.

By acquiring rights to the Western goods in high demand, you could form a pretty efficient distribution structure where you had a vast network of retailers purchasing your goods and services without getting involved in any of the ground operations. We sold our goods through absolutely legitimate purchase and sales contracts as a foreign entity right at the pre-clearance warehouses.

As for goods we were exporting from Russia, we purchased them legitimately as a foreign company and sold them to our Western clients via a FOB mechanism, meaning that legitimate goods were delivered to the terminal in Europe or the United States and picked up by the buyer there. This eliminated the need for us to warehouse, transport, or transfer goods.

What we offered Russian companies was access to the Western market and reliable payments for domestic hard commodities. For large Western brands that had no on-the-ground operating interests in Russia, we offered sales and a new revenue stream. Our prices in Russia were unbeatable because we were buying original product directly from the source.

I spent a lot of time understanding how US businesses worked while my partners in Russia or Georgia understood the domestic market there as well as having a solid network in Switzerland. It was extremely rare at that time to have US and Swiss business networks, knowledge and command of the relevant foreign languages, and good legal counsel to structure contracts with Western companies.

We positioned ourselves as a Western company that understood local challenges and knew how to find solutions. The key ingredient we offered was providing a pathway for legitimate business. Doing so was, in and of itself, an insurance policy against local corruption. We no doubt could have had greater profits with less legitimate businesses, but the long-term risk was too high for us. We chose peace of mind over greed. However, what we did wasn't easy; you needed strategy and discipline; you had to manage the clash of ideas, ideals, and, from time to time, utterly different ideologies.

My associates—Mamuka Mikashavidze, David Antelidze, and Gia Chavdia—formed a very successful financial services company in Switzerland that became a go-to company for many of the Russian elite to access lucrative investments abroad as well as keep their money safe.

We engaged this Swiss company in financial transactions related to the distribution contracts with US brands. Our network was well organized and extensive, ranging from the US to Switzerland to Russia to Georgia, and was growing fast. It sure was an exciting time. We were on the rise with many new business ideas and projects. Even bigger financial success seemed inevitable. Sadly, the honeymoon ended when the Russian default rocked Russia.

I remember I was having dinner at our New York apartment with David Antelidze when he got a call. The voice on the other end said, "It's all over. We need to close the bank in Moscow." David slammed his cell phone on the floor and looked at me with devastation and defeat. Words weren't needed; I knew the tough times were here. I knew that a new, uncertain chapter in Russia's history was about to be written. Two years later, Putin came to power and that same chapter is still being written today.

Yeltsin and his government had collapsed. Just before the Russian default, our good friend, after attending one of the private dinners with Yeltsin, told us that Yeltsin walked in heavily buzzed and sat down. The first words he said were "My friends, Mother Russia is dying."

We knew things were getting out of control, but we never imagined the country would fail so spectacularly. David flew back to Moscow to salvage what he could.

Over the next several months, Mamuka Mikashavidze and I explored several different projects in Russia. It quickly became clear that conditions would need to stabilize further before we could do anything. Manufacturing facilities in Russia were bankrupt, and Russia's worst nightmare came true; oil, which buttressed the Soviet economy, had fallen to eighteen dollars a barrel. These were difficult circumstances for any hope of recovery.

Of course, the chaos and despair in Russia did create great opportunities for a whole new group of characters, such as Boris Berezovsky. Berezovsky had a degree in applied mathematics, studied engineering, and conducted research on control and optimization theory about which he published many books and articles. Berezovsky first found wealth in the Soviet auto industry. In time, as privatization occurred, Berezovsky became a Russian oil magnate. Along with other Russian oligarchs, he bankrolled Yeltsin's 1996 campaign for president. While Yeltsin was in office, he was called the Godfather of the Kremlin. However, once Putin assumed power, Berezovsky became a rival.

Back in early 2000, I met with Berezovsky in New York. He had already split from Putin and was living in London. One day his associate called my landline and asked that I see them for dinner, which was set in Manhattan at Nello's, one of my favorite restaurants on Madison and Sixty-Third.

Berezovsky arrived with his associates and light security. After an enormously expensive dinner where we enjoyed some very expensive wines, vintage Chateau Margeaux and Petrus, I'd hate to admit who paid the bill.

During the dinner, he asked me to move closer to his corner. Nearly whispering, he looked straight into my eyes and told me, "You need to meet my friend Bardi, he's from Tbilisi. We are not done with Russia. In no time I'll be back there. Vova won't last," he said, referring to Putin. Berezovsky had revenge in his eyes.

However, I knew about Bardi, and as much as I thought Putin needed to face a strong challenger, I didn't see Berezovsky or Bardi as a better alternative.

As Berezovsky spoke to me about his plans for a new revived Russia, I asked, "What about Georgia?"

Berezovsky answered, "I am working on that. Your motherland," he said, "is the key to Russia." At the time, Berezovsky was enmeshed in a lawsuit against Forbes for defamation. But once that was done (he was confident he would win), he told me he was going to Georgia.

It was a conversation that I will never forget. He was a beyond-powerful man of Russia's nineties who was obsessed with getting his nearly absolute power back.

After dinner, Berezovsky wanted to go to one of New York's hottest nightclubs, which a friend of mine then owned. So we went.

Berezovsky loved the club and the whole New York nightlife atmosphere. Excited, he talked to me loudly, shouting over the music blasting at the club. Berezovsky said he could use a partner like me in the US. He wanted to buy the Versace villa in Miami and build the most exceptional hotel and spa there.

Berezovsky was extremely smart, but I wasn't interested in partnering with someone of such a high profile. I hoped that once his initial excitement died down, he would forget about the Versace villa and me. Well, he didn't. He requested another meeting.

We went for dinner at a trendy Vietnamese restaurant where I told him, as much as I hated to disappoint him, given that I knew nothing about hotels or spas, I would have to pass on the opportunity. He nodded quietly, no words, just a thousand-mile stare. I couldn't tell whether he was thinking, *How dare he refuse me?* or if he was considering how to better ensnare me. Who knows? No more words were said.

Berezovsky departed the next day. I went to our house in Litchfield, Connecticut, and while flipping TV channels with my family, I suddenly saw his image displayed on ABC's *Nightline*, which was devoting a whole evening's program to him. Berezovsky was described as one of the most powerful personages in Russia, really the first true oligarch, with an extensive and powerful criminal network. He was characterized as one of Putin's most formidable opponents.

I was not the only businessperson at those dinners and evenings with Berezovsky, but suddenly I heard that people were saying that Berezovsky was my uncle or my godfather (he wasn't either), and that he and I went way, way back—when in fact our acquaintance was recent and rather limited.

Berezovsky was one of the last standing Russian oligarchs of the late nineties who possessed both immense wealth and major political power, and who was both super intelligent and merciless. Once he left Russia, he was determined to be accepted in the West and did all sorts of deals— with none of the negative press I received for just one real estate deal with developer Donald J. Trump. Go figure.

Berezovsky died under suspicious circumstances in London in 2013.

A Short Window

IN THE EARLY 1990S, most of my friends thought that we only had a short window of opportunity in Russia. The generally held belief was that, eventually, Communist hardliners would make a comeback and things in the Soviet Union would go right back to normal, under the Kremlin's control while a new evil infrastructure took hold, arranged and stratified to benefit whoever was then running the show.

During that initial time, the InterContinental Hotel in Moscow was the center of all the action. Foreign businessmen congregated in the lobby. The InterContinental was still off-limits to non-foreigners, but I understood it could be deal central for me. I just needed a way to get inside to have meetings in the lobby. The doormen had been warned not to let in anyone who wasn't truly a foreigner.

Now, as I mentioned earlier, I had served in the Soviet Internal Forces. And I knew that the Internal Security Services had offices in the same building as the InterContinental. And I still had friends who worked there.

What I did was have a friend meet me outside. He would handcuff me and then lead me inside, telling the doorman I had been detained for whatever reason and needed to be processed in their offices. Then, once in the elevator, the cuffs would be taken off, I would pay him twenty-five rubles for his trouble, and I would head to the InterContinental lobby.

This worked fine until the doorman recognized me and noticed that I was being detained a little too often. However, he understood that I must have friends in the security services, so he decided that I was okay and allowed me to bribe him directly for my entry. That was how you got your foot in the door there.

And let me tell you: it was worth it.

There were opportunities that came our way that turned out to be very lucrative. And others that were too good to be true. And some downright dangerous.

So, for example, I was sitting in the lobby with a German businessman. He was asking me in detail about doing business in Russia, the people I knew, my network, if I had to bribe anyone, and if so, how I was going about doing that.

My instincts have always served me well and they were screaming at me to tell him nothing about how we operated our business. I just shared general thoughts with him.

He smiled, saying, "It's like the ocean of opportunity." But, he said, "that ocean is shark-infested. And I'm afraid that if I dip my toe in the water, it will be bitten off!"

My English wasn't great, so we spoke Russian. After a while, he said, "You know what, I'm very interested in talking to you more." He claimed to have a huge business in Germany. He asked me if I could help him purchase substantial quantities of lumber and oil. At the same time, he wanted to provide agricultural and supermarket products for Russia. He asked me if I knew any lobbyists for large supermarket chains, by which he meant criminals providing protection for them.

After our meeting, I called my friend Sergei. I told him it sounded like a potentially great contact. But something about him bothered me. He claimed to be German and spoke Russian with a bad German accent but occasionally he used words that showed a much more sophisticated knowledge of Russian. I wasn't sure we could trust him. I wondered if he really was a German. Something didn't feel right.

Sergei told me his family was having a big gathering that night at their beautiful apartment in the heart of Moscow located on Ostrovsky Pereulok near Metro Krapotkinslaya, one of the oldest Metro stations. It is in the Khamovniki District, the "golden mile" that is Moscow's most expensive residential area.

Ela and Sergei Sergeivhich Kiparisovs, Sergei's parents, were part of Moscow's elite as highly respected scientists. His father was a principal of Lomonosov University. Really well connected, Sergei and his friends grew up all over the world. The rumor was always that his parents had friends who were major KGB officers.

Soon after the dinner started, the doorbell rang. Sergei's mother welcomed into the dining room a well-dressed man in his late forties whom I immediately recognized as the German I had met. He was seated at the other end of the table, but I turned away so he didn't see me.

Once he started speaking in fluent Russian, I was in complete shock that my suspicions were confirmed.

I quickly whispered into Sergei's ear, asking him who the man was. Sergei silently patted himself on the shoulders twice (which was the sign of someone being a ranking KGB officer, a "spook"). I became very concerned. My mind started racing immediately, circling back to my conversation with him. How much had I said to him? Did I tell him anything that could get me in trouble? He suddenly caught me looking at him. We nodded at each other quietly.

I told Sergei that I had an early flight to Tbilisi and I had to go. As I left, I saw the man I can only call "the German" watching me. I was afraid he would get up as well and race to confront me. But he didn't and I never saw him again. Much to my relief.

My partners and I dodged a bullet. He was a certain ticket to arrest, imprisonment, or being forced to do the security services' bidding.

Still, while at the InterContinental I did meet a real prospect, a very important executive from an oil company, which, in time, became Eni, the Italian oil conglomerate. We ended up doing a deal with him, and he became a very important client.

Now, you might wonder, what did my partners and I have to offer an experienced and sophisticated international oil conglomerate? Well, in essence, we could do what they could not. As an example, let's say you have a contract for oil, but that oil is in Siberia at Novorossiysk. You have to get that oil to the Black Sea. There is only one pipeline to there, and you have to know the head of Novorossiysk's oil terminal or your oil will never, ever end up there. The deal may be made in Moscow, but you need to go to Novorossiysk to make sure your oil gets transported.

The secret to success in these deals was in being able to manage the logistics down to every detail. Your Western client's tanker could not sit idle. You needed to set and keep a schedule so that the oil tanker berthed at the right moment, the oil was unloaded successfully, and the tanker then left for its destination—all with military precision. Keeping the Western client happy was way more important than the size of the profit.

We had to learn to do swap deals, as they were called. In order to get access to the pipeline, you needed to reserve time, and the pipeline was booked way in advance and was nearly impossible to access. If you needed access sooner, then you needed to swap dates with the company that had guaranteed access when you needed it.

Beyond that, the purchase and sale of oil requires substantial funds, borrowed, loaned, and repaid. We needed serious and reliable banking and credit facilities. We made it so that all payments at that time were done in Switzerland.

A relationship of trust with the Swiss bankers was developed that led to having several other foreign clients, as well as issuing letters of credit, so we didn't have to use our own money.

While this was going on, Moscow was in turmoil. Many of the families that had been powerful under the Soviet regime and their children, who were my contemporaries, found themselves unable to succeed in, much less cope with, the new environment. They couldn't adjust because they had once had everything they didn't have to do much for. Their parents were well connected, very powerful, and suddenly all of that was vaporized like it was never there. And there was a new playing field. No one needed them anymore.

In this lawless era, business was up for grabs. That was when the Russian Criminal Elements made their move.

When you're asking about how business was done in Russia, the simplest answer is that business was done in a way that made money. No one really knew what was or wasn't ethical. This was not New York, London, or Zurich, where rules had been established by years of doing business and a framework of laws and regulations. This was a newly born free society where the rules were made on the fly and nothing was guaranteed except that today's rules would change tomorrow without any advance warning. Steve Miller's "Take the Money and Run" would be an exact description of those times in Moscow.

Oddly, the old Soviet constitution was still in place, but no one knew what was Russian and what was Georgian. What was fair? What was ethical? In business, did the ends justify the means? No one knew, but everyone was trying to grab what they could while it was still there.

That is why you saw the rise of tough guys during the Yeltsin era. During the chaos of the Yeltsin years, the Thieves-in-Law threatened to take over all business in Russia.

The Thieves-in-Law

EARLIER I MENTIONED PUSO, one of the legendary bosses of the Thieves-in-Law, a real Soviet kingpin. Allow me to explain further. As you may know, while official Soviet society was under the rule of the Communist leaders, a parallel criminal society was forged inside the Soviet prisons: the Thieves-in-Law.

Thieves-in-Law was an elaborate code with its own rules, regulations, and hierarchy. There were criminal groups and bosses, and bosses of bosses. And then they too had bosses. The chain was long, but at the end it was all going to the top like a pyramid.

Otari Kvantrishvili was a Georgian organized crime boss who became the face of the Russian criminal world in the 1990s. Kvantrishvili was so powerful that he was chosen to mediate among warring criminals or rival gangs. His word was law.

He had many friends in high places, including some who were very popular with Yeltsin.

In the early 1990s, Kvantrishvili was in the process of becoming legitimate. A former champion wrestler, he had formed a political party, Athletes for Russia, and was considering running for office. He coached Dynamo, a wrestling team popular with the military. And he had become director of the Sports Academy, a company that was the agent for selling titanium, oil, cement, and other resources abroad that Boris Yeltsin himself had given freedom from taxes for a two-year period from 1993 to 1995.

When I went to Moscow in 1992, my friends met me and took me to his nightclub. It was called Manhattan Express. No one could get in, only the elite of that time.

This was the wildest nightclub I have ever seen in my life.

Otari Kvantrishvili was at this big table with a great amount of alcohol and an enormous amount of caviar. There was a group of around twenty people there, Russians, Georgians, Armenians, and some Russian Israelis. They were discussing how to divide up Moscow, who was going to get what.

Kvantrishvili was saying to one person, "You're going to get billboards, because that's good business." To another, "You're going to get real estate for this part of Moscow." Moscow was huge, a city of twelve million people, so there was plenty to go around. Although Kvantrishvili was powerful, I realized then that there was a lot of hype to his power as well; not everything they were planning was going to actually happen.

I was introduced to Kvantrishvili. I was surprised, but he knew all about me. "So you are in America, right?" he said. "That's good. We need one from America. That's great that a Georgian is actually in New York, because I can never fucking go there. They don't need me. I can never get out of here. So, maybe you should be my man in New York in the future."

Let's be clear: I had no intention of being his man in New York or anywhere else. I was going to have nothing to do with him. But that wasn't something I could say to his face in the moment. Not only because it was supposed to be an honor to be his man, but also because he didn't like being refused anything.

I didn't know what to do: how to respond, how to decline his invitation. As luck would have it, I never had to.

On April 5, 1994, at 5:45 p.m. following his well-established routine, Kvantrishvili left the Krasnopresnensky Baths, surrounded by his bodyguards. However, a sniper perched in a building two hundred yards away fired three shots that ended Kvantrishvili's life.

The gunman disappeared and no one ever definitively took credit for the murder.

Kvantrishvili's funeral three days later was held at one of Moscow's most famous cemeteries, Vagankovskoye. From accounts at the time, it seemed like all Moscow was in attendance. Actors, athletes, Olympians, and celebrities of all sorts.

There were more fancy foreign cars parked there than anyone had ever seen in all of Moscow.

Kvantrishvili's death caused huge chaos in Moscow. There was no one to control the people who were out of control; no one to mediate among the criminals. The government couldn't do it. And these guys were running businesses that were important to Russia.

So, business in Moscow changed again.

"Moscow Belongs to Us"

I WENT BACK TO Moscow in 1994, when I needed to leave the US in order to get my green card. There was one beautiful hotel overlooking the Kremlin, the Kempinski. This had become the center for Russian and foreign dealmaking. And it was also, not coincidentally, the center of all KGB activity and that of other spy agencies.

When you were sitting in the Kempinski and talking business, you knew that Russian and other foreign agents were listening. American agents, too. Because everyone knew that Russia was in play. Don't forget that Russia had tons of nuclear and chemical weapons. There were plenty of bad actors trying to get their hands on plutonium or other weapon systems. And because of these heightened concerns, there was a whole swath of deals and transactions and money made that the officials could no longer be bothered about.

And in this moment of opportunity in Russia, many became rich.

So, for example, when I visited Moscow in 1994, my friend Sergei Kiparisov and my other friend Sergei organized a dinner for me, Russian-style, taking over half a restaurant for us and our friends with a long table laden with caviar and bottles of vodka.

"Moscow belongs to us," Sergei bragged (as he occasionally did when the vodka was speaking). "We own Russia. We make so much money, I really don't know what to do with it." I was impressed. At this time, I was mostly doing music in New York but had done my first few deals in Georgia and Russia.

"I'm starting a pharmacy chain," Sergei explained. "Because we have the real estate already." He wanted me to be a partner. "Maybe you can help me with American pharmaceuticals and over-the-counter products." I told him it was a good idea but not for me. I didn't have those relationships and wouldn't know where to begin.

Sergei was fine with that. However, he asked me to follow him outside. There was something he wanted to show me.

I followed him out of the restaurant to the street where his driver/ security person was waiting beside a large black car, one of the first

Cadillac Escalades in Russia—because the bigger the person, the bigger the black car.

At this time in Russia, there were a lot of out-of-work former soldiers or KGB agents. Many got jobs as security people because they were licensed to carry guns and knew how to use them. They were also trained in threat assessment and improvising solutions when things went bad.

Sergei had two more cars also parked there. He asked me to get in the Escalade. When I did, I saw that the entire back seat was filled with cash. American dollars. There must have been $2 million there.

Sergei explained that the back seats of the other cars were also filled with cash. "We don't trust the banks," Sergei explained. What they did instead was bought these cars and filled them with cash, and then used them as their private safety deposit boxes, protected by their security men. And each time they made a lot of new money, they bought a new car. Sergei said he was now up to a fleet of a dozen cars.

"Instead of paying the bank's fees, I'd rather buy a new car. I can sell them later," Sergei said.

Was this really a secure way to hoard money? I can't say. But it is an example of the creative solutions people had to come up with to be successful in the New Russia.

People who were successful needed to figure out what to do with their money. Many of them bought real estate. The wealthiest among them began to convert their cash into tangible assets and bought real estate in London, and cars, and yachts. Instead of paying taxes, they were paying for protection for their money and assets.

Putin

THE FIRST TIME I heard of Putin was from Anatoly Aleksandrovich Sobchak. Sobchak was a brilliant man. He was born in Siberia but studied at Leningrad State University and attended law school at Stavropol before returning to Leningrad State University to complete his PhD and teach law, eventually becoming Head of the Department of Common Law in Socialist Economics.

In 1989, during Perestroika, after election laws were changed to allow independent candidates, he was elected to the Congress of People's Deputies of the Soviet Union, the highest state authority during the period of 1989 to 1991. During this time, as one of the few legislators with a deep background in law, he drafted much of Russia's new laws and legislation, including its new constitution. He also was one of the founders and a cochairman of the InterRegional Deputies Group, along with the famous dissident scientist Andrei Sakharov and Boris Yeltsin. Together they worked to remove the Communist party from the ruling structure of Russia.

Sobchak was also appointed Chairman of the Parliamentary Commission to investigate the April 9 tragedy in Tbilisi. In traveling to Tbilisi and in the process of his committee's investigation, he met several close family friends who even went to St. Petersburg to meet with him, which was a very big deal among our friends.

Georgia loved Sobchak because he criticized the Soviet forces for their behavior against the Georgian people. I still get this warm feeling when I say his name. I met his daughter, Ksenia, briefly at the Russian Easter event when I was in Moscow in 2005. She is a politician and has been a TV anchor and journalist. She is a smart and ambitious young woman who could well be the future of Russia.

It was during that time that I first heard of Putin. Turns out that when Sobchak was involved with Leningrad State University, he worked closely with then administrator of international affairs, a young man named Vladimir Putin.

Under Yeltsin, Sobchak was appointed to the Presidential Commission and was very involved in drafting a new constitution. Yeltsin also appointed a new head of the KGB: Putin.

In April 1990, Sobchak was elected to the St. Petersburg governing council, then became its leader, and then became St. Petersburg's first independently elected Mayor. Between 1991 and 1996, Sobchak transformed St. Petersburg into a cultural magnet for tourists and upgraded every aspect of the city. Putin was his deputy mayor.

Once out of power, Sobchak was indicted on charges of corruption relating to the privatization of apartments held by him and his family members. Rather than face imprisonment, Sobchak fled to Paris, where he lived for two years until 1999, when Putin assumed power and struck down the charges against Sobchak. It was a vivid display of their close and unbreakable bond.

Sobchak returned to Russia to enthusiastically support Putin. In 2000, in the midst of a Putin election campaign, he went to Kalingrad where he died suddenly in what remains to this day suspicious circumstances. Two of his aides later died as well, all of which indicates possible poisoning. Putin attended the funeral and stood by Sobchak's wife and daughters.

—

So, BACK TO PUTIN. When he was head of the KGB under Yeltsin, we understood that the madness in Russia had to end. Clinton missed a historic opportunity to rescue Russia and forge a lasting partnership which could've guided Russia and Russians to a somewhat balanced capitalism and democracy.

Instead, chaos reigned. People were starving and they were starving for leadership. As much as the average Russian loves alcohol and vodka, Yeltsin was an excessive example of that. Even for them, he was too much. Things had to change.

I will never forget a conversation I had with Sergei. Sergei had this beautiful, beautiful apartment in Moscow from his father. It was in a monumental Old Russian Soviet building, quite solemn, and they had completely renovated the interior.

Sergei told me, "They're bringing back Putin. He's going to rule the country." The reason was simple: "Because it's impossible. We can't do anything. Nothing's guaranteed, nothing is permanent, nothing is insured. Everything is up for grabs every hour, every day.

"It's really hard to live like that," Sergei said. "I don't trust anyone, and no one trusts me. This is terrible." The mayhem in Russia had been very good for him. He had profited enormously from the chaos. But even he'd had enough.

Putin was also very smart in recognizing that the vast majority of the Russian populace had become nostalgic for elements of their lives under the Soviet Union—when there was law and order.

Take Sergei, for example. He was in a rare position of privilege. He could leave Russia and fly to the United States and spend an evening in Atlantic City gambling away $100,000. But despite the tremendous freedom he already enjoyed, he was more comfortable with someone like Putin.

The reason, he said, was because Russian pride was gone. "Before Westerners have eaten Russia up, we need somebody like him."

This is what Americans and the rest of the Western world fail to understand: Putin didn't really impose himself on Russia. Russia demanded to have a Putin.

Putin understood that his number one job was to restore Russian pride—in other words, to Make Russia Great Again.

—

When Putin first came to power, Russian businesspeople were enthusiastic believing he would introduce a market economy. Through my business partner, Mamuka Mikashavidze, I met several Russian businessmen who worked closely with Putin's presidential campaign.

They believed in Putin. They were very smart: educated, cultured, and multilingual; they were master chess players and they thought the same of Putin. These were the caliber of people supporting Putin in the beginning.

They dressed in nice suits, nice ties, and they had great aspirations for the Russian economy. They saw America as a potential partner, not an enemy.

When I was in Moscow, they said to me, "Why don't you take an office where we are? It will be a great office for you."

"Where are you?" I said.

"We are at Number Three Red Square. Come here. We'll do business." I said sure, that would be a dream come true. The office looked out on the Red Square at the Kremlin across the street.

Having that address on a business card was something I never could have imagined. The building was next to the GUM department store.

Three Red Square was also former home to the offices of Putin's election campaign. Putin had smart people working for him, but he needed smarter people to run the Russian economy. So Putin started making millionaires and billionaires out of the businessmen he trusted. Or the ones he once trusted.

So, for example, Three Red Square was managed by Sergei Pugachev, who is now in exile. They used to call him "Putin's Banker." In fact, he was part of Yeltsin's inner circle and is sometimes credited with having suggested to Yeltsin that Putin succeed him.

At one point my partners and I wanted to buy the building, but to do so we needed to meet with Pugaschev. He was a Russian giant. A Rasputin with red hair and piercing eyes. We quickly understood that the deal was too risky and that the building, at some point, would revert to his ownership.

We decided against pursuing the deal. I was going back and forth from New York to Moscow working on a number of deals in Russia, especially deals in the energy sector—not in fossil fuels such as oil and gas. I had a bold plan to bring wind power, the energy of the future, to Russia.

But before that, I had a major deal fueled by that rarest of commodities, Star Power, powered by one of Hollywood's brightest lights, Jennifer Lopez.

J-Lo Goes Moscow

THE GEORGIAN BUSINESS COMMUNITY in the United States is not that big. We all know each other by name or by reputation. So, I was not that surprised when, in 2002, I received a call from Irakly "Ike" Kaveladze. He told me that he was working with the Crocus Group, a successful Russian Real Estate construction and development company. Its owner, Aras Agalarov, was in the States, Kaveladze said, and Agalarov would like to meet with me at their New Jersey offices.

Aras Agalarov was born in Baku, Azerbaijan, in 1955. Agalarov spent the greater part of his first thirty years in Baku, attending school and then working for Trade Union organizations, which led, in 1988, to a position at the All-Union Research Central Union of Trade Unions in Moscow. The following year he established Crocus International as a Soviet-American joint venture.

Emin Agalarov, Aras's son, was born in 1979 in Baku but raised in Moscow. He attended high school in Switzerland and college in New York. In 2001 he was named Commercial Director of the Crocus Group.

Crocus International began life as an importer of premium luxury goods to Russia, and they were still in this business when our paths crossed in 2002. They were in the process of building shopping malls outside Moscow and intending to expand from there.

The Alagarovs had heard that I had success in bringing American brands to Russia and the former Soviet Union, and suggested we might collaborate—first, I helped him bring the legendary American musician George Benson to the Grand Opening of the Crocus City Mall, and secondly, he suggested that Crocus had the best real estate and retail locations, and we would bring retail brands there. It seemed like we might work well together.

When I eventually made a deal with Jennifer Lopez to launch her own fashion and retail brand in the former Soviet Union, we made a deal with the Agalarovs to have the first J-Lo Store in their Moscow mall. The deal was successfully launched at the Agalarov's mall. We had hoped to bring the business and develop our own retail locations throughout Russia, Central Asia, and eventually Europe. Politics, however, got in the way.

The Ideologist

OUR NEW OFFICES ON Romanov Lane eventually became the home of the J-Lo distribution operation. And the showroom was absolutely stunning, amazing. We set up the management and the sales team there. Buyers from stores throughout Russia and other former Soviet states would come to us to place orders.

The Agalarovs had one J-Lo store in their mall and the other one in the center of Moscow, but they wanted to control all J-Lo retail and distribution locations. Our team preferred to sell to individual retailers wherever they were—and we wanted to be able to launch our own stores.

Our idea was to own the commercial real estate ourselves. The way we were going to make the real estate more desirable or higher value was by putting celebrity retail shops in them, of which J-Lo was to be the first. We were working with a number of local banks, including the bank of St. Petersburg, to secure the financing.

Once again, we were making great progress in establishing American brands in the former Soviet Union and establishing legitimate businesses without corruption or criminal influence.

Unfortunately, what we couldn't control were the politics—and, unfortunately, we found ourselves at the mercy of two competing national narratives and two large personalities: Saakashvili of Georgia and Putin of Russia.

As I mentioned earlier, Saakashvili became president of Georgia in 2004. I met Saakashvili in New York when he went there for the first time as president of Georgia. I believe my publicist, Melanie Bonvicino, and I were the first ones to put Saakashvili on American TV in a major interview with Charlie Rose, who was rocking the PBS channel then. Saakashvili brought a measure of stability to Georgia and immeasurable optimism to its citizens. By the time I ran into George again in 2004, he told me that there was a buoyant spirit in Tbilisi, and that Georgia was coming back stronger than ever. George believed that we would survive as a country and that a day would come soon when Georgians could be happy again. I chose to believe George.

Saakashvili spent his first few years rooting out corruption and cleaning house. Then, one day in 2006, he arrested five or six Russian spies. Without fully understanding that he was doing so, Saakashvili had sparked hostility between Russia and Georgia.

After the arrest of Russian spies, Putin said, "They're not spies. This is sabotage. Return our citizens, or I want every Georgian out of Russia. Arrest them, take them in, and deport them."

Suddenly, as Georgians, our whole operation in Russia came under scrutiny. Russia knew I had a company that had traded in oil and other commodities. Suddenly Russian authorities thought it strange that I was bringing an American star's fashion to Russia. Was I a Georgian-American spy?

One day, our offices were visited by one of our retailers. A very friendly, gentle guy who had seemed perfectly nice. Then he offered us a loan if we needed one.

"No, thanks," I said. "We're okay."

Then he said, "I know you also do business in renewable energy. There is an important professor here in Moscow that I know who is a genius in that, and he wants to meet you. You should meet him."

I said the professor should feel free to visit us here in the offices whenever he wished.

"He's not going to come here," he said, "but it would be actually good for you to meet him. I think it will be necessary for you to meet him." This was no longer a request. It was an order.

After he left, I called a friend, a Georgian lawyer who lived in Moscow. He recommended I go and said he would accompany me.

—

THE PROFESSOR'S OFFICES WERE located in a building that was directly behind the infamous Lubyanka Prison, the former KGB headquarters (where, among others, Raoul Wallenberg was held).

The professor met us in a windowless conference room. He was an interesting-looking person who wore thick glasses. He was not so much intimidating as a slightly nervous personality. He began talking in this very friendly tone, but I had the feeling that at any moment he could pounce.

He was asking me about my businesses and my connections to Moscow. I assumed he thought I was some sort of American agent. Putin was about to have an election and they were suspicious as to why I would want to bring an American business to Moscow at just that moment. I told them I felt the time was right because Russia was going to open up to the West even more, and we wanted to be the first.

This went on for a while. Then he said, "Listen. You know, I understand you're doing these things. But I know also this is not your real business. We're doing many things in Russia," he said. "We have this brand-new technology to turn natural gas into oil…" And then he added, "But you have to also know that your people will never win."

"My people?" I said. "You mean Americans?"

"Yes. You are American," he said. "You're not Georgian anymore. I see that even when you are advocating for Georgia you are doing it for America—not Russia. I spent a lot of time in Seattle. I was just a biologic institute worker, you know what I mean?"

"No," I said. "But why don't you tell me?"

This was taking a much darker turn than I expected. My lawyer was shaking.

"I'm an ideologist," the professor said. "That's what I do. My ideologies are like the Gospel. Everyone who is important in Russia reads my books about Russian ideology and about what Russia is. How important Russia is to the world. That we're sent by God."

This was strange. But not as surprising as it sounds. In the early years following Communism, there was a void that needed to be filled, an ideological one, and even a religious one. Many people, even Solzhenitsyn who returned to Russia, sought to infuse the national character with a Russian identity and a Russian religious one. The Russian government knew that they, too, would need an ideology about Russia—with a religious dimension—to capture the hearts and minds of the Russian people.

The professor said, "I have spoken to God. And the first words he spoke were in Russian. You must know that Russia is the center of the universe." I did not know if he was speaking metaphorically or literally. But there was great intensity and fervor to what he was saying.

"I'm going to give you my book, *My Conversation with the Almighty*," he said. "What I discuss in this book is followed by the people running the country. They all listen to me."

Then he became Dr. Evil again and said, "Your guys will never win. This election is going to be done right and proper." He wanted me to admit I was working for the Americans and against the Russians. It seemed he wanted to crack me. I wasn't sure anymore if I would ever be allowed to leave the room.

I decided right there and then that I would push back. That I would not be bullied. That I would stand up to him.

"You know who my grandfather was?" I said. "I actually carry his name, Giorgi. My grandfather was one of the best friends of Joseph Stalin. And Lavrentiy Beria. So don't tell me about my people and your people. There are no my people and your people.

"My grandfather was the pride of the Soviet Union that you and your people destroyed. You have taken what Stalin and Beria did and wiped your ass with them. So don't blame me for that." He was taken aback by that.

But if our whole conversation was some sort of test, then I felt that, at that moment, I had passed. After that, the professor turned nice again and we spent that next hour talking history, philosophy, and religion. He was extremely knowledgeable about the history of religions, about Russian history, and even Georgian history. We talked a good bit about Queen Tamar (a celebrated twelfth-century ruler of Georgia). He had an amazing mind, an extremely high IQ no doubt. And I must admit I enjoyed our conversation.

He gave me a copy of his book. I read it later. It was crazy talk about Russian superiority. But crazy like a fox: intellectual and spiritual, but his religion was Russia. And what he was telling me was that Putin's Russia wouldn't be like Yeltsin's. The days of alcoholic excess were over. From now on it would be focused ideology on restoring Russian pride and Russia as the world's superpower.

Our conversation ended with him telling me that he was all for business in Russia. And then, abruptly, he stood and said, "Chaika is here. I have to go."

Chaika was the attorney general of Russia, at that time one of the most feared men. And as we were leaving the building we saw him. That, too, was slightly intimidating.

It's the strangest thing, but when you have gone through something intense, and that is potentially dangerous, personally and professionally, and come out the other side unharmed, you feel incredibly well—giddy, almost. That is how I felt after leaving the ideologist. The air I breathed seemed somehow fresher, everything smelled better. I had a goofy smile on my face, and I had to say to myself, "Maybe life is not so bad, not so bad."

After that, things started to go well for me in Russia. A number of good things, seemingly unrelated, happened. I can only assume that it was no coincidence.

So, for example, positive articles about me appeared in the Russian press. On the front page, I was touted as an example of a Georgian who was bringing businesses to Russia, investing in Russia, and working with the Russians (as opposed to Georgia itself that was arresting innocent Russian citizens).

That lasted for a while. However, as the situation between Georgia and Russia got worse, so did my situation there. Every day there were reports of Georgians being made to leave Russia.

Putin himself came out and spoke out against Georgia and Georgians. And Putin seemed to have adopted the professor's ideology: the Georgians were becoming Americans, and thus were Russia's enemies.

Soon after, there was a radio report critiquing me and my business, not for bringing money into Russia but for taking money out of Russia (the radio report was based on an article by a journalist named Kashin who, three years later, would be beaten to near death).

The next day, no one showed up to work at our offices. I was sitting there wondering what to do, when *CRACK!* The door was busted down by three Russian security agents. They tossed my offices. I protested and one of them grabbed me by the neck and started strangling me.

They broke things and took papers and files away. My business visa was about to expire, and I doubted it would be renewed.

Soon after, I left Moscow.

8

Back in the Grand Jury Room

In the Room

THE MUELLER TEAM HAD a definite narrative they were hoping to have me affirm, and Prosecutor Rhee was aggressive in pursuing it. The Mueller Team's focus was almost entirely directed at establishing a connection between me and Russia. They wanted me to draw a line that extended from my Russian network to Trump. The more they brought up Russia, the more I talked about Georgia. It was like an arm-wrestling match.

I was informed that Michael Cohen had described me to Mueller as having deep ties to Russia.

It was clear that all they cared about was Russia. They wanted me to admit to being Trump's connection to Russian money, to the infamous kompromat video of Trump in Russia, and to have me confess that Russians I knew were using me to gain leverage against the president. It was preposterous and ridiculous. I made clear that I was no such thing, and I refused to let them make me out as such. I wasn't even a Russian. I was an American, and I was born in Georgia.

I wasn't afraid to talk about my contacts in Russia or my knowledge of Russia. When I did, I quickly realized based on their questions that none of the Mueller's prosecutors really knew much about Russia or understood how Russia really worked.

They never understood that to the Russians, I was always a Georgian. They would never treat me like a Russian national. I could do business there, but it was always as a Georgian. They would never let a Georgian American be the conduit between the Russian government and an American president.

Rhee continued to insist that I was connected to Russia. She told the grand jury that I came from "a prominent Russian family."

That was the moment when I decided I needed to reassert myself and take control of this narrative by saying, "No, that's absolutely incorrect."

That threw her completely off guard.

I explained that my family was not a prominent Russian family. My family is a Georgian family, and there's a big difference between Georgians and Russians.

She seemed nonplussed.

I again had to explain to everyone sitting there that the difference between being Georgian and being Russian is even more stark than the difference between being American and Russian.

Georgians have been suppressed, repressed, beaten down, and isolated by Russia for a long time. Since independence, every single day the borders of sovereign Georgia are encroached upon by Russia as they try to expand the contested Georgian territories they've occupied since 2008.

My family, my business partners, and I have defended Georgia's interests against Russia for years, and that's who I am. The only reason my family was in Russia in any way, shape, or form was because Georgians were under the thumb of the Soviet Union. But today Georgia is a sovereign nation. And to call me Russian is to absolutely misrepresent my heritage.

She pushed back, saying I had strong ties to Russia: My grandfather was a great hero in Russia, was he not? My father was a famous scientist who lived in Moscow, did he not? I had spent time in Moscow as a youth. Had even gone to school there. I spoke Russian. I was educated by Russians, and I served in the Russian military. So, in what way was it incorrect to say that my family was prominent in Russia, and connected in Russia?

We went back and forth on this for some forty minutes, by which time I was parched and thirsty. There wasn't even a glass of water at my table. I don't know if that was intentional to break me or make me rush my answers. But at that point, I said "I need to get up and have some water." And I made a kind of joke and said, "Everyone should have some water," which was a human moment with the jurors.

After I had my water and returned to my seat, the questioning resumed, this time with a focus on Michael Cohen, Donald Trump, and the Trump Tower Moscow deal.

9

Trump Invests in Georgia

Ivana Trump Hotel

IN 2008, A MONTH after the bloody Russian invasion of Georgia where the West stood silent as Russian tanks were butchering innocent Georgian lives, George Ramishvili, my good friend, and I founded Silk Road TransAtlantic Alliance (SRTA), a US company with a mission of strengthening US-Georgian relationships so that Georgia would be less vulnerable to another brutal Russian invasion.

Over the following years, SRTA was successful in launching Georgian entities for a number of iconic US brands including National Geographic, CNBC, and CNN. Bringing the Trump brand to Georgia was a brainchild of SRTA as well.

In 2009, Saaskashvili was still president of Georgia. He had made developing Batumi, a city on Georgia's Black Sea Coast, into the Monte-Carlo of Caucasus and Central Asia one of the signature projects of his administration.

Silk Road had acquired a property in Batumi, and George and I started thinking about a strategy for developing this magnificent site as a hotel or residences and how to market it internationally.

My good friend Camilla Olsson is a master in PR, connecting some of the most powerful people. When on the rare occasion there was someone I wanted to contact whom I didn't know, I asked Camilla, who was never more than one degree of separation from anyone.

For example, when I wanted to bring Roberto Cavalli to Georgia, Camilla organized a meeting in the middle of a New York winter storm. In no time, Roberto and I got along. I knew his creative and business-driven personality would be open to the idea of traveling to Georgia to add his magic touch to the Batumi development. He agreed. Soon after, Roberto came to Georgia on his private plane.

Camilla and I had met Ivana Trump, Donald's first wife (and mother of Don Jr., Eric, and Ivanka). I wondered if we might develop an Ivana Trump Hotel on the Batumi Riviera.

I asked Ivana if she would be interested in branding a hotel in her own name, if that wasn't a problem because she is a Trump.

Her answer: "Absolutely. It's very interesting."

First, I visited Ivana in her beautiful Manhattan townhouse. She was a gracious host, and served us an elegant high tea with a strong black tea and delicious sweets. She was there with her lawyer and we discussed a potential deal.

At the conclusion of our conversation, I invited her to Georgia so she could see the property, learn about Georgia. She accepted.

George Ramishvili and I hosted Ivana for three days in Georgia. Her trip was not without incident. To arrive in Georgia, Ivana flew first to Kiev, Ukraine, where her luggage was lost, including two (very expensive, as she described) chinchilla fur coats.

Ivana was upset. She is a wonderful woman, but you definitely don't want to be there when she's angry. She was very blunt: "If I can't get my chinchilla coats back ASAP, I am canceling my trip and going right back to New York." I told her that going back to NYC abruptly would've been very disrespectful to me, my partners, and to the president of Georgia (with whom a meeting was set up). She didn't seem to care about any of that. I was not sure whether she was testing me and my partners on how powerful we were or making a point that she's a tough customer to deal with in business, but whatever it was, she succeeded. We took her demands very seriously. I also liked her very much and hated to see her so deeply disappointed in my native country.

I can't tell you exactly what happened, but we called someone who called someone who spoke with the president of Georgia who in turn called someone in Ukraine who spoke to the president there, who called someone…and I don't know how, but Ivana's luggage and her two fur coats were found and sent to Georgia in time for our appointment with the president.

There is an old saying that no person is happier than one who has lost something and found it. With the return of her coats, Ivana was in a fantastic mood for the rest of the trip.

We had a number of important events organized for Ivana's visit. She met with President Saakashvili. We also took her to Batumi to see the site for the residential tower.

Ivana and I had a nice, quiet dinner the night before she departed. It was fascinating to hear Ivana talking about her experience working with her then-husband, Donald J. Trump, and how involved she was in his hotel and casino businesses. She even spoke of how supportive she was of Trump when it mattered the most. She also explained that she was very hands-on with their children, Donny Jr., Ivanka, and Eric. She often took them to the Czech Republic to show them life in the Eastern Bloc. She's a real character, tough but very glamorous.

She loved everything she saw of Georgia. Afterward, she said, "I would love to collaborate."

When I came back to New York, my partners and I were concerned that even though Ivana was an absolutely amazing person, smart and savvy, she didn't have enough experience building the sort of large-scale real estate projects that the Batumi Riviera site required. Although we never moved forward with Ivana, the time spent with her and her description of Donald Trump building his business (in which she definitely played an important role) led me to think of Donald Trump himself and consider having a Trump-branded property in Georgia.

In early 2010, George and I discussed various projects that we might work together on. "We're thinking about how best to develop the Riviera site in Batumi. We want to build a residential property but more like a high-end residential property." I started to think about whether there were US real estate and hospitality brands we could bring to Georgia for this project that would be meaningful.

We wanted to signal that Georgia was open to investment on the highest level, whether from Asia, the Middle East, Europe, and, of course, America. We wanted to increase tourism from foreigners outside of Russia and the former Soviet countries.

At the time there was an embargo with Russia—which was hampering Georgia's economic development. However, if Georgia could find trade and investment success with the Western countries, it would be the best defense against the Russian embargo.

For a few days I pondered what we could do. Then it came to me: Trump. The Trump brand was perfect for global visibility, recognition, and publicity. I believed then (and I still do today) that a Trump Tower in Georgia would set the stage for luxury international brands and foreign investment. I shared my idea with George Ramishvili and he immediately liked it. George knew it was a massive undertaking but he knew it was worth it.

Our thinking of the Trump brand was not as strange as it may sound. Trump's *The Apprentice* had been on TV for many seasons. And often, as I walked from my office to have lunch, drinks, or business meetings at one of my favorite spots in Midtown, the St. Regis Hotel, I would pass Trump Tower, seeing tourists from around the world taking pictures in front of it. Trump's name was global, but his business operations were mainly limited to North America. It was time to bring him to the former Soviet region.

We started to think about how to make a Trump Tower in Georgia possible. To be in business with Donald Trump sounded like a wild adventure. On the one hand, his TV celebrity status was something that had nothing to do with real estate, but at the same time it was his iconic real estate projects that made him a credible TV authority. One thing I knew for sure was that Trump pretty much guaranteed global recognition for Georgia.

Enter Michael Cohen

I MIGHT HAVE FOUND another way to get to Donald Trump about the potential Trump project in Georgia, but my good friend Camilla Olsson knew him and his entire family well (she knows half the world), so when I asked her, she said, "Absolutely. I will connect you with Michael."

"Who's Michael?" I asked.

"Michael Cohen is the right hand of Donald Trump. I think it's better you talk to Michael first before meeting with Donald."

"Okay," I said.

Camilla did a group text introducing me to Michael.

Michael responded quickly. Two hours later my wife and I were walking in Manhattan when Michael called me and said, "You should come now to Trump Tower. Let's meet now."

"I'm with my wife," I said.

"It's okay," he said. "You should bring her too."

I remember the call vividly. At the time, I thought Michael's eagerness to meet was because Camilla had vouched for me as a serious partner who could deliver.

Today, with all we know, and all that I know, it is clear there were other factors at play. Michael was looking to prove his worth to Donald Trump—he was working in an environment at the Trump Organization where Trump was dismissive of everyone other than himself and his children. The only way to truly earn Trump's respect was to deliver and deliver big.

My wife and I walked over to Trump Tower and went up to the twenty-sixth floor.

Michael came out to greet us. I asked my wife if she wouldn't mind waiting in the reception area while Michael and I talked in his office.

But Michael said, "No, no, no. Bring her in." He insisted. He led us to a boardroom.

Michael Cohen, at first impression, struck me as a loud, fairly aggressive guy. There was nothing about him that signaled to me, at that moment, that we were going to become friends of any sort.

We were joined by a gentleman whom Michael introduced as an associate of the Trump Organization named Felix Sater. Michael said Felix knew a lot about the former Soviet regions, so it would be good to have him there.

Felix Sater, short, dark, in a good suit, had a face that looked permanently tired. Although born in Moscow, his family immigrated to the United States when he was eight, and he speaks English without any trace of an accent. If you have spent time in Russian or amongst Russians, he looks familiar, like an uncle at a wedding that no one really knows.

I wasn't completely comfortable with having Sater there, given that I didn't know him. I didn't think it appropriate to share my partners' business information with him.

I decide to speak only generally about the deal I was proposing without going into much detail. I explained that Silk Road had this property in what was going to become the Monte Carlo of Central Asia, and we were looking to develop it into a luxury residential tower that would be home to international investors—and that I believed that branding it as a Trump Tower would signal to the international community the seriousness and standard of luxury of our development.

Michael immediately liked the idea and wanted to know more.

He told me how much he knew about Russia and the Soviet Union and how many Russian friends he had. And, he added, he had a deep understanding of the culture of Georgia because he had a Georgian nanny.

"Wow. Really?" I said.

"Yes," he said. "Her name is Nazy and, basically, she raised both of my children." He knew Georgian food, about Tbilisi, and about the Black Sea. That small detail sealed the deal for me. Michael's respect for Georgia convinced me his interest was sincere.

"I'm definitely interested," Michael said. "The only thing is, I need to bring it up to Mr. Trump because it's going to be a tough case to sell."

I asked Michael to have Sater leave the room because I wanted to discuss the project in greater detail. I was honest that I wasn't comfortable doing so with Sater in the room. So he left, and I never saw him again in my life—other than seeing him on TV.

Michael and I talked further and then he said it would take him a couple of weeks to get back to me. I left feeling positive about the meeting. I had big dreams and I wanted to see them through.

However, thinking back to that first meeting at Trump Tower, it's still hard to believe that Michael and I would both become part of such a massive and controversial public investigation—one that would land Michael in jail. Sometimes life is more surreal than surrealism itself…

The Deal

WE WERE CONVINCED THAT the Trump brand was a great fit for our vision for Georgian real estate and for Georgia as a whole. Now all we had to do was convince Donald J. Trump.

I heard from Michael Cohen about two weeks after our first meeting at Trump Tower.

Michael began the call in his unapologetic and aggressive style and went right to the point: "Mr. Trump wants to explore this a little further. But the thing is," Michael said, "I need to go to Georgia first to scout the locations. Otherwise the deal is dead on arrival."

I wasn't sure why Michael was being so aggressive, but I had no objection to his visiting Georgia. On the contrary, I thought his doing so would be a positive step forward.

"Not a problem," I said.

I arranged for me and Michael to fly to Georgia together. However, at the last moment, my wife, who was pregnant, was experiencing complications, and she asked that I remain to take care of her.

I explained the situation to Michael saying we could postpone until later, or I would arrange his trip so that George would meet him in Georgia and take him to all the potential development sites. I promised him first-class treatment.

Michael decided to go without me. George and Silk Road hosted and accompanied him to Batumi, and saw all the potential locations and all the development occurring around it.

Michael called me upon his return, saying, "There are a couple of really good spots, so let's get into a letter of intent. We need to see that you are serious."

Michael cautioned me, however, saying it was a tough sell to Trump and that when he raised the subject, Trump's response was, "The only Georgia I'm going to is in Atlanta because it's too damn far, the other Georgia."

We received the letter of intent, which was 99.9 percent about protecting the Trump brand. Donald Trump was not mentioned in the agreement. However, Donald Trump would be the sole signatory from the Trump Organization to the letter of intent. As part of the letter of intent, Silk Road put up a reasonable fee for all the legal work required to arrive at the long-form licensing agreement.

After several months of back-and-forth between the Silk Road team and the Trump Organization's lawyers (as supervised by Michael Cohen), we managed to get the terms of the licensing agreement agreed upon, after which Michael told me Mr. Trump was on board.

George and I thought that there was great significance to the signing of the letter of intent (LOI), so we arranged to have the signing of the LOI in Trump's office. The president of Georgia was in town then, and he asked for an opportunity to attend the signing along with Mr. Trump. It all came together rather quickly.

—

THE TRUMP ORGANIZATION'S OFFICES on the twenty-sixth floor of Trump Tower were not very light and airy. They were rather dark. There were very attractive women seated at the front desk and many smart women working in the back office. The offices had plenty of gold or polished brass accents that were shining. However, in terms of décor, there was not so much art on the walls as there were framed news articles, magazine covers, pictures, and portraits of Donald Trump. Everywhere you saw pictures of Donald, throughout the office hallways and particularly in Donald's own office.

There's a bench where one waits. And then you go through glass doors and on the right is Donald's office and that of his long-time assistant, Rhona. To your left, there's a corridor where you get right into the corporate side of the Trump Organization, including the offices of Alan Garten and Allen Weisselberg. Michael's office was down another hallway in the back.

Donald's office is, actually, not very big. It looks out north over New York toward Central Park. There is all kinds of memorabilia in his office of one kind or another—90 percent of it referring to Donald himself.

Donald was very charming. I remember when Saakashvili and I arrived, as part of Saakashvili's staff there was an attractive older woman from the Georgian Press. Donald joked that she could be in the Miss Universe pageant representing Georgia. She answered that was funny because her daughter was actually Miss Georgia in the Miss Universe pageant he had held in Moscow. Donald got very excited; he called for the book from the pageant. It was brought in and we opened it to see her daughter. I thought the signing was off to a great start.

Donald may have a bad reputation in the press regarding women, but I can say in my dealings with the Trump Organization, Donald had a lot of women in his organization whom he trusted deeply and who were very loyal to him.

Among them was Amanda Miller, who was head of PR and marketing for the Trump Organization. I had a lot of dealings with her. She was very instrumental there, and Trump thought the world of her. She also worked closely with Ivanka, I believe. Some days I was on the phone with Amanda several times over press-related matters, and she was always tremendously helpful and efficient.

—

THE SIGNING BEGAN WITH Trump asking Michael what the document was exactly—as if he didn't know what was going on (I doubted that, but I also don't think that Trump was aware of every detail in the document; he trusted Michael). Michael opened the folder and, in short order, described the terms of the LOI.

Trump then smiled and said, "This sounds great! I guess we are going to Georgia!" We all laughed.

That broke the ice. Trump was very cordial and charming to the Georgian press and was very friendly with the president. He commanded the room, bringing that sense of success to all of us. There is no question that Trump can be very convincing, firm, and charming at the same time. At one moment, he even dialed Melania on the landline and put her on speakerphone. He told her he was sitting with the Georgian delegation and the president signing a deal to build the first Trump Tower in the former USSR and that Georgia was a true miracle.

All I can say is that Trump knew how to galvanize people around the deal. You felt like you were doing something big. I felt like we were at the start of something very significant happening for Georgia. It felt very different than any other big deals we've done for Georgia, and I think this was because the fate of the deal was in just one person's hand: Donald. Without Trump's engagement in the deal, it was nearly worthless.

George and Trump executed the LOI and the deal began. At the end, Trump shook my hand, looked me in the eye, and said, "Great job, let's get this spectacular tower built in Georgia!" I couldn't agree more.

The signing was televised in Georgia. The Georgian public was impressed and thankful to Trump for choosing Georgia as his next destination. It was a very big deal even then, and at the time Trump was only president of the Trump Organization.

Once the letter of intent was in place, we began to negotiate the formal agreement. It was a tough agreement, and I quickly realized that my personal lawyer, George Nicholas (who was a great lawyer), was not enough to negotiate the Trump Organization's monster of a licensing agreement. I had to reach out to my law firm, Paul Hastings, who recommended David Klein, one tough cookie, who was one of their best intellectual property lawyers and who was, not surprisingly, very expensive.

David and I took to showing up at the Trump Organization twice a week to sit with Michael Cohen and other Trump Organization attorneys, all of whom were tough negotiators. And like that, we negotiated that agreement for six months or more. Silk Road and I had to go through the agreement sometimes page by page, line by line. It was not easy. Or inexpensive.

George Ramishvili and I spoke almost daily about the developments during the negotiation process. He felt the magnitude of the deal for Silk Road and for Georgia. Michael was the one with whom I interfaced most. Michael would be told by Trump's attorneys what the hot issues were at any given time and he would take them to me and David Klein to work them out. In most cases every single clause was an epic battle.

One such clause was the "bad boy clause, a guarantee," meaning that the guarantor, in this case Silk Road's shareholders, was held liable for any financial losses that the Trump Organization incurred as a result of the property or problems with the financing; and in the event Silk Road ever wanted to bring a partner into the deal or desired to transfer the agreement entirely to someone else, the potential partner would be intensely scrutinized and would have to be approved by the Trump Organization, otherwise Silk Road had no right to transfer the agreement either entirely or even partly to someone else. There were many other restrictions in the agreement which we had to negotiate hard.

The popular perception as told in countless press accounts is that Donald Trump is hungry for deals and for making money. But my experience is that the Trump Organization considers every detail of a deal closely. And if Trump himself is not happy with any of the terms, the deal does not move forward. Also, in my experience, he isn't doing this just to protect himself. Rather, he wants to make sure that any deal he does is given the best shot to succeed. He cares whether the financing is in place, the land has been secured, the contractors are in place, and so on.

Trump cares about his name and the value of his brand; and he certainly wants to make sure that others are not just using his name for their own publicity purposes. The deal is not final, in my experience, until Trump agrees it's final.

Michael acted as the loyal warrior for the Trump Organization throughout the deal. He was fierce in never giving any concessions, and he was totally focused on delivering a deal to Trump—not just a deal, but a great deal—that would meet what Michael called "Trump standards."

For my part, I wasn't going to deliver a bad deal for myself and for my partners at Silk Road. So Michael and I fought like cats and dogs. It wasn't pretty, but no dealmaking in NYC is pretty—but as long as the results are, who cares about the process? We are big boys; no hard feelings, right?

We were ready for signing. I met Michael at his old office, which was located a bit farther from Mr. Trump's office but still on the twenty-sixth floor. After a long discussion about the logistics, and back-and-forth with Mr. Trump, Trump agreed to hold a press conference to announce the signing of the Master License Agreement.

The event needed to be big and loud. The very first Trump deal in former Soviet territory was worthy of bells and whistles. We knew that President Saakashvili was very eager to attend the signing. We invited all the American media to showcase Georgia as a viable country for foreign investment and Silk Road's vision for the Trump brand.

Like Trump, Saakashvili was a master of creating media events and loved the publicity, particularly from US media. Saakashvili was not going to miss an opportunity to stand with Trump at Trump Tower on Fifth Avenue.

Even at that early date, it was common knowledge that Trump had been playing with the idea of running for president, so Trump presenting himself on a world stage with a foreign leader, making an international transaction, was too good a showcase for Trump to pass up. With Trump personally involved, I knew that Georgia was going to be put on the map. I was very excited at the possibility, but I also understood that I would still have to manage every detail leading up to the event.

Michael and I arranged to use the lower level public area of Trump Tower for the press conference. We set up the space with microphones on a table flanked by flags and with a huge backdrop that said, "Trump invests in Georgia."

Now, it is true that Trump was not actually making any investment in Georgia. He was, in fact, being paid to use his name on Silk Road's property in Georgia. The banner had been the Georgian president's idea, and while Trump initially objected, he agreed in the end. Trump was never shy about the fact that this was just a licensing deal. Trump himself had told me that these licensing deals were the smartest thing he'd ever done to protect his business and his brand from possible losses while guaranteeing them revenues. He didn't do these deals with anyone, he told me, only with partners that saw the Trump brand "as large and valuable as he did."

The Trump Tower Press Conference

ONE OF THE MOST memorable moments in my dealings with Donald Trump is from March 10, 2011, the press conference and the signing ceremony of the Trump Tower Georgia deal.

We had negotiated long and hard and managed every detail along the way to get to this press conference. In my mind, this was Georgia's comeback after the Russian-Georgian conflict of 2008 painted Georgia as a country under siege, unstable and unworthy of foreign investments. This was a game-changer, at least on the surface.

It gave me a great opportunity to watch Trump work the media. Michael stoked anticipation among the media for the signing ceremony by hinting and leaking that Trump might or might not have an announcement about his possible presidential run.

To that end, our press conference was set up to look like a presidential press conference with American and Georgian flags on each side. Sitting there would be the freely elected president of the Republic of Georgia, and next to him a presidential-looking Donald Trump. All this was catnip to the press and a huge crowd had assembled to cover the event.

*Left: My great
grandma Ariadna*

*Right: My grandpa Giorgi
"Gulo" Rtskhiladze*

1988 Soviet Internal Forces

1989 Soviet Internal Forces

1987 Soviet Internal Forces

Mom and Dad at my live show, 1996

My mom and I at my New York City office, 1999

In the minutes before the event, I was upstairs in the offices of the Trump Organization tending to last-minute drama. As part of our agreement, Trump was to be paid a licensing fee. Michael and the Trump legal team demanded that the licensing fee be released before the signing. Otherwise, Michael informed me that Trump would cancel the ceremony.

I was told by Michael that Trump was waiting upstairs in his office for confirmation of the payment, knowing full well that the president of Georgia was already in the building ready for the ceremony.

It was a slippery slope, a very tricky moment, I admit. It needed to be managed with surgical precision. A slight tilt in the wrong direction could've blown up the whole deal. Was Michael bluffing? This was typical Michael behavior that usually ended in a compromise, but the stakes were much higher here. I thought about my answer hard, and I decided that I needed to push back. I told Michael, "Fine, if the trust between us is so low that you cancel this huge event over this, then so be it."

As I said this, I was standing right in front of Donald Trump's office. Out of the corner of my eye, I caught Mr. Trump stand up and fix his suit and tie. He was clearly pumped up, ready to put his magic touch on Georgia and deal with a foreign dignitary, who was Putin's worst nightmare, as an equal on the world stage. In that moment, I realized that there was no way that Trump would let this opportunity go.

I am not saying that Trump needed the deal or Georgia to promote Trump, but one thing was for sure: this deal had too many unique benefits for the Trump brand for him to pass on it.

Trump, in the end, is all about Trump and his brand. Whatever he believes is best for him and his brand is what he believes to be true and urgent at any given moment. That is how he ran his company. That is how he behaved in this deal and it worked in his favor, so who am I to doubt or judge his instincts?

Everyone around me at that time was very vocal in saying there was no way Trump would agree to a public signing ceremony in the Trump Tower lobby to announce the deal. But he did.

Or that he wouldn't without asking for an extra appearance fee. Which he did not.

Or that he would let us hoist a banner that said, "Trump Invests in Georgia." But he did.

I had spoken to Ivana at length about Donald and how he did deals, and I'd been negotiating with Michael for almost two years; I understood that what mattered to Trump was his brand.

At that moment, Trump came out of his office. Michael told him that the money had yet to be released from the escrow account to the Trump account.

Mr. Trump nodded, looked at me disappointed, but said nothing, letting his facial expression talk. Although I was pretty positive that he wasn't canceling, I decided to speak to my partners immediately. I told them that we didn't want to risk canceling the event over this, and that Silk Road had to release the funds eventually one way or the other. Their concern was simple: "What if we release the funds and he cancels, or doesn't appear personally at the event?"

"No way," I said. "He wants to do this press event." George thought about this for a second and he nodded, confirming the release of funds. In a split second, we told our attorneys to release the funds.

As the elevator door closed, I saw Trump standing with his head of security, Keith Shiller, talking in his ear. Trump was nodding like he was making an important decision. As I was riding down the elevator, I was still wound up inside, thinking, *What if he doesn't come down?*

Seconds later, I received a text from our lawyer, saying, "The funds are released from escrow."

A few minutes later, I was standing in front of the stage, along with my partners from Silk Road, all of us waiting for Trump to come down the now famous escalator.

I saw Michael Cohen and others from the Trump Organization entering the venue, which I took to be a good sign. But minutes passed and there was no sign of Trump yet.

Surely if Trump wasn't going to show, Michael would have said something? I wondered. *But maybe even he doesn't know? Trump can change his mind and not tell anyone, that's for sure.* I knew I'd done my best and beyond for Georgia, and the rest was just destiny.

Then, suddenly, Donald Trump and Ivanka appeared on the escalator, descending to us. I breathed a deep sigh of relief. And so the press conference began.

At the press conference, Michael opened the event (which you can see on YouTube) and started his speech by referring to "my good friend Giorgi" (even though I asked him to not to mention me), and then he mentioned me about three more times in the speech.

The pictures of Trump, Saakashvili, and George Ramishvili all shaking hands appeared over and over in the press to the point where Saakashvili and Ramishvili were both getting recognized on the streets of New York. The building of a Trump Tower in Georgia was described as a $350 million project. That, too, was "huge." I was excited for my friend, George, it was a big day for Georgia and he did all in his power to deliver it.

The event was tremendously successful. Georgia got extensive positive coverage, particularly on CNBC and NBC (*The Apprentice* being an NBC program).

—

WHAT I RECALL MOST from the press conference was Trump being asked, perhaps for the first time, questions about foreign relations—about Russia, Putin, and what seemed crazy at the time: the notion that Trump might run for president. The press asked, "Mr. Trump, how do you see the Russia-Georgia relationship?" "What do you think of Putin?" and "Mr. Trump, are you considering running?"

When they asked the Georgian president what he thought of Trump's chances for president, Saaskashvili answered very diplomatically given that Obama was still in the White House: "If he ran for president in Georgia, he would probably win." Everybody laughed.

It was clear to me that Trump got exactly what he wanted out of the Georgian deal for his company and his brand.

We had a big celebratory dinner scheduled that evening at the Four Seasons restaurant. Something told me that Trump wasn't going to show, as he had already done his part. I was right because just before the dinner, Michael Cohen came up to me and whispered, "Listen, Mr. Trump can't come, he's got some urgent thing he needs to deal with concerning Melania."

I wasn't happy but I wasn't going to complain. Donald Trump had delivered big for my country and Silk Road. In his place, he sent Donny Jr.

Trump Goes to Batumi

ALTHOUGH REPORTERS WERE ALSO eager to belittle Trump's net worth by saying that he didn't own the buildings that bore his name, and that they were just licensing deals, when it came to the Trump Tower Batumi, suddenly it was as if Trump and the Trump Organization were the main owners of the project, involved in every financial aspect.

Of course, Silk Road now had to actually build the project. Silk Road hired an architectural firm. The architectural renderings were done in collaboration with Michael Cohen and John Fotiadis, the Trump Organization architect. Once we were discussing the design and building details, Don Jr. and Ivanka became involved.

We had several meetings at which Ivanka and Don Jr. were present. I found them to be smart, savvy businesspeople. And, as young people, they were clearly well brought up. I definitely saw the influence of Ivana on them, who had told me she taught them that being a Trump wasn't a calling card; they had to be good people. She used to take them to her native country, the Czech Republic, so the kids were brought up aware of the universe outside of the US.

As to Georgia, they weren't really familiar with the region. However, since Czechoslovakia had once been under Soviet Rule, as Georgia had been, they were familiar with that mentality.

Once Silk Road had the architectural designs from Fotiadis, Michael and I were going over them. We went to the reception area of the twenty-sixth floor about two doors down from Trump's office and were talking when, suddenly, Trump himself appeared.

I shook hands with Trump and Michael said, "We got the Georgia project designs." Michael opened the design on his phone and we started showing Trump the Batumi Tower designs. He seemed to really like them. One thing I will say was he was always listening.

"So, what do you think?" Mr. Trump said to me, looking straight in my eyes.

"It's amazing," I told him. "It will be biggest thing Georgia has ever seen. This will get attention all over the world." Seizing the moment, I added, "Georgia is just the beginning. I believe we can do more in the former Soviet Union. Next one could be Kazakhstan, and after that, Russia. Why not?"

Trump never interrupted what I was saying. I was well aware that, in the end, only Trump could move this project forward. Michael didn't have the power to do so without him.

Trump seemed to respond favorably to my thinking bigger and seeing this as more than just one deal. Michael kind of bragged to Mr. Trump, saying that I had great connections in Russia, to which Trump just nodded and said, "Good, good."

Trump didn't strike me as a person who had great knowledge of Russia, but when we were talking, he told me, "I'm finishing my new book, and I have a page or two about Russia in there."

"I'd love to read it," I said.

That aside, Trump did not appear that interested in doing projects in Russia. At this point, he was only focused on making our Georgia project a success. After that, if there was a deal in Russia, he would look at that. But as far as I could tell, it wasn't really on his radar.

Trump glanced at the hotel renderings once more, nodded, and said, "Great, looks great." I took that as Trump giving us his blessing to go ahead. But he was rushing to go somewhere and the minute Keith Schiller, Trump's security person, was there, Trump shook my hand with a very tight grip and left in a hurry.

I am not ashamed to admit that in addition to wanting to do something great for Georgia, I was pursuing the Trump brand because I saw big money in doing so. Without question, Trump was very appealing to that part of the world.

What I also liked about Trump was that while the negotiations were brutal, with no breathing room, no mercy, always a "take it or leave it" attitude, at least you knew where Trump stood when it came to making money. It was very obvious that making lots of money and building something great were equally important to him.

Trump didn't seem to care that Georgia was largely unknown to Americans. It may have been an advantage. Trump liked that he was going to put Georgia on the map the minute he announced the project. He knew the project would get lots of publicity all over the world and, when it did, he wanted the designs for the tower to look spectacular.

As for the money, in a typical Trump licensing deal, he received an upfront fee and a percentage of the gross apartment sales or hotel revenue.

I felt good about where Silk Road came out on this deal. The numbers were quite fair for Trump licensing deals. And it was good for me as well: I planned to make 1.5 to 2 percent on each sale.

Imagine, if you will, that if we did two towers in Georgia, two towers in Kazakhstan, we're talking about an incredible amount of money. For the developers, the total portfolio could have been worth $850 million. Maybe close to $1 billion in total investment.

Not too bad, right? If only…

That didn't turn out to be the case. In the end, all that happened was that Trump became the forty-fifth president of the United States, and I remained just an ordinary American citizen. That's all.

—

BUT BACK TO THE Batumi Trump Tower. I told Mr. Trump that he needed to come to Georgia. I pressed Michael on the point. More than once. Again, I had to work my magic, manage details, get Trump excited, deal with Michael's passive-aggressive mood swings. Just when I thought it was done, the trip was off the table the next day and I had to start the discussions all over again. I knew how important Trump's visit was for

Georgia and Silk Road, and I wasn't about to quit. Trump himself told me once, "You never ever quit, no matter what, right?"

And then a miracle occurred. Michael said, "Okay, I just spoke with Mr. Trump and it's a go!"

Michael and I traveled to Georgia together for the advance planning. With Silk Road, we discussed the logistics of what needed to happen when and finalized ideas for where to hold the press conferences and what the right backdrop should be. There were a thousand little details but Michael worked efficiently. As long as his boss was made to look good, he was happy.

However, upon our return, Michael flipped out. I don't know what happened, but he said, "No, Mr. Trump is not going to come."

It was already December. All the plans for Trump's visit to Georgia had already been made. Everyone in Georgia was expecting Trump. So we went back to making the case for Trump to come to Georgia again.

It was a lot of hard work, but we got them to agree. So, when I finally got word that Trump was "wheels up" and on his way to Georgia, I breathed a great sigh of relief. I was exhausted. I believed that the project was off to a fantastic start and my work was done. We had delivered Trump and the Trump Batumi Tower Project to Georgia.

My attitude was to let my friends and partners take it from here. After all, the formal deal was between Silk Road Group and the Trump Organization, and the signatories to the deal were George and Mr. Trump. Let them celebrate.

I went to Turkey to decompress and relax. I got word that they had landed safely in Tbilisi. There was a large reception at the Presidential Palace for Trump hosted by the president of Georgia. I knew that George was there, so I was relaxed.

George and Silk Road definitely deserved the celebration. They had stood strong throughout the entire process; George never wavered, never backed down. He was like a rock for me during and after the deal. That's just the kind of person George Ramishvili is—that is what has made Silk Road resilient.

Silk Road's success is, in many ways, the success of a generation of Georgians determined to work for Georgia's independence and, after that was achieved, to put the country on a solid footing. No matter what the obstacles, they persevered. George was smart, tenacious, and willing to have his business pivot to wherever he found opportunities. Silk Road's success was also the success of Georgia, and that of our generation of Georgians.

George and Silk Road have become an inspiration to young Georgians not only because they have been successful but also because in the face of success, Silk Road chose not to loot the country, as had occurred in other former Soviet Republics, but to invest in Georgia.

Philanthropy continues to be a new and novel concept in the former Soviet Republics and even in Russia. But George and Silk Road support Georgia in many ways, including sponsoring the Georgian National Ski Team and creating the first public-private partnership in Georgia to restore the historic Tsinandali Estate with its historic gardens, vineyards, and wine cellar and transform it into a museum, public park, and a cultural center with a boutique hotel and a thousand-seat indoor-outdoor amphitheater.

In September 2019, the Republic of Georgia, in partnership with Silk Road, launched the Tsinandali Festival, a classical music festival that follows the example of the Verbier Festival (and is led by Verbier's founders, Avi Shoshani and Martin Engstrom) featuring performances and workshops by world-renowned musicians along with the creation of a Pan-Central-Asian Youth Orchestra.

—

GEORGE WAS MORE THAN capable of hosting the Trump party in Georgia. However, at the reception, Trump, Cohen, and Schiller were all asking, "Where's Giorgi?" They all expected me to be there.

So the next day I got on plane straight to Batumi to meet up with them.

Batumi was the main attraction where the Trump Tower was going to be built. We had a massive, Trump-size press conference with a visual presentation of the architectural renderings of the tower. It was a bright clear day.

Standing in a giant open lot with a beautiful, large backdrop of the Black Sea and a rendering of the impressive-looking tower, President Saakashvili, Donald Trump, and George Ramishvili took their places on a gray platform podium. George spoke first.

President Saakashvili spoke next. Donald Trump listened via a simultaneous translator held to his right ear.

Donald Trump then took the podium, saying, "Well, thank you very much, Mr. President. It's an honor to be here…It will be something very special. I have to start by congratulating George and their entire team because I've gotten to know George very well over the last year. And he just doesn't stop. He wants to make this special. He wants to make it great and that is why with Michael Cohen and my entire staff we decided to go forward…and it's becoming even greater than we ever thought."

Trump continued on for a few minutes and then shook the president's hand again as they made their way to a draped item. Trump cut the ribbon while George and President Saakashvili removed the covering, revealing a cornerstone with a brass plaque that read "Trump Tower Batumi."

After the ceremony, we had a major luncheon with President Saakashvili.

At the lunch, Trump and I talked about New York back in the day and some of our mutual friends. We discussed various businesses we had each been involved in. I told him about Wind Farms as an alternative energy business, which I was a proponent of and had invested in. He didn't like them (apparently there are wind turbines offshore next to Trump's golf course in Scotland). I told him why I was doing it, and why there's money in it. He listened very carefully, and then he said, "That's not too bad."

As we were walking out of lunch, I told him I had hosted his first wife, Ivana, in Georgia, to which he joked, "Oh, that's how you probably know a whole lot about me." I replied, "Well, maybe," and we both laughed. It was very friendly. All in all, we had about an hour-and-a-half conversation.

Let me be clear: I don't agree with everything Trump says or does, particularly during his campaign and as president. However, I find it mystifying when people say insulting and offensive things about Trump, calling him ignorant, racist, senile, or incapable of sustained interest or thought. That definitely was not my experience. Quite the opposite.

In my interactions with him, Trump was savvy, sharp, flexible in his approach (the way he adjusted to the Georgian situation), and, at times, somewhat sentimental and nostalgic. For example, he spoke to me about the Ziegfeld Theater in New York, how much he loved that place and how heartbreaking it was for him to see that they were going to close it. He wanted to help out, even by putting money into it, but for some reason it didn't work out. I was surprised that Donald Trump, a man who has built so many skyscrapers, was pouring his heart out over a New York movie theater building.

Before departing from Georgia, Trump showed us his new plane. George and I got on the plane, and we all sat down in its very comfortable seating area.

Michael offered me a lift back on the plane, which I would have enjoyed. But I had to decline because I wanted to visit with my father so we could visit my mother's grave.

However, once Trump had departed, we were all very satisfied. The announcement and press conference had been a huge success. We received tremendous international media attention and a number of business inquiries about the project.

And then, upon his return to New York, Trump called in to the Fox News program, Fox & Friends, and praised Georgia:

"I was in the Republic of Georgia over the weekend," Trump said. "You have to see a place that's booming. It's unbelievable. This was a Russian satellite for a period of time, broke away. Leaders are going to that country to find out what they're doing."

"What's the industry there?" one of the anchors asked.

"It's everything. But one of them is tourism. And what they're doing, they're building a place, Batumi. It's going to be one of the great places of the world within four or five years. I see what they're doing."

"What's your interest there? What are you investing in there?" the female correspondent asked.

"I'm doing a big job there. A big development there. It's been amazing. It's been amazing. Ten percent growth in that country as opposed to one to two percent growth that we have in this country. But I think ten percent is a very low number."

Whatever media Trump did, he praised Georgia. It was like Georgia received $10 million of free publicity. And Trump didn't have to do that. It certainly wasn't in the licensing agreement. He's just a natural salesman, and I think he genuinely liked what he saw of Georgia and wanted our project together and Georgia itself to be successful.

The Other Cohen in Kazakhstan

MANY MONTHS AFTER TRUMP'S Georgia visit, as Silk Road was ready to unveil the model apartment, George called Michael to suggest Trump return to Georgia for the launch of the model house of the Tower Project.

Michael Cohen's response was, "Sure, he will come to Georgia again. But this time it'll cost Georgia at least three million dollars." At this point, Michael said, Trump deserved an appearance fee such as he was paid by Macy's or other brands.

I have no idea whether Michael had consulted Trump before asking for the fee. My guess is that he did not. Michael was always trying to push his boss's case for earning more—and always wanted to gain favor from Trump by bringing him deals and more money. Michael didn't earn a penny from licensing or endorsement deals, as he so often told me. He was just wanted the best (or the most) for his boss.

I had to get involved in the discussion about Trump's follow-up trip to Georgia. I shared my idea of a second Georgia trip with Michael at a meeting while we were both in the Hamptons. The notion of paying Trump that much was ludicrous, so I let the whole matter of his returning to Georgia drop.

Michael often talked about his relationship with Trump, sometimes with exuberance and braggadocio; other times, Michael expressed unhappiness that he was working so hard for Trump for very little money.

Occasionally, he would rant about Trump treating him like shit. But a minute later he was back to himself, praising Trump.

Once during our negotiations, I told him I didn't care if this was the Trump brand or any other brand, all I cared about was whether the deal made sense or not—not about the Trump name on the building. Michael flipped out and shouted back, "You don't even know what you're talking about. Trump is the most photographed person in the world, you understand that?!"

If that wasn't true then, it certainly is now.

Michael and I fought a lot and our arguments often got heated, but I always felt his expressions of friendship were genuine.

—

STILL, MICHAEL WAS ALWAYS badgering me about progress on the tower. I had a lot of pressure from Mr. Trump and the Trump Organization. They kept saying, "You are responsible." And they didn't want Mr. Trump to look bad because the tower was not being built. Nonetheless, the project ran into unforeseen problems concerning local approvals and the financing we needed.

At the same time, while the Georgia project was going on, Michael and I were already working on the next chapter: Kazakhstan.

The US ambassador of Kazakhstan helped me set up important meetings in the country. We had the prime minister of Kazakhstan and the mayor of Nur-Sultana (then called Astana), the country's capital, join us for a meeting. I managed to have Mr. Trump write a personal letter to Nursultan Nazarbayev, the president of Kazakhstan, saying they would be delighted to do a tower in Astana, which was sent to him prior to the meetings in Kazakhstan (the president stepped down in 2019).

Astana's main architect and city planner was directed to find us a selection of possible locations in Astana, including one we liked next to the Presidential Palace in the center of Astana. And they approved the location.

We met with the Prime Minister, who asked us, "How much would it cost?"

Michael answered, "Three hundred fifty to four hundred million dollars."

The prime minister replied, "I like it."

The funniest part of the meeting with the prime minister of Kazakhstan had nothing to do with the proposed Trump Tower, but instead Michael's last name, Cohen—and it's not what you think.

Cohen is not only Michael's last name; it is also the last name of Sasha Baron Cohen, the producer, writer, and star of the film *Borat*, whose full title is (in case you forgot) *Borat: Cultural Learnings of America for Make Benefit Glorious Nation of Kazakhstan*. Not the favorite film of Kazakhs as it portrays their country and their people as backward, uneducated, racist, sexist, homophobic, and all-around idiots.

So, when the prime minister looked at Michael's business card, he stopped, took a deep breath, and left the room for a brief moment. Michael and I looked at each other, puzzled.

When he returned, he asked Michael bluntly, "You are not related to the Borat guy are you?!"

Michael laughed and said, "NO, I am not, don't worry, nor did I enjoy the movie."

We all laughed. The meeting resumed in a more cordial fashion after that.

We saw great opportunity in Kazakhstan. Astana had been chosen as the location for the 2017 World Exposition. There was tremendous development going on for that event. They were building new futuristic hotels, conference centers, and office structures.

"Trump Tower is the one you should build for the expo," I said.

Michael was his usual brash self. "We have to announce it now," he told the prime minister. "This is going to be the biggest deal, the most spectacular tower in Asia, if not in the world."

After we returned to the United States, we had architectural designs made for what we called the Trump Diamond, a really spectacular design. As for our business plans, what's the saying? "Man plans, God laughs"?

In the 2013 presidential elections in Georgia, Saakashvili was voted out and there was a total change of power.

The new administration announced they would no longer be directing their energies toward developing Batumi, and would concentrate instead on Tbilisi, the capital.

As for the Kazakhstan Tower, we were still pursuing that when on June 16, 2015, Donald Trump announced his candidacy to run for president of the United States. Suddenly, building a Trump Tower that would be ready for Astana's 2017 Expo no longer seemed feasible.

And once Trump was elected president, everything changed, and I mean EVERYTHING…

10

Meanwhile, Back in the Grand Jury Room

Abramovich's Party

I WAS GLAD TO step outside the grand jury room and take even a few minutes' water break. It was incredibly draining to be so "on," thinking through and second- and third-guessing every question and answer.

My lawyers, who were waiting outside, took me back to the waiting room and told me to make it clear to the jurors. "Listen: I'm innocent. I've done nothing. I've never done anything purposely or deliberately to be part of this whole fiasco."

And, right on cue, there was a knock on the door. They were ready to return me to the grand jury room. I left my attorneys once more.

—

AFTER THIS BRIEF BREAK, I was feeling a little more prepared, a little more experienced. I had broken Rhee's rhythm and now stood better able to defend myself.

Still, I was caught between my lawyer's advice—which was to say little, give short answers (preferably yes or no), and avoid back-and-forth with the attorneys—and my own inclinations to be truthful and explain things completely.

Either way can be extremely dangerous. If you don't explain fully you may leave them with the wrong impression. And if you talk too much, say too much, you may open a whole other Pandora's box.

The lawyers would have liked me to either give a definitive answer or respond with "I have no recollection of that." "I have no knowledge of that." "I'm going to have to think about it." "I can't remember." "I don't have any comment on that." The second time I went in, I was like, "Okay, now I'm going to be different."

Mueller's team, I was now told, wanted to explore what "favors" I had done Michael Cohen.

But the pressure was still there. I couldn't help but think that I was participating in something really huge and historic—and that there was the possibility that I could be recalled and that next time, I might be coming in as a person of interest in my own right. That was concerning.

As for the jurors…I was slightly puzzled. My attorneys had warned me that the jurors could be very aggressive in their questioning, sometimes even more so than the prosecutors. However, no juror asked me a single question. Not one.

Either the prosecutors were doing that good a job, or perhaps what I had to say was not as relevant or important as they had hoped. Either way, it was not what I expected.

Prosecutor Rhee started in again, picking up where she'd left off about the favors I had done for Michael Cohen.

At first, I wasn't sure what she was talking about. She then explained that on several occasions Michael had asked me to help him with something—and that I had endeavored to do so. She pointed out that some of the people Michael had asked me to help him with had Russian names. Was there a reason why I had or had not done these favors for Michael Cohen to the people with Russian names? And what was my connection to these Russian names?

The prosecutor asked for a document to be brought in to her, which was somewhat dramatic. When the door opened, a man came in—who for a second I thought was Steven Mnuchin, because he looked a little like him.

He handed Rhee a document that, after examining it, she handed to me to, as she put it, "Refresh your memory." After that, she asked for the document back, which was, as far as I was concerned, a little over-the-top dramatic.

What the prosecutor showed me was a text from Michael asking me if I knew Roman Abramovich.

It's a big question that has a complicated answer. Abramovich is a Russian-born billionaire who was one of the first oligarchs, making a fortune that began with recycled tires and rubber ducks (I kid you not), then spread to oil and other investments. He is the owner of the Chelsea Football team in England, and he recently became an Israeli citizen.

And yes, I had met him. But I didn't really know him.

I could well have used one of the stock phrases my attorney had prepared me with because, as he put it, "I am going to fight tooth-and-nail with Mueller's team not to put you in the hot seat."

Which was reasonable. But I didn't listen to my lawyer's advice. Instead, I went with my gut—which told me to explain the complicated situation honestly, truthfully, and then the investigation would have no more need for interviewing me.

I told the grand jury I really didn't know Abramovich. I had met him but hadn't seen him in many years. But I had friends, old friends from my school days, who knew Abramovich, which was a normal thing. It would be like someone who'd grown up in New York City and had friends or family in the real estate business knowing someone who knew Donald Trump.

Mueller's team led me through a series of text messages with Michael. Michael's said, "My daughter wants to get into Abramovich's party, can you do that?"

It's really silly, right? Abramovich is known for throwing lavish parties. Cohen's daughter wanted to attend—to be on the list. Could I help? That was all it was. Michael wanted to make his daughter happy. What's wrong with that? Michael assumed I knew Abramovich or knew someone who knew him and that I could help. Which, in principle, was true.

In fact, it happened twice that Michael asked me to help get his daughter into some event. He asked because he considered me a friend. In the first instance, I texted Michael back that although I had met Abramovich, it was a very long time ago in Moscow when he was celebrating that Chelsea, his soccer team, had made the UEFA Champions League final.

However, it was New Year's Eve, and my friends in Moscow were already at their own parties. In the end, I couldn't reach anyone and was of no help.

The Mueller team didn't really care about whether I could get Michael's daughter into a party. What they cared about was my Russian connections. Who I knew and why. And, more importantly, how I knew them. What the prosecutor was trying to establish was that I was a back channel for Michael or Trump, that I was one of their possible conduits to Russia.

The other possibility they were exploring was that in some way I was so beholden to Michael and Trump personally or for some financial benefit or necessity that I might do anything to protect their reputations. Which sounded serious but, really, did the fate of the republic rest on getting someone's daughter into Abramovich's party? Really?

Moscow Connections

PROSECUTOR RHEE AND MUELLER's team seemed inordinately interested in my involvement in a potential Moscow Tower.

Associates in Moscow knowing that I was doing business with the Trump Organization sought to propose doing a Trump Tower in Moscow. In order to secure the best possible location from the city of Moscow, they suggested that Trump write a letter to the mayor of Moscow about his interest in the project.

My friends drafted the letter (in Russian), which said that such a project would strengthen ties between the US and Russia. Neither the letter nor the project saw the light of day.

What I didn't understand until much later is that any contact a presidential candidate has with a foreign official, such as the mayor of Russia, is suspect and could be a channel for corruption, illegal payments, and even financial blackmail.

Which sounds, at first impression, outlandish.

But consider if you want to give someone a large bribe, isn't one way to arrange for them to profit hugely in a real estate deal? Or paying them an inflated licensing fee? Or what if the real estate went south and now the person owed millions, which the other party was willing to loan them or forgive the debt?

Suddenly, a presidential candidate, president-elect, or president (or his family and relatives) doing real estate deals seems like a minefield worth avoiding.

So it was easy to see why Mueller's team wanted to explore this. But it was hard to see what actual connection or relevance there was in asking me about it.

That Infamous Tape, Again

BACK IN THE GRAND jury room, Jeannie Rhee turned to what she no doubt saw as a smoking gun, a text exchange I had with Michael Cohen about tapes of Trump in Moscow. To me, these were innocuous—gossip I was teasing him about. It meant nothing and I meant nothing by it. But that is not how Rhee saw it or hoped to characterize those texts.

On October 30, 2016, ten days before Trump became president, I sent Michael a text that said, "Stopped flow of some tapes from Russia but not sure if there's anything else. Just so u know." Michael did not seem to know about any rumors of these tapes. I told him I knew nothing about the content of the tapes, just that someone at a party in Moscow was bragging about them, and I wanted to give him a heads-up. I told him that it was most likely nothing, just some "stupid people."

Again, to me, this was nothing. However, to a seasoned prosecutor this was a gold mine of potential collusion, obstruction, corruption, blackmail, and bribery. However, the riches here turned out to be nothing more than fool's gold.

The questions this text exchange raised were: Were there in fact tapes? And was that plural, as in "tapes," rather than a single "tape"?

If, in fact, that tape (or those tapes) existed, what was on them? Was it the lurid scenes described in the Steele dossier? Was it kompromat?

Honestly, I had no idea.

When I used the word "flow" as in "stopped flow," was that a reference to the alleged content of the tape—i.e., a reference to possible urination having been filmed?

In saying that I had "stopped" such flow, did that refer once again to the contents, or to measures I had taken to suppress, obstruct, or stop the distribution of such tapes?

The prosecutors wanted to know who had called me with the information, who had given them the information, and what follow-up contact with either I had.

There were all very serious, very important questions. However, I was forced to disappoint Muller's team and Prosecutor Rhee because I had no such information.

I had been told someone heard a rumor. I didn't believe the rumor, and I was never presented with confirmation or anything that would substantiate the rumor, but I was in business with the Trump Organization and Michael Cohen, and I thought it best that he know what people were saying about his boss, if not for Trump or Michael Cohen's sake then for the benefit of the deals we were hoping to close.

Rhee and I had a very aggressive back-and-forth. It became clear to me that her plan was to dominate the "Tape Topic" so as to turn this into a real "Wow!" moment for the grand jurors (and, potentially, for the Russian Probe investigation).

She wouldn't let it go, coming at me from many different angles. I must give her credit; she was successful in making this seem like a potential collusion, but again she also knew that in reality it was going to lead them to a dead end. Despite aggressive and loud questioning, with Prosecutor

Rhee using expressive arm gestures to emphasize her points, she did not succeed because there was no "there" there.

No kompromat. No collusion. Nothing more than a rumor that was as difficult to grasp as a wisp of smoke.

Still, Rhee kept at me. I must admit hours of being interrogated, called Russian, and being accused of potentially hiding information about kompromat on the US president was wearing me down. But I kept telling myself, *I know who I am!* The Russia I know is utterly different from the way Prosecutor Rhee is portraying it to the grand jurors. In fact, I did believe in a better, prosperous Russia. Russia that could've been good first, for the Russians and everyone else too, including both the United States and Georgia.

11

In the Media Maelstrom

We Can't Let The Deal Die!

DECEMBER 8, 2016, I went to a breakfast for Donald Trump, held at Cipriani's midtown location on Forty-Second Street. It was meant to be a farewell from Trump to the Trump Organization and persons close to it, to acknowledge his status as president-elect and launch his transition to president of the United States.

Michael Cohen was there, as well as Anthony Scaramucci and all of Trump's team. Michael and Keith Schiller saw me and called me over to them. Michael was warm and Keith, as always, shook my hand firmly and hugged me. Michael introduced me to Anthony Scaramucci. At the time they seemed very close, joking and looking happy and excited about everything Trump. It's so strange and sad to see what happened to all of that excitement. Both would fall from grace in ways that were painful to watch no matter what one thinks of them.

Trump gave a very well-structured speech directed at his base—a whole room of dedicated Trump believers. Trump was funny and, I must say, very presidential.

Trump even addressed any possible "Never-Trumpers" in the room, who then joined everyone else in cheering for him. At that moment, it looked as if Trump would indeed bring the whole country together and that his presidency would be a boon for all Americans.

After the event, I waited for Michael, who was very busy dealing with a million different people. Michael seemed very much to be Trump's guy. He was shaking hands with everyone, scheduling meetings and calls. Once he was done, he joined me and we decided to walk together from Forty-Second Street to Trump Tower on Fifty-Sixth Street, where Michael was still working.

It was a chilly day. We walked on Madison Avenue. Michael was very, VERY excited, and who could've blamed him? His boss, his favorite person in the world, had just become the president-elect of the United States. Michael was committed to doing absolutely everything in his power to ensure Trump was victorious. Although he told me that Trump wanted him to come to the White House but that he didn't want the job because it paid very little, I sensed that deep inside Michael was dreaming about being in the White House working for his old boss. Then Michael went on to make a case that he was better off being Trump's lawyer because he could do a lot more for Mr. Trump by being outside than inside the government. Even if he left the Trump Organization, he said, he was better off.

I remember telling him that he was a free man now and he should consider doing his own business deals and that I had some good ideas for us. He stopped and looked at me. His face looked tired and weary, but his eyes still bristled with excitement. "Let me just lock and load, and we will do big things, I promise!"

Just as I was about to ask what would become of our Batumi deal and the other potential deals, Michael suddenly received a call from Trump, which took up much of the remaining time. All I could hear was "yes, sir," "sure, I understand," and "I'll take care of it once I get to the office."

When we arrived at Trump Tower, Michael said that he'd be in touch soon to update me on the Georgian deal and to discuss all the other business opportunities he was about to explore.

That night I got a text message from Michael to call him. I was walking in New York with my wife and sister. I called Michael immediately.

"The deal is being canceled," he told me. "It's not even up to me. It's been decided much higher up than me, at the top."

"We're going to have to save the deal," I said. "We can't let it die. No way!" All of Georgia was watching this deal. Losing it could be a serious blow to Silk Road's reputation in Georgia.

"The deal cannot be saved," Michael said. "A default notice has already been sent out." Basically, the Trump Organization wanted to blame Silk Road for the deal being canceled. It made me angry. I was pissed. I felt totally betrayed by Trump, Michael, and the entire Trump Organization. Silk Road had done no wrong to be treated like that, canceling the deal because it was no longer convenient for Trump as president-elect. It was not right; it was not fair on so many different levels.

At that point, Silk Road was out over $4 million, including the license fee, and it didn't feel like anyone at the Trump Organization gave a damn about that. Honestly, at that moment I felt stabbed in the back, disgusted, and really damn pissed off at everyone there, including Trump himself. I couldn't believe that after all that my partners at Silk Road and I had done for the Trump brand, we would be iced out like the deal never existed.

I understood Trump was under a great deal of pressure and could no longer devote as much attention to our projects. Still, you don't just dump your partners who put faith in you and your brand. A whole lot of time, energy, and money went into securing the very first deal for a Trump-branded property in the former Soviet territory.

There's no question that the Trump Batumi deal elevated the Trump brand's image in the entire region. Suddenly Azerbaijan, Kazakhstan, Russia, and other former Soviet republics were convinced that doing a Trump-branded project was not only possible and lucrative, it also could provide global exposure for their respective countries. These countries were desperate to make positive headlines in the Western media and the Trump brand had suddenly become their golden ticket.

This extensive rollout of Trump-branded buildings across Central Asia could've brought many skyscraper deals and lots of money to the Trump Organization. Michael Cohen wanted more than anything to deliver this for Trump (and himself). However, his overly aggressive style did not always play well with the wealthy and powerful individuals from that part of the world, and he was never empowered by Trump to actually sign and close the deals. That was left to Mr. Trump. And my friendship with Michael meant that I would never go behind his back directly to Trump.

Over the years, I observed that there were two very different Michael Cohens. One was creative, sharp, and quick to act, someone who would go out of his way to do anything for a friend. This Michael was very positive and could accomplish great things. The other Michael was unhappy, desperate, depressed, and would do or say anything to get what he wanted. That Michael complained that he received no respect, no loyalty. The problem was that Michael could flip from one to the other in the blink of an eye.

Similarly, Michael's relationship with Trump was an emotional roller coaster, fueled by an Oedipal love/hate relationship in which Michael alternately looked up to Trump as his god, his idol, someone he would give his life for. Then, a minute later, Trump was the guy who didn't appreciate the massive amounts of work Michael was doing, who would dump Michael in a New York minute if he didn't perform the impossible for him.

This is the same Michael Cohen who announced he "would take a bullet for Mr. Trump," and then a few weeks later announced that he had "made a mistake in being so loyal to Mr. Trump." But, knowing the two different sides of Michael, I wasn't surprised. Let's put it this way: Michael changing his mind about Trump didn't change my mind about Michael.

The Side Letter

THE WAY THE BATUMI deal was structured, Silk Road had to reach certain milestones—the building needed to be up and running by a certain date—or the Trump Organization had the right to walk away (keeping the payments they'd received thus far). And when that date arrived, it's true that the building was not up, nor had the contracted milestones been achieved.

This was the reason Trump Organization claimed that Silk Road was in breach, and why they had sent a default notice, which was sure to be followed imminently by a termination notice.

However, Michael and the Trump Organization had forgotten about one very important detail. It was something over which I had negotiated arduously with the Trump Organization at the time.

There was a side letter to our agreement, signed by Trump himself, which I had asked my lawyer to draft on my way to the signing ceremony at Trump Tower.

I had dictated the terms to our lawyer from my car as I was driving to the event because I saw trouble in paradise ahead for Georgia. The gist of the letter was that if there were changed conditions in Georgia (political, economic) that were beyond our control, the deadlines were tolled for Silk Road until such time as conditions improved. Right after the side letter was drafted by my lawyer, I sent it to Michael for his review—right from the car. My wife, who was accompanying me to the signing, was witness to all this madness.

I knew that Michael would flip out and fight me tooth and nail to talk me out of it. Michael called me immediately. He was yelling; I was yelling. My wife was shaking her head and poking me to focus on driving the car.

During that vocal and vigorous argument, Michael and I canceled and restarted the signing ceremony probably ten times. He hung up twice on me and I did once on him. But somehow, by the time my wife and I arrived to NYC from Connecticut, Michael had Trump's blessing and had agreed to sign the letter before the signing.

It had been smart to get that letter signed. Georgia had undergone great political and economic change—in November 2013, Mikheil Saakashvili was voted out of power. Making Batumi a world-class destination had been Saakashvili's signature initiative. The new administration in Georgia was no longer interested in so great a commitment as investing in Batumi. At the same time, Georgia was also still suffering economically—reeling from the 2008 global economic collapse.

For Silk Road, both of these represented a significant change of circumstances that warranted putting a hold on the project, as provided for in the side letter.

Before Saakashvili left office, his people delivered one more serious blow to Silk Road by not approving their acquisition of real estate adjacent to the Trump Batumi site that included marina and beach access, which was part of the master plan Trump had agreed to and was essential for the success of the project.

A Trump Tower in Batumi had publicity value for Saaskashvili, but once it could no longer deliver for him, he had no interest in furthering Silk Road's plans. Which was too bad, because it demonstrated that he put his own success over that of his fellow Georgians, the Georgian economy, and Georgia's international reputation.

—

I KNEW THAT THE side letter was our best legal argument against the Trump Organization canceling our deal. It was clear to me, even then, that the Trump Organization was moving very fast and methodically to get foreign deals like ours off the books before January 20, the day of Trump's inauguration.

Given this turn of events, I put in a call to George. "You are going to have to get on a plane and come here," I told him. I explained the situation to him and said we needed to go together to talk to the Trump Organization. "We have a situation here and it's a lot worse than we thought."

Keep in mind that, at this point, neither we nor our deal was in any way on the press's radar. There had been inquiries from *The Wall Street Journal*, *Forbes*, and others fishing around for updates on what was happening with the Georgia deal, but no one was pursuing the story.

For more than twenty years, my publicist Melanie Bonvicino is whom I've trusted in my most challenging moments. She's always been a person who delivers the goods in a time of crisis. Melanie is like a bunch of crisis PR agencies in one. She is resilient, never takes no for an answer, and always has ten strategies for accomplishing the goal in case things go south.

Many of the deals Melanie and I have worked on were deals that seemed impossible. To me, that's just the nature of business in New York. The competition is incredible so there are no easy deals to be done, only "impossible" ones. When a business partner told me, "There's no way you can make that happen," Melanie always looked at me and said, "I love doing this!" And she always managed to deliver.

Melanie and I discussed different options for legal representation and a potential PR strategy. After all, given that we were considering a lawsuit against the president-elect, we needed not just a great lawyer, but a lawyer who was intimately familiar with how the Trump Organization operated its real estate deals. Finding a powerful PR angle to tell our story and the reason behind the lawsuit was no less important. Melanie delivered, yet again, and we engaged David Hryck and his partner Gil Feder of Reed Smith as our attorneys. (Gil had extensive knowledge of working on Trump real estate deals for the last decade or so.)

Once George arrived in New York, we went to see David and Gil at their law firm.

"Looking at the side letter, we have a very, very strong case," Gil and David said. "They're breaking the contract, and if they are breaking the contract and are pulling out of the licensing deal, they're going to have to pay you back your deposit or payment." The changed circumstances in Georgia, as he saw it, stopped the timeline for meeting the milestones—but once they were running and we failed to meet them, they could terminate the deal and keep the $1 million fee.

"How sure are you?" I asked.

"We'll get you your million dollars," Gil said. "We could even ask for more," he added, given that Silk Road had already spent over $4 million on the property and the deal.

"Let's go ahead," George and I said. "Even if you have to sue, we have to sue."

David and Gil cautioned us. "This is not just some real estate deal where you are buying an apartment. Do you really understand that you're going to be suing the sitting president?"

It was pretty heavy. But we agreed and Gil then sent a letter to the Trump Organization.

After the letter was received, George and I got calls immediately from Michael Cohen. By then, George was on his way back to Georgia and I was on my own. We were at a crossroads; either the deal proceeded or it died along with our entire shared vision for the Batumi Riviera site, and the whole of Georgia for that matter.

Michael and I talked more and decided to meet to work this out. We scheduled a meeting at Trump Tower. Having meetings there was no longer as easy as it sounded. By this time, there was tremendous attention in the press on Trump's potential conflicts of interest. Every time you turned on the TV, whether it was CNN or any of the other cable news networks, all you heard about were Trump's potential conflicts. There was also tremendous scrutiny of every person who went in or out of Trump Tower to meet with the president-elect or went up to his offices.

A Women's March was being organized. There were protesters every day outside of Trump Tower. Trump's own security had been increased as well as the Secret Service and the NYPD maintaining a large presence there.

It certainly was a new reality. I was living with lots of uncertainties and was pursuing a plan to sue the president-elect of the United States.

A Very Expensive Press Release

ENCOURAGED BY OUR LAWYERS' belief that the side letter gave us strong legal grounds against the Trump Organization canceling the deal, I arrived at Trump Tower with Melanie and David. It was no longer just Trump Tower; it was the office of the president-elect of the United States. It was difficult to get past the gauntlet and even enter the lobby. Once inside, we were told that I alone could go upstairs. My lawyer and publicist had to stay downstairs.

"Listen, this concerns a legal matter, I need my lawyer there," I said.

"No, he's going to have to stay. Sorry!" was the answer I received.

I got in the elevator alone. For some reason, as it rose it stopped at every floor. I had been in that elevator dozens of times before and that had never happened.

Finally, I arrived on the twenty-sixth floor. When the elevator doors opened, I was met by officers with German shepherds and FBI agents at the ready.

After identifying myself, I was then led to Michael's office.

As I walked down the corridor of Trump's old office, I saw Alan Garten, Trump's chief legal counsel. Despite many years of dealing with the Trump Organization, I had never met Garten before. Nevertheless, Garten had just been quoted in what was an unflattering article in *The Wall Street Journal* filled with false innuendos and unverified rumors about the Batumi Trump Tower deal and my close friend and business partner George Ramishvili and the Silk Road Group.

The Wall Street Journal had run an article on December 23, 2016, by Alexandra Berzon, Nathan Hodge, and Georgi Kantchev, with this inflammatory headline and subhead: "Trump's Firm Winds Down Some Deals That Prompted Complaints of Conflicts; Organization wants to sever ties with Georgian developer with alleged ties to a now-outlawed militia."

In the article they wrote:

> "In recent weeks, the company has backed away from a partnership with links to an executive tied to a now-outlawed Georgian militia and a financial-crimes investigation, moved to extricate itself from problematic development contracts and settled high-profile lawsuits.

> "Four years ago, Donald Trump publicly celebrated his partnership with former Soviet Republic of Georgia developer Giorgi Ramishvili. Now his company is trying to end the relationship.

> "Mr. Ramishvili has missed milestones in its attempts to build a Trump-branded luxury apartment complex in Batumi, a resort city near the Black Sea, and the Trump Organization sent him a default notice, a Trump attorney says.

This article misrepresented Silk Road and painfully mischaractarized Ramishvili. The truth is that Silk Road and George played a major role in Georgian's successful revival.

> "The developer allegedly has a past that makes him a highly unusual—and potentially problematic—partner for a US president, the *Wall Street Journal* has found. He allegedly was linked with the Mkhedrioni, the now-outlawed militia that thrived in the lawless early years of independence, according to Georgian media reports and two former members of the group. In addition, in 2013, investigators launched a high-profile probe of Mr. Ramishvili and his company, Silk Road Group SA over allegations of money laundering, according to Maya Mtsariashvili, a former Tbilisi chief prosecutor..."

> [*Author's note: Again deliberate body blows based largely on distorted facts and wild rumors.*]

In response to the article, the Georgian Ministry of Justice provided a letter to the *Journal* saying that the investigation was terminated on February 14, 2014, "due to the absence of a crime." Despite the *Journal* having quotes from the president of Georgia and the former culture minister that George was a legitimate businessman, the *WSJ* implied otherwise. Here's what the *Journal* said:

> "Alan Garten, general counsel for the Trump Organization, said the recent actions were approved by Mr. Trump's sons, Eric Trump and Donald Trump Jr., without Donald Trump's involvement. They are part of the normal course of business and don't reflect a shift in business approach, he said." Garten said they had done extensive diligence on the deal and that they did not question Mr. Ramishvili. The move to cancel the licensing deal wasn't related to anything about Mr. Ramishvili, Mr. Garten said. "Extensive diligence was done on this deal..."

> [*Author's note: This was true, the Trump Organization vetted all of us: Silk Road, Ramishvili, and me.*]

The article went on to discuss various Trump deals in Brazil and Azerbaijan that were also being dismantled.

While I was in Michael's office, just as we were about to have what I knew would be a difficult conversation, there was a hard knock at the door.

"Come in," Michael said.

The door opened and a female FBI agent with a large German shepherd came in.

"We need to go through the room," she said. Michael nodded. She loosened the leash and the dog jumped on me, sniffing all over. Not finding anything, they left. It was certainly a strange way to start a meeting. If the intention was to intimidate me, it wasn't going to work.

"We have to get this deal back on track," I told Michael. I demanded that David be brought upstairs because I needed to stress the strength of our legal case.

"Listen, brother, you know you can't win this," Michael told me. "You can't sue the president. Imagine what will happen to the US relationship with a small country like Georgia." Michael turned serious. "It's not gonna be pretty, I can tell you that much," he said.

"It's not just about Georgia," I said. "It's about being fair to Silk Road." I demanded that the deal needed to go forward. "We don't have to build it now. Let's not cancel it. We can postpone this for six months or a year, or until after Mr. Trump is out of the White House. Why can't we do that?"

Michael explained that it was no longer even up to the Trump Organization. He stood up, grabbed some papers, and handed them to me. It was a copy of the "Emoluments Clause."

The Emoluments Clause is a provision in the Constitution that restricts members of government from receiving gifts (and payments) from foreign governments. Because Trump is an international business figure, from day one of his election the press had seized on the Emoluments Clause. Those who were against Trump were searching for clear violations of the law while those who were Trump supporters said it didn't apply. But here was Michael Cohen, perhaps Trump's greatest supporter, saying it applied to our deal in Georgia.

"Even if we wanted to build it, we just can't, he can't," Michael told me. "It's a major conflict of interest."

I wasn't convinced that Michael really believed that. "Silk Road is not a government but a private corporation so there's no violation of the clause," I said.

Michael knew I was right, but Michael loved to argue, especially on behalf of his client, Donald J. Trump.

Michael knew about the problem we were having with the adjacent land in Batumi and he brought that up, too. I said we had a work-around for that.

"Listen," he said, "whether we like it or not, *The Wall Street Journal* didn't help either."

"The bottom line," Michael said, "is that Silk Road had four years to build the damn project and it didn't. They are in violation of missing the milestone."

"The 'missed milestones' claim isn't accurate," I said.

"You can't win," Michael said. "When *The Wall Street Journal* reports that your partner is part of a criminal organization and that Silk Road was investigated for money laundering—whether it's true or not—how can the president of the United States be in business with them?"

Although we had sought to have that false allegation corrected, Michael was not wrong in saying that the *WSJ* article had tainted Silk Road. Michael added that when the *WSJ* had called him to corroborate the article he had said, "Have you ever met the guy? He's the nicest person I know." But it didn't matter; the damage was done.

I knew well that George was never part of a criminal or outlawed entity. That such a respected publication would say so, based on rumors and without hard evidence, was appalling. George was a decent and honest person, a good son, a wonderful husband, an incredible father to four amazing children, and was dedicated to his business and to his country.

I will never know why the *WSJ* published these attacks. There are two theories that come to mind. First, at that moment, the *WSJ*, although a conservative right-leaning newspaper, was still in the camp of the traditional conservatives who opposed Trump such as George Will, Bill Kristol, and Peggy Noonan. Perhaps they were attempting to tar Trump using whatever dirt was at hand. That still doesn't explain who supplied the dirt. The Trump Organization or members of Trump's campaign inner circle seemed a good guess, but Michael denied it, and as I said, I will never know.

No matter. At that moment, I had to admit that *The Wall Street Journal* had made our deal radioactive. And this was just the beginning. There would surely be more articles to come in other news outlets. The writing was on the wall: this was going to be really, really bad for our deal, our partners, and for me personally.

I pressed Michael to let David upstairs as we were now discussing legal issues. Michael agreed, and soon David joined us. David was taking notes of our conversation when, in the middle of the meeting, Michael received a phone call. He picked up, and all of a sudden got very quiet and spun his chair around 180 degrees so his back was now to us.

All Michael was saying was "Yes, yes, sir."

I am not sure who was on the other side of the call, but it sounded exactly the way Michael spoke with Mr. Trump.

Once Michael was done, he spun back and nodded with a slight smile, saying, "We gotta get this thing done, Giorgi."

"We will," I said, "but if the deal has to end, it has to end fairly. Silk Road must come out dignified."

"What is fair to you?" Michael asked.

"First of all," I said, "Alan didn't have to take a swipe at Silk Road in *The Wall Street Journal*. That was uncalled for. So, we have to fix that."

I insisted that Alan now join our meeting. Michael asked him to come in.

Once Alan was in the room, I had a chance to recap what had been said and demanded that Silk Road get a fair treatment not only because of my personal relationship with Michael or the Trump Organization, but because Silk Road did nothing wrong. I was emphatic in saying that we had a side letter signed by Mr. Trump and that, according to our lawyer, it meant we would prevail if Silk Road sought to enforce the agreement.

I made clear to Alan how angry I was about his public comments. He said he appreciated that I was angry but that he didn't know anything about the side letter, and if he had, he would have refrained from any such comment.

Clearly Michael knew about the side letter—he had fought tooth and nail over it. Clearly, Trump, who had signed the letter, knew about it. But Alan seemed genuinely shell-shocked to find out that the side letter existed.

David seemed pleased with the change of dynamic in our favor, but it was clear that the Trump Organization no longer wanted any part of this deal. They would do whatever they had to, absent returning any money, to walk away.

The best solution I saw at that moment for restoring Silk Road's damaged reputation was a joint press release by the Trump Organization and Silk Road, rebutting *The Wall Street Journal*'s negative claims about the deal and regarding the business.

We needed the Trump Organization to state clearly and definitively that Trump was cutting ties with SRG due to his election and not due to any allegations against Silk Road. That, to the contrary, he held Silk Road in the highest esteem.

I had to sell this to Michael and Alan, who seemed desperate to get this deal off their books. They both also told me that looking at the toxic environment around Trump, they wouldn't be surprised if they were each called before congress for some type of hearings (at the time I didn't make anything of this, but looking back now, perhaps they already knew what was ahead).

I made it very clear that unless the Trump Organization actively helped restore Silk Road's reputation, we would initiate a suit based on the side letter. We would do so, win or lose, as a matter of principle.

Negotiating with Michael and Alan was intense, and they were very aggressive. But they understood that I was resolute and was not going to be intimidated by them or by the fact that our discussions involved the president-elect.

In the end, they understood that they had to give something to get something. They agreed on the press release, which was a small but at that time important measure of vindication.

The Trump Organization was going to have to issue a joint press release that stated the truth: that Silk Road is a great company and that the Trump Organization and President Trump hold them in high regard and that we have mutually canceled the agreement because of the current changed circumstances. We started throwing different ideas around for the press release. David was quick to write all of them down and what he read back to me sounded powerful.

At the end of the day, that was a very expensive press release, but at the same time, it was worth it in terms of crisis management. Silk Road had ongoing loan agreements with a number of banks and those agreements were at risk because the *WSJ* article implied there was something wrong with Silk Road.

—

AFTERWARD, I WOULD ALWAYS wonder about the timing of the *Wall Street Journal* article. Was it possible that the Trump Organization, in wanting a reason to exit the deal, had planted the article just to get rid of us? I don't know. But the timing was strange and certainly worked to that purpose. At any event, after the *WSJ* article, the media was zeroing in on me, Silk Road, and George Ramishvili.

The Oncoming Media Storm

UNFORTUNATELY, THIS WAS ONLY the beginning of our problems with the American media. A shitstorm was coming, of that I was sure.

In spite of the Trump Organization press release speaking to Silk Road's good reputation, and the corrections in *The Wall Street Journal* where the Georgian government itself spoke of Silk Road's good standing, Melanie and I understood that the American press was coming after us.

I told my wife that we had to expect more bad news from the press. She was upset. She couldn't believe the press in America would be so mean or cause harm to people who had done no wrong.

I called George to warn him, telling him that the *Wall Street Journal* article that appeared surely wasn't the last we'd see.

"Something bad is going to happen. Be prepared," I said.

—

I CONVENED A MEETING with Melanie and our other PR executives. I told them we needed to work up a strategy because we were going to get killed in the press. "We are in a partnership with the president-elect, a sitting president—who the press wants to bring down. They'll take us down first. It's only going to get worse." I wasn't wrong about that.

Within days, my phone rang with a 202 area code (Washington, DC). The call was from Rosalind Helderman, a *Washington Post* reporter. I had no idea how she got my number, but she told me that with Tom Hamburger, another *Post* reporter, she was pursuing a story about Trump's potential foreign conflicts among his ongoing real estate deals. She asked me about the status of the Trump Tower Batumi.

I told her that we were ready to proceed but that the Trump Organization was reevaluating the project in light of Trump's election. Mostly, I wanted to make sure that Silk Road was portrayed fairly. The article, which appeared on November 25, 2016, concerned potential conflicts from Trump continuing foreign deals in places such as Buenos Aires, Batumi, and even India. As for the Batumi Trump Tower, the article mentioned the challenges the project had faced but implied they could now be resolved. The article came to no definite conclusion about whether the deal in Batumi would move forward. As far as I was concerned, that was a win for us.

—

AT THE SAME TIME, I also wanted to be prepared on the legal front should any of the reporting prove to be false or defamatory. I went in search of a great first amendment attorney.

Melanie reached out to Alan Dershowitz. He said he was interested but nothing ever came of it. She ended up introducing me to Rodney Smolla, Dean of Widener University of Delaware Law School, an expert on the first amendment whom we hired. Smolla has argued before the Supreme Court and has written numerous books on freedom of expression, as well as an influential treatise on the law of defamation.

We weighed suing *The Wall Street Journal*, but after they published their correction, we decided against doing so.

Nonetheless, articles critical of me and Silk Road kept appearing. I began to think perhaps we needed someone experienced in both law and publicity, based in Washington, DC. One name came to mind: Lanny Davis. I met with him and he gave me some advice, but as we were no longer interested in suing *The Wall Street Journal*, we tabled working together at that time.

In the midst of all of this, Dan Alexander from *Forbes* contacted me. He said that he thought Silk Road had been hammered in the press and that it would be important for me to tell our side of the story. I asked if he was willing to fly to Georgia to tell the true story. He said "absolutely" and even sent me a page of bullet points on what and how he would cover the story. It looked quite fair.

I knew Dan was an open Trump-hater, but I thought that didn't matter because we were no longer in business with Trump. Plus, I honestly believed that Silk Road was doing so much good in Georgia it deserved unbiased coverage. So, I arranged for him to fly to Georgia with me.

That July, we traveled together to Tbilisi. We gave him total access to Silk Road. He interviewed George at length. We went everywhere, including Batumi, because I knew we had nothing to hide.

Spending so much time together, of course we talked about Trump and the challenge facing my partners of marketing a Trump Tower after the Trump brand was gone.

The article, which appeared on August 1, 2017, was very different from what I hoped. The title itself was damning: "Exclusive Investigation: Inside the Wild Plan to Create a Fake Trump Tower."

Not finding any improprieties with Silk Road, instead Alexander chose to target me and George as hucksters who were going to build a fake Trump Tower without the name but still capitalizing on the Trump association and all the high-profile media publicity that came with it. The article made it seem like this was some high-flying, high-spirited flimflam job where we intended to erect a building that would traffic in how much it looked like a Trump Tower to lure investors and tenants; and that we were keeping open the possibility that if, at a future date, Trump wanted to rejoin the project, he could do so and that his original pre-negotiated percent of sales commissions would be honored. I was referred to, in a mocking tone, as "the former King George" or just "King George" (which was a stage name I used briefly). The gist of the article was that Trump's foreign conflicts of interests persist even in "fake" projects.

Once again, with the best of intentions, I had been hoodwinked by a reporter following his own sensational agenda rather than the truth. It was as if someone visited the Louvre and believed the graffiti on one of its building's walls was the art and not the treasures inside.

It was really damaging to my reputation, and certainly to our hopes of salvaging the tower we wanted to build in Batumi to make that city the Monte Carlo of Eurasia.

Like it or not, I was now a public persona.

Kevin G. Hall of the McClatchy Newspapers (the *Miami Herald* among others) contacted me saying he was writing a story, and "it's going to be a bad story." Hall was looking into Michael Cohen, Donald Trump, and a possible Russian connection. That our deal had been in Georgia seemed to make no difference. Each instance of bad press was a snowball, and it was clear we were about to be buried in an avalanche.

The New Yorker. *Yes, the* New Yorker

I HAD BARELY RECOVERED from the *Forbes* article, which weighed on me, when I received a call from Adam Davidson, a contributor to

The New Yorker. He is, for the most part, a financial reporter, and part of the successful podcast *Planet Money*.

My conversation with Davidson told me that he was a serious reporter who had sources on the ground in Georgia and in the US. (What I didn't know was that he was working with Columbia Graduate School of Journalism and their students in doing some of the extensive international financial reporting he was undertaking.)

None of this was good for Silk Road's or my private business. I was in the middle of several very complex deals in the renewable energy, media, and film industries that were close to being consummated. In addition, I was my wife's business partner in two ventures she was launching: a fashion brand as well as a film project she was going to star in.

However, due to the vicious media storm directed at me and my partners, I had no choice but to step away from all of them. Being a Trump foreign business partner became a liability in ways I never imagined.

For example, my wife had a photo session for *Spirit and Flesh Magazine* where the legendary Sharon Stone was wearing my wife's dress for the editorial. The photo shoot went well. However, during the lunch following the shoot, it came out that I had had business dealings with Trump. Just like that, she ended the lunch quickly, left, and we never heard from her again.

As for Silk Road, the European Bank for Reconstruction and Development (EBRD) had agreed to explore the possibility of issuing bonds of $200 million. We were also hoping to close a deal with the Overseas Private Investment Corporation (OPIC), a self-sustaining US government agency that helps American businesses invest in emerging markets such as Georgia. We had a fully executed agreement with OPIC, which would have made Silk Road a significant partner for Georgia. Instead, the deal was canceled. I still can't fully understand what happened. But I am here to report that it did.

—

AND THEN OTHER SHOE fell: the *New Yorker* article, "Trump's Business of Corruption" (or "No Questions Asked," its title in the print version of the magazine) by Adam Davidson appeared in the August 21, 2017, issue asking, "What secrets will Mueller find when he investigates the president's foreign deals?"

Davidson's article, which he wrote, as mentioned above, with the help of several journalism students at Columbia University, delves deeply into the Batumi Tower deal, Silk Road and its partners, and gives the impression, among other things, that Trump's motivation for the Trump Tower deal could possibly have been money laundering, either for his own benefit, Silk Road's, or both, and that Silk Road's partners may be connected to Russian partners who may themselves be connected to Putin.

If the above sounds vague, it is because the article is a collection of theories and possibilities lacking real knowledge or facts. Professors, attorneys, and tax experts in New York give opinions about Silk Road's corporate structure, its transactions, and its partners—but if one reads the article closely, it is just one theory after another, none of which are proven. Nonetheless, these theories are used as building blocks to a conclusion that is also neither proven nor supported by actual fact—and so it is simply false.

The immediate post-election hunger to find Trump guilty of corruption, money laundering, and/or having ties to Putin was so great and so urgent to certain members of the press, and at *The New Yorker*, that my reputation and that of Silk Road, its principals and partners, were just collateral damage along the way.

Rachel Maddow, she of the arched eyebrow, devoted an hour to Adam Davidson's article on her primetime MSNBC program. Maddow insinuated, implied, and assumed Grand Guignol looks of skepticism and mockery regarding the legitimate businesses of Silk Road and its partners and our very real attempt to build a Trump Tower in Batumi. She floated Davidson's theories uncritically, adding her own stamp of approval as to their veracity when in fact she had done no independent fact-checking or investigation of her own. In truth, Rachel Maddow only gives the appearance of being a journalist; she is instead an entertainer, a talk show host.

The damage to Silk Road and my reputation from this double-barreled shot of innuendo was so great that Silk Road hired Kroll Investigations to assemble a factual rebuttal.

The resulting fifteen-page October 2017 document, "A detailed response to recent media allegations against the Silk Road Group," states in its opening section that "the *New Yorker* article levels several damaging allegations against SRG [Silk Road Group] which have no basis in fact… and are not backed by any concrete evidence." It goes on to say that the Davidson article "is based on speculation, circumstance and innuendos, and conveniently disregards facts…that do not fit its chosen narrative."

The response identified two main allegations: that SRG had an improper relationship with the Kazakhstan-based BTA Bank that allowed it to benefit from preferential access to funding and, after the bank's collapse, an inexplicable write-off of SRG's liabilities; and that SRG was an instrument in laundering the proceeds of crimes from the large-scale fraud perpetrated by BTA Bank's disgraced former chairman.

The report was quick to address these two false claims by stating that BTA's bank loans to SRG were made properly as confirmed by audit reports from Big Four accounting firms; and that, following the bank's collapse, SRG settled its obligations to BTA, in a legal manner, acceptable to the Kazakh authorities who investigated the bank's collapse, the successor management of BTA, and the Georgian government, which launched its own investigation into SRG's loans and also found it blameless.

The financing mechanisms viewed with suspicion by Davidson and the professors and experts he sought out are explained in detail in the report. They are complex and convoluted. Why this was the best vehicle for these investments is not relevant (they may not be)—what is critical is that auditors, regulators, investigators, and prosecutors examined these transactions multiple times and found no wrongdoing. *The New Yorker* looked suspiciously on Silk Road's venturing into new industries, ignoring the successful management team they had assembled to do so.

The *New Yorker* article states that the Batumi Tower development deal "for which Trump was reportedly paid a million dollars involved unorthodox financial practices that several experts described as 'red flags' for bank fraud and money laundering."

As to the claims of fraud and money laundering, the report points out that Davidson's claims rests on the opinion of a Case Western professor that SRG's corporate structure is conducive to the obfuscation of funds. Although Davidson treats this as conclusory evidence of malfeasance, it remains a theory, and an incorrect and false one at that. "Not one piece of evidence is referred to in the article substantiating a very serious allegation," the report states.

The New Yorker goes on to insinuate that if the Trump Organization were paid with shady funds of questionable origin, then the US president could be exposed to Russian blackmail. Yet there is no reason or evidence to characterize SRG's relationship to Trump in these terms. Trump's fee was paid by SRG in 2011, more than two years after the BTA loan funds were invested by SRG; and they were paid out of SRG's earnings from other projects.

Finally, Davidson, in what I can only imagine was a desperate attempt to get his article maximum publicity, made the outlandish and improbable attempt to connect Trump to Putin through Mukhtar Ablyazov, the former chairman of BTA who fled Kazakhstan when BTA was nationalized and is accused of bank fraud and looting the bank's assets.

The New Yorker tars SRG for being partners in a bank with Mr. Ablyazov when in truth SRG, BTA, and others were partners in a bank— they were not personally involved. The entire article was a patchwork quilt of innuendo after innuendo, followed by speculations and assumptions, all based on nothing more than vicious derogatory stereotypes of corrupt foreign actors—basically the thesis was that if you are a successful businessperson in the former Soviet Union or have dealings in Russia, you must be doing something shady and there must be something wrong with your business and your partners' backgrounds.

Despite being a highly experienced investigative reporter, Davidson knew that anything negative about Trump would sell magazines—the more controversial the better, all the more so if your thesis leads back to

Putin. Davidson's article was a conclusion in search of facts rather than the other way around.

I went out of my way, meeting with Davidson no less than three times. I elaborated in detail about the relationship between Trump and Silk Road, as well as between Cohen and myself. Honestly, was there anyone who knew this transaction and the parties involved better than I? But I could tell Davidson cared more about the theories he was spinning than the truth I was offering.

The facts were clear: the Georgian prosecutor's office investigated Silk Road Group in connection with BTA Bank and other transactions and found no evidence of any wrongdoing.

The *New Yorker* article as spun into infotainment on Rachel Maddow was very damaging for Trump and Silk Road. George and I were made out to be villains—partners in shadowy and dubious Trump-affiliated enterprises—and to be a front for Russian and Kazhak money laundering that somehow established a link of corruption from Trump to Putin. That was as ridiculous as it was false. However, in many ways, we are still dealing with the consequences of these false reports.

Finally, after the article came out, Melanie and I had a follow-up meeting with Davidson and his editor at *The New Yorker*. We had a heated discussion. I promised to provide them with a binder of facts showcasing Silk Road Group and the findings that there was no wrongdoing on any of our part. They both said that if we provided that, "we would be open to issuing a correction." We provided all the information I've listed above.

I am still waiting for a full correction to appear in *The New Yorker*.

Power Lunch

AFTER THE ARTICLES IN *The New Yorker*, *The Washington Post*, *The Wall Street Journal*, *Forbes*, and the McClatchy Newspapers, I decided that George and I needed to be more proactive in responding to the false claims that were damaging our reputation.

We accepted an invitation to appear on CNBC's *Power Lunch* with Michelle Caruso-Cabrera—a program that is watched by many in the business community all over the world.

Michelle and her cohosts asked very tough questions about a possible Putin-Trump conspiracy. However, George and I were able to refute *The New Yorker*'s allegations, and we made it clear that the Trump Tower Batumi deal was never anything more than a licensing deal. Trump had no real involvement beyond receiving a licensing fee. Furthermore, we made it clear that there was no impropriety with regard to BTA Bank.

As to why the deal was canceled, George explained, "It was a new reality. Mr. Trump became president. It was a different situation and we, amicably, agreed to stop this contract."

Asked on *Power Lunch* about the allegations in the *New Yorker* article, I answered, "First of all, I hope less people read the *New Yorker* article because it's just untrue....When reporting something, it would really help to be honest about facts, and the article has really neglected the facts."

I was also able to address the BTA allegations: "The BTA Bank-Silk Road relationship ended in 2008....The deal with Mr. Trump and Trump Organization was signed in 2011."

Finally, when asked about Mueller's investigation, I told the program's hosts that I had not heard from anyone about testifying against the president in the Russian probe (which was true at that point—the FBI hadn't even raided Michael Cohen's office yet). I had no idea at that point that I would be called before the grand jury.

George announced on the program that although Trump was no longer involved, Silk Road Group was moving forward with plans for the tower using the same architectural concept Trump had approved. And when asked, George added that he would be happy to team up with the president again in the future.

As good as appearing on CNBC was for us, even better was the article that appeared on CNBC's website by Catherine Campo on Friday, October 20, 2017, whose headline stated, "Silk Road Group executive refutes *New*

Yorker article about Trump deal." This has proven tremendously effective because when you Google "Silk Road" this still comes up high in the search.

Many of the principals and executives at the banks and financial institutions we deal with actually watch *Power Lunch*. If they didn't watch it live, they watched it afterward online. So that interview gave comfort to the business community about Silk Road.

For a few weeks, I breathed a sigh of relief and made my peace with the aftermath of losing the Trump deal.

However, my peace was short-lived. Soon after I visited Michael in his hotel room, his home and office were raided by the FBI.

A few weeks after that, there was that knock at the door of my Connecticut home where, as I recounted at the start of this book, I was questioned and hand-delivered a subpoena to appear before Mueller's grand jury.

Although all this was supposed to be confidential, CNN vans soon appeared outside my home, and their reporters started questioning my friends and neighbors about me. Then *The Washington Post* mentioned me by name in an article, saying that I would neither confirm nor deny whether I was interviewed by Robert Mueller.

Here is the paradox of modern times: Most people I know no longer subscribe to newspapers, and if so, just their local paper. Most of the people who subscribe may not even read the entire paper. However, when my name was mentioned in several lines of an article in *The Washington Post*, somehow everyone knew about it and had read it. Maybe the newspaper has Trump to thank for that. But gossip and false reports fly around the Internet gaining strength, regardless of truth.

I can't tell you the number of people who contacted me to ask, directly or indirectly, out of friendship or out of gossipy desire, why Mueller would even want to interview me.

The times were so toxic that many business contacts didn't want to have anything to do with me as long as there was even the possibility that I could be called before Mueller, much less once I had indeed appeared before the grand jury. The economic impact on me and my family was real and severe.

Where Suspicion Grows

IT HAS ALWAYS PUZZLED me that the Department of Justice would see anything wrong in a global real estate developer like Donald Trump and his right-hand man Michael Cohen entering into what was not so much a real estate deal as a licensing deal for his name, for which Trump could make a quick fee and get a percentage of the unit sales.

It seemed fairly straightforward, and without Trump having any real other role in the transaction, I saw no opportunity for corruption, collusion, bribery, or money laundering, as had been alleged, nor any chance of Russian influence. And I was sure that is how most businesspeople looked at Trump's dealings.

However, the June 9, 2016, meeting at Trump Tower with the Russian attorney, attended by Don Jr. and Jared Kushner, was clearly more problematic. There was specific mention of information damaging to Hillary Clinton being proffered, and even talk about the Magnitsky Act and Russian adoptions. Making the situation worse, the meeting was with a Russian attorney, and that was set up by Emin Agalarov, who had himself been contacted by a music publicist, Rob Goldstone.

Despite all that, the meeting didn't appear all that serious and nothing came of it. But once you opened the Pandora's box of Russian actors trying to establish contact with the Trump campaign, well, then everything and everyone concerning Russia became suspect, including me and my business ventures.

The problem seems to me that the United States has never had an international businessman such as Trump as president. They'd never had to consider what constitutes a conflict of interest, what is improper, and what is the normal course of business. And Trump, despite vague claims to the contrary, never stopped doing business. No matter which of his children were the public face of his enterprise, he never relinquished control (or the right to make money from those deals).

Why shouldn't the Trump Organization, a commercial entity, have full authority to continue to do business, look for deals, and, yes, make money just like every other corporation or partnership? I don't really see the crime. And if anyone finds a quid pro quo in any of the deals in which the president played a role, let them prosecute it to the full extent of the law. That's the American way.

However, the media's frenzy to convict Trump of wrongdoing—and their sloppy, unverified, and often false reporting regarding Trump's pursuit of foreign deals—was all smoke and no fire.

What is inexcusable and downright wrong is smearing people with unverified innuendo and portraying them in a derogatory fashion just because they had the temerity to do business with Donald Trump before he even became the forty-fifth president of the United States. (I do exclude fair and honest reporters because I know they are still out there—I just wish that I or my partners were lucky enough to meet some.)

I remain particularly rankled and offended that I was characterized repeatedly as a potential Russian actor or conduit. They seemed to conveniently forget that I am an American citizen.

As one of the persons who had business dealings with Donald Trump and the Trump Organization and who was one of the persons who proposed a potential Trump Tower Moscow deal, I certainly didn't deserve to have my life turned upside down.

President Ronald Reagan is credited by most Americans with bringing down the Communist Soviet Union, but he did not do so alone. It was the actions of people in those republics who gave their blood and lives to bring down what President Reagan called "the Evil Empire." Everyday citizens' resistance and their dreams of a better life played a major role. Those of us who dreamed of freedom in secret, and those like me who fled their countries of origin because of Communist oppression, all had a part in making that dream come true. And in the case of Georgia, it was the Silk Road Group and all its partners that made a huge difference—and also, I believe, benefited the United States greatly.

This is why my partners and I so resent being accused by the FBI and the Department of Justice, as well as the press, of colluding with Russia or helping Putin in the disruption of the US democracy.

12

What Russia Could Have Been

Moscow after the Fall

WHEN I RETURNED TO Moscow some years after the fall of Communism, I witnessed the crime, corruption, and absolute disorder that rocked the lives of millions. Post-Soviet-style democracy and capitalism was nothing but a battle ground, a Darwinian struggle for survival.

It was soul-crushing to see what Moscow had become: a city where miles and miles of people waited in line for a loaf of bread or a roll of toilet paper; where I watched frightened thirteen- to fifteen-year-old girls being shoved into foreign cars by loud and violent men dressed in fake Versace leather coats who were flashing guns just to make a point; where the smoky casinos were packed with new waves of Chechen businessmen wearing uniforms of Adidas tracksuits who checked their fur coats at the door along with two or three guns. It was crass, cruel, and merciless, and it was a Russia that most Americans knew nothing about.

So much so that the rest of the population felt terrorized, afraid, and full of despair. You can't blame the Russians for succumbing to their worst impulses—the Soviet State had starved them for decades and now placed out an all-you-can-eat buffet for them to compete over.

My generation was witness to thousands of our own losing their lives as a barely sober Boris Yeltsin took the barely nascent dream of democracy and capitalism and drowned it in the corruption, greed, graft, and incompetence of his administration, creating chaos and a vacuum into which the Russian security services and a former KGB officer, Vladimir Putin, would reassert control of the Russian nation.

It didn't have to be this way. For this I don't reproach the average Russian citizen trying to survive in a chaotic time, or making the most of the opportunities presented, but I hold responsible both Putin and the leaders in the West such as Clinton, Obama, and Merkel.

—

WHEN THE SOVIET UNION dissolved, what the West should have done is develop a well-thought-out strategy regarding Russia that would have supported Russian pride rather than offending it; that would have kept the average Russian above the poverty line and secured Russia's dangerous nuclear arsenal.

Instead, the United States and US-based corporations decided to follow the Russian State's lead in looting the country's natural resources, most notably their oil and gas, which helped to create the class of Russian oligarchs. As the average Russian was plunged into chaos, the desire for a strong leader grew, creating the opening Putin seized.

I don't fault Putin for seizing the opportunity, just for what he did or didn't do with it.

—

JUST FOR A SECOND, let's play devil's advocate and imagine what would have happened if Putin had decided to pursue a different path after the breakup of the Soviet Union. He certainly is smart and a savvy enough politician and a tremendously gifted leader who could've executed a number of different strategies instead of the one he was most familiar with.

Russia has the largest territory and is the largest market in the region with the most well-developed infrastructure of railways and roads. The

Russian language is spoken by all its citizens, as well as those in the former Soviet satellites and Communist bloc countries, not to mention China.

If only the Russian government had focused on building a real market economy, accepted a real democracy, and established an open society living under the rule of law, there's very little doubt that Russia could've been a global economic force rather than an oil-and-gas-dependent struggling economy where the general population is largely living on a prayer.

With their brilliant computer programmers and coders, mathematicians, and scientists, Russia could have taken a dominant role in information technologies, biotech, and medical advances rather than in cyber war and spy games. With a prosperous and peaceful nation, Russia might have brought a lasting stability to the Eurasian region rather than division and military conflicts that isolated Russians from their formerly friendly neighbors.

With Russia as a viable economic competitor to the United States, their world prominence would be assured and there would be no need for Russia to support murderous regimes such as Bashar Al-Assad in Syria or that of the Venezuelan dictator Nicolás Maduro.

Russia could have united those in Georgia and Ukraine who share the Orthodox Christian faith rather than creating such conflict that the patriarchs are declaring their independence.

Even if Russia had decided to remain a Communist or a Socialist republic, look to the accomplishments of China and even of Vietnam to see what Russia might have been. But that's not the path Putin chose, unfortunately and in many ways tragically.

There's a saying, "*Russiu Umom Ne Ponyat*" ("you can't understand Russia with your brain"), which speaks to the fact that there is no accounting for how Russia will act.

We can't control Russia, or Putin, but we, as Americans, can choose to be proactive in finding political and economic solutions for Russia to consider, not only as regards Russia but also as regards the entire region of former Soviet States. Whatever the solution is to contain Russia or improve the West's relationship with Russia, it must work for all former

Soviet countries. Georgia, Ukraine, Kazakhstan, and other former Soviet States must be supported in finding their own success as democratic, free-market modern countries. Otherwise, willingly or unwillingly, they will fall right back into the horrifying post-Soviet syndrome and there might be no coming back from it. I surely hope that President Trump seizes every opportunity he may have to bring peace and prosperity to one of the most important regions for world peace, the former Soviet region.

What Michael Cohen Told Me

OVER TIME, MICHAEL COHEN and I had developed a close relationship. We had several dinners with his wife and mine. He called me "brother," and I was okay with that. And I take friendship seriously.

Michael and I had discussed Russia in general, of course. He never seemed pro-Russian to me, but unlike other friends I had, Michael never saw Russia as a hostile power to America. His impression of Russia was a very rich bunch of guys who could afford everything and anything. And Putin for him was the guy who ruled those money guys with an iron fist.

Still, Michael never struck me as a guy who would conspire with Russia and betray his country. Michael was, however, the guy who would go way above and beyond to do whatever he could to enhance the image of his boss, Donald J. Trump. Michael saw Trump as president before Trump started running. To Michael's credit, he was proven right.

—

IN 2011, MICHAEL TALKED to me about whether Trump should run for president. I said he definitely should.

"He's got *The Apprentice*," I said. "He's got his name on buildings and country clubs nationwide. He's a great salesman, maybe the best ever. He's definitely a showman. I think he should run. And I think he will win."

Michael said, "Yeah, I think he would win too."

Michael then created a website, "Should Trump Run?" That was how it all started.

After Michael started a "Trump for President" organization and website, he was constantly giving me updates: "You know how many people are looking at the website? This is great, we've got everybody excited." Another time, Michael told me, "He would be number one right now if he ran as a Republican."

We had many of these conversations over the years. I didn't think Trump would ever run if he thought he had no chance of winning. But if he did run, I was pretty sure he would win because of his absolute and complete commitment to winning no matter what and at any cost.

I saw these qualities during my encounters with Trump. They stand out from the minute he shakes your hand till the end of your interaction with him. There's not much room for anyone else when Trump enters the room, and when he leaves, the room feels empty and boring. Like it or not, Trump is a natural-born leader.

—

When Trump was already in the White House and the Stormy Daniels controversy broke, Michael and I texted each other and we agreed to meet to talk as friends. Obviously I had no idea at the time that he was under criminal investigation; I'm not sure that Michael knew himself.

I went to the Regency, his hotel. He was staying there because there had been a flood in his apartment and he had to move out during the repairs. He looked worried, understandably so. The entire country was talking about him and the Stormy Daniels hush money payment which the *WSJ* had reported on just a few days before.

Michael didn't want to sit in the restaurant on the lobby floor (home of the "power breakfast"). He asked me to come up with him to his hotel room.

When we arrived, his son and his wife were there. They are wonderful people.

Michael was always proud of his children. He would often tell me about his son's great talent in baseball as well as his daughter's academic achievements.

We sat in his hotel suite's living room. It was a very friendly conversation. He told me about the ridiculousness of the situation and how badly and unfairly the media was treating him.

He said he had an iron-clad confidentiality agreement with Ms. Daniels, and that every time she talked to the press, he was going to charge her $1 million for breaking it.

I told him that, as a friend, I assumed that "you were not thinking very straight because this looks pretty weird." I told him that I knew he was more than just a lawyer to Mr. Trump, he was a friend. A friend to Mr. Trump, to Melania, and to their family, and that, whatever he did, I was sure he did it from his heart and out of friendship to protect them from scandal and unpleasantness.

He was very sincere in his response. He confirmed to me that the only reason he did what he did was exactly that; out of the respect and love he had for Mr. Trump, as he always called him—never Donald—as well as for Melania and Mr. Trump's entire family. He paid the money out of his home equity loan, he told me, because he didn't want his wife to know that he was paying monies to a porn star.

Never in this conversation did he say or imply that he paid Stormy Daniels at the direction of his former boss, Mr. Trump, to buy her silence about their affair. As I said above, Michael was doing this to protect Mr. Trump, as well as Melania and the family.

I told Michael that I thought it best if he went on TV to personally tell his side of the story instead of sending his lawyer to defend him.

Michael was upset and nervous, but he still had that hopefulness in his eyes. He was confident that things would turn back around and that he'd be back on top again. He suddenly stood up, removed both his cell phones from the table, and placed them in a different room, far from the living room where we were sitting. I thought it was strange, but I also realized it meant that he wanted to tell me something important.

Michael quietly said that he couldn't care less if the media and the public were against him and were laughing at him. He said he was going to be the one laughing when it was all over. The only thing that mattered to him, he told me, was that the president was on his side and was genuinely worried about him. (He didn't say Mr. Trump as he always used to.)

In a hushed tone, Michael said, "He just called and asked me, 'How are you doing, Michael? Do you need anything? Can I do anything for you?'"

Michael was pleased that there was no change in his relationship with his former boss and current client, the president of the United States, Donald J. Trump.

Our conversation continued for a short while, and then I left. I had this strange feeling that this might be the last time I spoke to Michael about any of this. However, I never in my wildest dreams would I have imagined what was to come next.

Shortly after our meeting at the Regency, I turned on the TV to see FBI agents raiding the exact same room that I had been sitting in.

I had no idea whether my conversation with Michael had, in some way, been recorded. And no idea, if it had been, whether that conversation was protected due to my business relationship with Michael.

My conversation with Michael had been a very honest, very friendly conversation. I knew that I had said and done nothing wrong. But I also realized that what I thought no longer mattered.

What mattered was what Mueller, his agents, and his attorneys thought.

Trump's Deal in Russia

THERE HAVE BEEN MANY reports in the media about Trump's more than thirty years of attempting to do deals in Moscow.

Trump had tried to build a tower in Soviet Moscow as far back as the late 1980s. As someone who has done business in Moscow since the 1990s, all I can say is Trump is lucky none of those deals happened.

Business in Moscow in those days, as I've made clear, was very tricky. Right after the fall of Communism, it was like the Wild West and the Gold Rush all in one. There was no credible internationally recognized system in place that could confirm or challenge the legitimacy and transparency of funds or the background of investors from Russia—of how the money was made and where it came from or where it went, or even who was the real beneficiary behind the corporate facade.

The only two sources at the time were either the Russian Security Forces (the former KGB or Soviet Authorities) or the Russian criminal underworld—neither of whom was in the habit of sharing information with Western businesses. You needed a trusted insider and, most often, that person would take over the deal themselves before helping you.

Russia was in such dire economic straits that the criminal underworld was allowed to flourish—as long as it was paying the authorities. Underworld figures were only exposed or arrested if they refused to pay or stopped paying.

All of which is to say that if Trump had made a deal to build a tower in Moscow in the 1990s, he would have had to partner with Russian criminal elements who, in the end, would have profited even if he didn't.

Conversely, the fact that Trump never made a deal or got a tower built in Moscow tells me that Michael Cohen never had direct links with the decision makers there or powerful enough connections to get a deal done.

A lot of suspicion surrounds Trump's connection to the Agalarovs. They are, as I've said before, very successful real estate developers in Russia. They hosted Trump and the 2013 Miss Universe pageant. Gossip would have you believe that if there is kompromat involving Trump, it comes from the Agalarovs and Trump's 2013 visit to Moscow; and that if there were a Moscow Tower deal to be done with Trump, the Agalrovs would have done it.

Another significant reason that the Agalarovs aroused suspicion is because it was Emin Agalarov, Aras's son, who was instrumental in setting up the June 2016 meeting between Donald Trump Jr., Jared, and the Russian attorney.

However, the notion that they did tape Donald Trump in Moscow and that there was anything salacious about his conduct there is all just uninformed speculation and rumor.

When it comes to Aras, the owner of the Crocus group, he has built a very successful residential real estate business by putting his own name on every property. In many ways, he is the Trump of Moscow. He is a very self-interested person, much like Trump. Aras is a great salesman and I'm not sure why he would step out of the limelight to have Trump's name on a building when he could easily have his own name there. Or why he would promote the Trump brand in Russia rather than his own. It just doesn't sound like him.

As far as I can tell, Trump never did do a deal in Russia, and so he was correct in saying he had no investments or active business in Russia. Trump was up-front about the fact that he was trying to do a deal in Moscow and that Michael Cohen was pursuing it. But it seems to me no final deal was ever signed, no building was ever built. And no deal was ever going to get done, in my opinion, because they never had the right contacts in Moscow to get it done.

I also question the value of the Trump brand in Moscow and Russia. Donald Trump, to most Russians, was a global celebrity, and like any Hollywood celebrity he had a value in terms of making a personal appearance. It makes sense that Crocus would stage the Miss Universe pageant and have Trump make a personal appearance—but the brand was Miss Universe, not Trump, and it was Crocus presenting it in Russia, which is how the Agalarovs like it.

Did Trump try his best to have business in Russia and did Michael Cohen try to deliver for him? Sure!

Should he have told the American people during the 2016 campaign that his company was still negotiating potential deals in Moscow? Of course!

There was no reason to hide that his company had a business to run and expand. But the facts are stubborn: Trump never had a signed binding final deal for any Moscow Tower projects.

Was Trump at some point promised a meeting with Putin? My guess is yes, he was.

Most celebrities coming to Moscow are promised a meeting with Putin, which, in most cases, never happens. On YouTube you can see events where Putin is present and American celebrities such as Sharon Stone are in the room. Trump, as an American TV celebrity, would certainly be told Putin wanted to meet him—whether he did or not.

I have no idea whether Trump has Russian investors in his various projects and businesses. If he does, he would not be the only businessman to have done so.

Has Russian money or money from Russian-funded corporations purchased Trump properties? Most likely.

Is some Russian money shady? Perhaps.

The problem remains, as I said before, that it is exceedingly difficult to verify the source of much Russian wealth—where it came from, where it goes, where it ends up.

On the other hand, is every wealthy Russian or former Soviet a shady businessperson somehow connected to the Kremlin? Of course not. That's absolute nonsense.

Adam Davidson's *New Yorker* article, "Trump's Business of Corruption," would have you believe that my partners and I are connected to the Kremlin and Putin, but that's just a fairy tale—an anti-Trump conspiracy theory. And one that did tremendous damage to my and Silk Road's business reputations. Once again, if Davidson or others actually knew anything about Georgia and Russia, and understood the enmity between the two, they would know how ridiculous Davidson's premise was in the first place.

A Moscow Tower

IN 2015, AFTER DONALD Trump had already declared himself a presidential candidate, friends in Moscow who knew I was connected to the Trump Organization suggested that they could build a residential Trump Tower in Moscow and that it would be a big success.

They wanted to be the first to build a Trump property in Russia, and they wanted exclusivity for the Trump brand in Russia. I told them that was not possible and not how the Trump Organization worked. They would never get exclusivity in Moscow or in Russia. But they could be first.

Real estate deals are often predicated on not spending your own money until you have the best deal possible—by buying a property under market value or having commitments already that exceed your costs. In the case of this Moscow Tower, my Russian friends did not yet own the property but wanted to make sure they got it in the best location and at the best possible price.

Their intention was to build the residential skyscraper in Moscow, and their idea was that if they could get a letter to the mayor of Moscow from the Trump Organization—stating that Trump was interested in building a tower with their company—then the mayor's office—interested in bringing a well-known US brand to Moscow—would give them the prime location they wanted at a favorable price.

Now, it makes no difference whether you are trying to erect a skyscraper in New York, Paris, or Moscow, you will need local government support at the highest level—otherwise you'd be wasting your time. To do so in Moscow's City Center you need permits and approvals, all of which run through the mayor's office.

—

SERGEY SOBYANIN, THE MAYOR of Moscow, is a very powerful man who is one of Putin's allies and is very close to him. I told my Russian friends to send me the letter that they would want written and I would pass it along. Which they did, and I did.

When I followed up with Michael, I said, "My contacts in Moscow are very eager to do the residential tower, and they're ready to engage right now, sign a deal and move forward." I wrote to Michael that, "If we could organize the meeting in New York at the highest level of the Russian government and Mr. Trump, this project would definitely receive worldwide attention."

"Of course. I'd love to make a deal with you," Michael told me. "We've done deals. I know I can trust you to deliver." But then he said, "Listen, I'm already talking with someone. Our deal is not yet signed, but I am pretty sure that we are going to complete the deal."

As time went on, the Moscow deal would come up. Sometimes, I brought it up to Michael, saying, "What's going on with the Moscow Tower?" and sometimes he brought it up, when there was either a positive development, such as the Trump Organization signing an LOI on the project, or a negative, as when Michael complained about the deal not getting done.

In early 2016, Michael gave me an update on the deal status and the LOI. Michael told me that some of the changes I'd negotiated with him on our deals were now part of their standard contract. That was in late January or February.

Then in April, it came up again. I had stopped by Michael's office. He was frustrated that things were not moving faster on the deal. Michael was angry. He was spouting off. "I know how Russia works now," Michael said. "I'm just gonna call the Kremlin directly to get this shit going."

I told him he was crazy. I told him you definitely shouldn't contact the Kremlin because, first of all, it's not going to get you the results you want; and second, it's just not smart.

Michael was adamant that he was going to do something to break the logjam. "I'm going to send an email," he insisted. At some point in our conversation, he asked me who he should send his email to.

"Who's the most important guy there?" Michael said. This was the way Michael's mind worked. His mindset was always that you needed to know the right person. When we were in Kazakhstan, he would always be asking me who was the right guy we should be meeting with.

"Who do you think has Putin's ear?" he said.

I told him that he shouldn't waste his time, but if he was trying to get to the Kremlin, he should write Dmitry Peskov, Putin's press secretary and his right hand.

I told him not to do so. But Michael was always going to do what Michael thought best.

CNN outside My House

To THIS DAY, I don't know who leaked the fact that the FBI had shown up at my home, or how the press found out Mueller's team wanted to interview me. I was concerned that having ıny name in the press as being part of the Mueller investigation would ruin my business reputation as well as that of my wife's. We were worried about ourselves, our children, our life in America. As each day blared reports of new indictments and guilty pleas, my wife worried about what might happen next.

Kevin Hall at McClatchy Newspapers published an article saying that a former associate of the Trump Organization who was involved in projects in Georgia, Kazakhstan, and Russia had been visited by the FBI. They didn't mention me by name, but anyone who knew me or was in business with me knew who they were talking about. And that was not good for either our privacy or my business.

Although I wasn't named, it only took a few hours before someone on Twitter started trolling me by name. This person, whom I'd never met, who didn't know me or my business or, let's face it, any of the facts, let loose a torrent of tweets about me. How I went to Kazakhstan with Michael Cohen; she connected it to the *New Yorker* article and everything else. And from there, the *WSJ* began to chase after me, and CNN continued to appear on my doorstep in Connecticut harassing my mother-in-law to confirm my identity and if I was investigated by Mueller. My wife and I really felt like we were under siege, again, but this time the Mueller subpoena was like a ticking bomb, which could've gone off at any time.

After CNN interviewed all my neighbors, it became intolerable. I wasn't going to be made a prisoner in my own home under siege from the media. So, along with my family, we decamped to New York and then to the West Coast, to LA.

I had to call my business partners, here and abroad, and tell them what was going on. They had to hear it from me rather than reading about it in the press. Although my telling them made little difference, suddenly people were concerned that if they continued to do business with me, they too might be called upon by the FBI or turn up on Mueller's subpoena list.

I decided to disassociate myself from my partners and projects in Georgia and in the US. That was not an easy decision. But I did not want to place them at any risk. And, of course, this had a huge negative financial impact on me and my family.

George stood by me. The rest of them…some were not so comfortable in continuing our association. An attorneys at one of the ventures asked me to personally indemnify the company. I quickly became an outcast.

Even my friends were curious to find out if I knew anything more. They knew all about the Mueller investigation. They knew all about Michael Cohen. But to me, they would hint or ask if I could tell them more. *Just tell us everything*, they would say. *You would tell us if you are guilty, right?* These were the kinds of questions I faced even from people who had known me and worked with me for years.

The more Cohen was in the news, the more my name surfaced. I stopped having dinners with friends and business associates because it all became too awkward. I didn't know what was coming next, and I didn't want to answer their questions or have them tarred with guilt by association.

Michael Cohen's Big Plans for America (and Mine, Too)

WHEN I TALKED TO Michael on that walk to his office on December 8, 2016, Michael told me that he believed that he could still represent Trump independent of the government or the Trump Organization. "I can do a lot more for him, I can protect him, and I can also start making money because I'm so close to the president."

For Michael it was not just about making money. "You know, there's so much to do for the country." For Michael, it was about doing good for the country—and doing it in ways that would also make him lots of money.

Michael's idea was to create a company and a fund to fix problems in America that needed to be solved (sort of like how Trump fixed the skating rink in Central Park, but on a national scale).

"One thing Trump wants to fix," Michael told me, "is the water in Flint, Michigan." Michael wanted to privatize water purification for Flint, Michigan. "If we fix that, we can be making money forever," he said.

There was also a power station in Alabama, Plant Gorgas, that had closed because of Obama-era regulations against coal-fired plants. "Mr. Trump wants to fix the power station," Michael said. "Let's find a way to buy this thing, invest in it, and make it efficient, right? It's a complete loss now!" Fixing the plant would be a blow to Democrats because Obama's war on coal forced it to close and Trump could show that it could be operated efficiently and profitably. That would be a big win for everyone.

Michael saw opportunity everywhere. To do good. To help America. And to make money, tons of money. Those were the conversations I had with Michael.

—

MICHAEL WASN'T ALONE IN having big ideas once Trump was elected. I had them too and discussed them with Michael as well.

We wanted to create a fund whose goal was creating a relationship of peace and prosperity with the Muslim world. I suggested a Eurasian Financial Fund by which countries such as Kazakhstan and some of the Arab nations would invest in American infrastructure. To show good faith from the Muslim world in the Trump era. We would also hold a financial conference at Trump Tower as part of creating the fund. I sent several proposals like that to Michael.

It was a time when everyone who knew or supported Trump was inspired by the great things we might do. We were all riding the wave of Trump's improbable win in the 2016 presidential election.

However, the next time I saw Michael, he was pissed and more than a little jealous that Scaramucci had gone to the White House to work so closely with the president. As Michael told it, he was the one who had first brought Scaramucci to Trump's attention.

Scaramucci had been raising money for Jeb Bush. And when Jeb Bush's campaign went south, Scaramucci promised to raise lots of money for Trump. Scaramucci joined the Trump Campaign Finance Committee.

After the election, Scaramucci was part of the transition committee. Just prior to the inauguration, Scaramucci attended the Davos World

Economic Forum as part of the Trump transition team. At Davos, he met with Kirill Dmitriev, CEO of the Russian Direct Investment Fund, to discuss mutual potential future investments—despite Russia being under sanctions at the time.

Over the next several months, Scaramucci would hold and leave several positions in the White House, culminating in his eleven-day tenure as White House communications director, one of the major fiascos of the early days of the Trump administration. Michael was frustrated over the damage Scaramucci did.

But Michael was more than a "fixer." According to Michael, he was responsible for several appointments in the Trump administration, including Jay Sekulow, President Trump's lawyer, and Ray Washburne, who served until March 1, 2019, as president and CEO of the Overseas Private Investment Corporation (OPIC), the US agency which invests in emerging markets.

Michael seemed to be involved in many serious and important tasks for Trump. It was more than handling Stormy Daniels. Michael had Trump's confidence in getting substantive and important tasks done. I watched Michael with Trump. There was a bond there. A closeness that Michael and Trump felt for each other that they would both come to tear asunder.

13

Final Rounds with Prosecutor Rhee

Was it Kompromat?

To Mueller's team, the Trump Tower Moscow deal was treated as more important than any of the deals I proposed in Georgia or Kazakhstan because it involved Russia. And that explains why it was so important to Prosecutor Rhee to make me out to be a Russian businessman.

Mueller's team was suspicious of any involvement of any Russian official's connection to a transaction that could potentially financially benefit Trump—all the more so when that Russian official is close to Putin. That I had suggested that a letter to the mayor of Moscow from Trump could help in securing a deal for a Moscow Trump Tower was, to Mueller's prosecutors, another smoking gun. But there was nothing there.

Rhee and her team were so eager to cry "gotcha!" that it is easy to understand why my innocent October 30, 2016, text messages to Michael Cohen regarding rumors of a tape of Trump in Moscow loomed so large in their imaginations—it must have seemed like a slam dunk piece of evidence for proving Russia-Trump collusion.

Kompromat was the prize they were after. If I had it, had seen it, knew it existed, knew someone who knew the tape existed, or even believed it existed, then I suppose the way they wasted my time (and that of the whole country) and the expense they put me to would have been justifiable.

Their only problem was that I wasn't going to just sit back and let them make a Russian piñata out of me. Perhaps because I was foreign-born and spoke with an accent, they thought I was dumb. Had they done their research, they would have known that Georgia is home to many chess grandmasters, and there was no way I was going to let them checkmate me.

Back in the grand jury room, I waited for Prosecutor Rhee to return to the kompromat. It didn't take long for her to come at it again from a brand-new angle.

It was exhausting and, frankly, surreal to be once again confronted with words and phrases I'd written off the cuff or in jest, now being treated as deadly serious, very suspicious, and part of an international criminal and political conspiracy.

For Rhee, I had to be validated as Cohen and Trump's Russian channel. She was quick to remind me again that my text exchange with Michael occurred ten days before the election and much before the infamous "Steele Dossier" leaked to the press, before anyone knew there even might be a tape, before, it appears from the exchange, Michael Cohen ever heard about it.

As I explained, not for the first or last time, my friend said it was a random person, not someone he knew, that was bragging about the tapes. It was no business of mine. But I thought I should give Michael Cohen a heads-up that this is what people were gossiping about. Not only because I thought Michael should know, but also because it could affect Trump's business reputation. And ultimately that could impact the deals we had and were hoping to do.

The prosecutor, strip-mining every fact she could from this, asked me, "Out of all your friends—and you have many friends, right?—how many friends do you have in Russia?"

"I have friends," I said. "I don't think there's anything wrong with having friends."

"You texted Michael. Why Michael?"

"We've established Michael was working for Trump. He was a friend of mine and we were still business associates at that point. It was pre-election and our deal was still ongoing. Given the damaging *Access Hollywood* tapes, I was concerned that more tapes from Russia would further damage the Trump brand and taint our deal in Georgia."

So, yes, I said, I was very concerned about damage to the Trump brand because we had invested in the Trump brand.

This led Prosecutor Rhee to ask, "Your interest was in Trump's brand, so would you do anything to protect the Trump brand?"

She asked again, "Would you do anything to protect the Trump brand?"

I answered that I wouldn't do anything. But if I knew the Trump brand was going to be harmed, I would want to know what to expect. And if I could take some preventive action to protect the brand, I would certainly consider doing that.

Prosecutor Rhee was very persistent in trying to make a case that I would I do anything to protect the Trump brand, and I would take preventive action to protect Trump, basically implying that I would do anything to help Trump get elected even if I had to destroy compromising tapes of Trump from the Russian trip—the kompromat.

She asked, "Did you ever tell anyone else about these tapes?"

"I think Michael Cohen was the only one," I said.

And then she said, "Let me show you an email you sent on that day."

Which is when I suddenly realized that I had indeed communicated with someone else about these tapes—Melanie, my publicist. I suddenly realized that Mueller's team knew what I did and what my emails said better than I did. It was scary. I knew that you could get steep prison time for lying or perjury. I was like, *WOW, she's good, somehow she was still able to put me against the wall!* I had to fight back, dig into my memory lane, and then I finally remembered. I said, "Yes, now I remember, I also traded messages with my publicist about this tape." I was breathing easier, again.

Melanie had sent me a link to a *New York Times* story about "The Dossier." Her comment was that she saw this as Crocus's handiwork. The optics looked like we knew something about the tapes and who might have made them and who had those tapes.

But again, that was false. Neither I nor Melanie ever saw proof that such tapes existed. To the contrary, we became convinced it was just a rumor. However, that didn't stop Melanie and I from having a little fun in some baseless speculation and gossip. We definitely didn't see anything wrong with it then.

As I explained to the prosecutor and the grand jury, I quit having any business relationships with the people at Crocus in 2005.

Nonetheless, Mueller's team pointed out, with some glee, that this was yet another of my Russian connections.

They asked how Michael met Crocus: Was it through Yuri Milner?

Yuri Milner is a Moscow-born entrepreneur who attended the Wharton School of the University of Pennsylvania and has since become one of the most sought-after venture capitalists and tech entrepreneurs. His many, many investments include a company called Cadre that was founded by, among others, Jared Kushner.

Perhaps Crocus met Michael Cohen through Yuri. I wasn't sure.

But I made clear (again) that I'd had no contact with Crocus in more than a decade, and that I had no idea how Michael was in contact with Crocus.

What I explained was that in 2013, Michael contacted me saying he was entering into a business relationship with Crocus. It was maybe 2:00 a.m. I told him to be vigilant with Crocus. I also recommended against Trump going to Moscow for the Miss Universe pageant.

Michael said, "Okay." But he didn't listen to me. And the rest is history.

—

As I explained to the grand jury, if you are a high-profile guest in Moscow, it's a fair assumption that you are tracked from the minute you arrive to the minute you leave. They don't let the guests go just anywhere. Mostly it is for security reasons; and sometimes it is to have a record of meetings for business; and, occasionally, there are more nefarious reasons.

Melanie had also met some of my Russian business contacts when I did business with them, and she understood how business was done in Russia. So when *The New York Times* wrote about the dossier, she emailed me, assuming as I did that the dossier, verified or not, could've been connected to Trump's Miss Universe Moscow trip.

And my response to her was "I told them not to go, but they didn't listen to me."

The prosecutors were desperate to paint a different picture—one in which I knew the tapes existed.

As I reminded them time and time again during the questioning, this was before there were any rumors about a tape, before *Buzzfeed* revealed the existence of the dossier, before anyone even knew that such a thing as a "pee" tape might exist. The mere fact of this—that I knew about the tape before anyone—was of great interest to Mueller's team, naturally, who wanted to know who told me there were tapes and, for sure, they wanted to get their hands on those tapes, if they existed.

My back-and-forth with Prosecutor Rhee was heated. I admit it made me angry, and I was raising my voice. But suddenly I realized that was exactly what Rhee wanted: to get me out of my comfort zone and cause me to say things I might soon regret.

I took a deep, deep breath and shut my emotions down. I said to myself, *Just follow your truth. You are innocent, you did nothing wrong.*

It sounds simple, but I realized all I had to do was repeat the truth: that I'd never seen any tapes, and that it was just a rumor from a random person. Doing so made me feel greater control and shifted the power in the conversation back to me. Now it was Rhee who was frustrated.

She wanted so badly for there to be kompromat. She wanted to find kompromat of any kind, even against me. Kompromat that would in any way, shape, or form possibly tie the president to Russia and prove collusion.

I was of no help to her.

But Jeannie Rhee isn't someone who quits easily. She wanted to take one last shot at those alleged tapes.

She asked if this was all so innocent, then why did Melanie immediately speak of Crocus? What was their connection to the tapes and what role did they play? I explained for what felt like the millionth time that as Crocus hosted Trump in Moscow for the Miss Universe pageant, it was natural to think of them or one of their associates as having documented Trump's visit, if such a record even existed. But the reality was that neither Melanie nor I had any evidence nor even a clue that was true.

However—and this is how prosecutors think—the fact that I would warn Michael and the fact that I was concerned about damage to Trump's reputation and how that might impact our deal—rather than that being proof of friendship or genuine business concern—somehow proved to the prosecutors that I was ready to do whatever it took to protect our business partner Donald Trump, including possibly lying or withholding information about the tapes.

I stuck to my truth. I made it clear to the grand jury that with me, what you see is what you get.

Then something strange happened. The prosecutors asked me to leave the room for a bit because they wanted to talk to the grand jury.

Now, what happened when I left the room, I have no idea.

Two agents led me out and took me back down the corridor to the little room where just one of my lawyers, the associate, was waiting. The agents told me, "When we need you, we'll call you back."

End Game

I DIDN'T WAIT TOO long. When I returned to the grand jury room, it wasn't clear what, if anything, had transpired, but there was definitely a change of attitude in the room. Rhee and Mueller's team were done with me, at least for now.

There were more than a few perfunctory follow-up questions followed by admonishments that I could be recalled and asked more questions by mail, email, phone, or in person.

And then suddenly it was finally over. I was thanked for my time and my cooperation. That also seemed more perfunctory than genuine.

—

I WAS THEN HURRIED out of the building because there was another witness coming and they didn't want us to meet. They asked me if I wanted to leave by the front entrance or the back.

They explained that "we have some people that actually want to go through the main entrance and get some pictures."

"No, thanks," I said, and chose the back exit. I wanted to avoid any press exposure. It's not like they were asking me if I wanted to walk the Red Carpet at the Oscars. The front entrance with the media waiting was a surefire way to tank my business and shame me and my family.

After two days of questioning for a total of almost ten hours, I was exhausted and completely spent.

Back Outside

WHEN I LEFT THE grand jury room, I felt good about several things. Mostly, I was relieved that there was nothing in our conversation that was damaging or imputed any wrongdoing in Georgia, or that could damage the US-Georgia relationship. That was very important to me. Next, I was satisfied that the Mueller investigation in my testimony saw no malfeasance in our Batumi Trump Tower deal or in Silk Road's dealings with Donald Trump.

Mueller's team had clearly examined every detail of our potential Trump deals in Georgia and Kazakhstan. But during my interview and grand jury proceedings, I made sure that there was no talk that Silk Road was anything but a serious and responsible business entity. In these ways, I felt that I had done justice to my friends and partners at Silk Road. That was also very important to me.

—

From the very beginning, I doubted that even such a masterful investigator as Robert Mueller would find collusion between Trump and Russia. As Lavrentiy Beria, the brutal former KGB chief, said, "It's hard to find a black cat in a dark room, particularly if it's not there."

14
Aftermath

After the Grand Jury

I APPEARED BEFORE MUELLER'S team twice, once in April 2019 and once in May 2019. Over the next few months, there was a small number of follow-ups between the special counsel and my attorneys.

One last thing: since my testimony, I've often been asked if at any moment during my questioning at the DOJ, or before the grand jury, I actually met Mueller himself.

All I can say is that Mueller was definitely in the building during the time of my testimony and nearby during my questioning. I don't know if he was sitting watching my questioning or testimony on some close-circuit audio or video feed, but I was made to believe that Mueller knew every word I said, and perhaps the answers to questions I wasn't even asked. However, I am not so sure about that now. Later, I will explain why.

—

FOLLOWING MY GRAND JURY appearance, Mueller's team continued to email my lawyers. For the most part, we answered by email. My lawyers wanted to avoid any further face-to-face meetings. On occasion, I went down to DC to see my attorneys and we worked our way through their questions which, for the most part, just rehashed what I had already told them.

Mueller's team was very persistent in wanting to find out a few things: Who was the person at the party in Moscow who overhead someone talking about the tapes? (I told them.) What was my connection to him? (He was a friend.) And who was the person who was bragging about the tapes? (Don't know. He didn't know them.) Who wrote Trump's letter to the mayor of Moscow? (I didn't know but assumed it was my friends in Russia.) And who translated it into Russian? (The translation was mine.)

So long as there were open questions, the Mueller team reserved the right to call me back in for questioning.

Just knowing that the special counsel can call you back anytime felt like standing in a minefield. This was all the more true as each day the news became more and more focused on Michael Cohen. In Soviet Georgia, I had experienced fear of seeing the KGB at our door or watching us. I never imagined I would know that fear again in the United States.

The impact on my family was greater than you can imagine. Our six-year-old son, Sandro, had friends in the neighborhood who suddenly no longer wanted to play with him or have playdates.

Worse yet, Sandro couldn't understand why CNN reporters outside of our home were flashing photos of me, asking our neighbors questions about his father. I didn't really have an easy explanation. I hope when he's older this book will explain it all to him. As for me, I will never forget my son asking me, "Daddy, why no more playdates? Is it because they're afraid of you?"

The press was relentless, calling me on my cell at all times.

Jennifer Forsyth at *The Wall Street Journal* was strategically persistent. She was very professional and, I must say, one of the nicest of the journalists I met. She said we should meet in person and talk, even off the record, because she knew things that I "would want to know."

I met with Jennifer. She didn't pressure me. But we played a kind of cat-and-mouse game where we circled around what she wanted to know.

She had very good journalistic instincts. She was very empathetic as well as smart and nimble. I completely understand how people fall into confidence with reporters and then are shocked the next day when they see what's written about them.

I can best compare dealing with journalists like Jennifer to going through a very relaxing, meditation-like experience where you are treated like a star, you are allowed to express yourself, release your anger and worries, you are assured that the only thing that matters at that moment is your truth and that the world needs to hear your story.

Reporters like Jennifer are great at showing their compassion and quest for justice. It doesn't take much for you to pour your heart out and forget that you are on the record. However, the next morning when you read the news story in the paper, it conforms to their spin, not to your truth as you shared it or how you imagined it would read. And that's when, shocked and angry, you call your very expensive lawyers to scream, "They took everything out of context!"

On those occasions when I found myself in that situation, my lawyers would calmly remind me that defamation is tough to prove and harder still to win. In the US, we have a free press, but talking to them can cost you greatly. Unfortunately, I've been in that situation too many times in the last two years. So I was extremely wary with Jennifer.

Jennifer and I spoke again by phone, and she asked me questions related to Michael Cohen that had nothing to do with Georgia, Kazakhstan, or Russia. She did ask me if I was called before the grand jury. I didn't know if she had that information from other sources but all I said was "I will neither confirm nor deny."

But what she did tell me was that the *WSJ* was doing an article about Michael Cohen and the Stormy Daniels case.

Stormy Daniels drew tabloid attention because she was a porn star. However, if Trump did indeed have an affair with her years before running for president or becoming president, well, that seemed like water under the bridge that was only being brought up now to smear Trump and hurt Melania. If Michael had bought her silence—even if it was $130,000—

didn't that occur all the time? It seemed hard to believe that the same Democrats who argued that Bill Clinton's affair while he was president shouldn't matter would now go after Trump about his over-a-decade-old story when Trump was a businessman.

Michael Avenatti, Daniels's attorney, did not impress me. He seemed to be more interested in publicity for himself than in resolving his client's legal problems, which made me think he was just a flash in the pan and would crash and burn. Which is what happened eventually.

However, the *Wall Street Journal* reporter made me realize that because of Michael Cohen's hush payment story, Stormy Daniels was a much more serious matter than I had thought. I saw how my honest and friendly conversation with Michael Cohen at his hotel room in March 2017 about the Stormy Daniels payment could now be of great interest.

What I did tell Jennifer was that Michael had said that whatever he did, he did it because he really respected his boss. He loved him. Being part of the Trump Organization was more than just work for him. To him, Donald Trump was a friend—more than a friend, a father figure. And Michael really, really respected Melania. He did not want her embarrassed or hurt. He wanted to make sure that the Stormy Daniels matter was kept out of the press. And that he had taken it upon himself to deal with this, even taking a home equity loan to make sure that it was kept quiet. Never in my conversation with him did Michael say or imply that he was directed or ordered to do so.

As more facts emerged over time about the payments and Daniels published her own account of the tryst, it all seemed too sordid and amateurish to be of national concern. But it involved Trump, so it fed the news cycle for weeks on end.

What I did not tell the *WSJ* reporter at the time was that Michael was also upset about being ceaselessly trashed in the press as a bad lawyer, a bad businessman, and a bad person. My advice to him was to take control of his narrative: "Choose a network and appear personally to set the record straight. Just tell everybody what happened in your own words."

I told him I thought he should so do right away. The sooner the better.

"Maybe you're right," Michael said.

But Michael is a very stubborn person.

I still wonder, if Michael had come forward immediately after the Stormy Daniels story broke and given a fuller explanation of the situation to the American public, whether things might have gone better for him.

Dodging the Trump Bullet

MICHAEL COHEN IS SOMEONE I've known and observed for almost a decade. I've seen up close what it takes for Michael to consider a deal ready to be shown to Trump. The proposal needs to be bulletproof. And more than legitimate. I've known firsthand how every detail is negotiated and scrutinized.

There was never a time nor a moment when Trump said, "Get it done no matter what, at any cost." Never. I worked on three different deals with Michael and it was a very diligent, thorough process. Very tough, hard work.

Michael rarely issued legal opinions. His lawyering was confined to finding deals, scrutinizing them, and negotiating them—but he did no drafting of contracts. Trump had other lawyers to draft terms—and I had my lawyers to review them. Michael Cohen was always the guy thinking about how to hype the Trump brand and delivering that to Trump so he could get a pat on the back. Michael was the person who personally defended, protected, and cared for Trump's interests.

I don't think Michael fully appreciated the threat Russia poses. He saw how the Russian oligarchs lived and he admired that. He wanted that for himself (as many would). I do believe there is a part of him that wants to do the right thing and be the hero—who knows? Maybe he'll get his chance again to do just that.

The values I was brought up with by my parents stayed with me throughout my life. My sister and I were always told that there are more good people in the world than bad, and that if you look for them, you will find them.

I'm not saying that I am a saint—far from it. I grew up on the streets of Tbilisi in a rough time. Over the course of my adult life, I've dealt with monsters and made deals with people I wish I had never met—but I did not do these things because I was determined to do bad things. To the contrary, I did them because I imagined that good would come from what I was doing. In some cases it did, and in some I failed, but I never lost sight of the difference between good and bad. This only made me cherish the good people around me, the people who stood by me no matter what, when it mattered the most. You find your true friends in times of trouble. My wife and I certainly found ours, and lost the ones we thought were true friends. But like they say, "You can't lose what you never had."

My plan of bringing Trump Towers to the former Soviet region has cost me greatly, financially and in business. The Mueller and House and Senate committee investigations have been very tough on me and my family, but none of this has made me bitter or angry. That is not who I am, nor who my parents and my country raised me to be. I will always stand up for myself, my friends, my partners, my country (USA), and my native homeland of Georgia.

Georgia's alliance to the United States remains strong, and I will do all in my power to see that the feeling is mutual.

On November 9, 2017, as I was pledging allegiance to the United States during my US citizenship ceremony, I meant every word. It seems like since I've become a US citizen, my allegiance to America has been tested to its limits through endless investigations and interrogations. But I can tell you one thing: through this painful process, my pledge to the greatest country in the world has only been strengthened.

Michael's Testimony before Congress

ON FEBRUARY 27, 2019, Michael Cohen testified before Congress. The day before, he had been disbarred from the practice of law. He had already pled guilty to campaign finance violations that would put him in federal prison for several years.

Like the rest of America, I watched Michael's testimony, spellbound. For me, the experience was bittersweet, and again, very surreal.

I had always been in favor of Michael telling his side of the story—but I had suggested he do so much, much earlier. Seeing Lanny Davis sitting behind him, I was concerned that this might do Lanny more good than it did Michael. I told Michael that in one of my last text messages to him, but he ignored it.

First, I felt so bad for Michael's truly beautiful family. This whole ordeal must have been awful for his wife and children. It pained me to know that Michael, whom I had worked so closely with for over a decade, was going to jail. And I knew that Michael must have been suffering terribly to be saying what he did about Trump, a man he looked up to and had praised so much for so many years.

As much as I tried to, I found it hard to believe Michael's claim that he lied or did other actions on Trump's behalf because he was blinded by him. There was no more aggressive defender of what he called "Trump Standards."

During his testimony, there were moments when I felt Michael did himself no service and, to my mind, they had Lanny written all over them.

So, for example, to hear Michael say about Trump, a person he so revered, that "He is a con man, he is a racist, he is a cheat"—Michael would never have said those words about Trump. As to why he felt he needed to do so, I imagine he had his reasons.

What I did feel was positive and good for Michael was that all of America got to see Michael as he is—not the super-aggressive Michael whom I negotiated against, but a sadder Michael who is honestly remorseful for himself and for his family.

That Michael said that he saw no collusion between the Trump Organization and Russia wasn't surprising, and as much as I had predicted, there was none.

Michael spoke of the payments to Stormy Daniels and Karen McDougal. Clearly Michael had placed himself in legal jeopardy with those payments, and his lies concerning them had led to a three-year jail sentence. Now, whether out of contrition or revenge, he was there to set the record straight and settle scores.

Michael spoke of the involvement of David Pecker and other executives of AMI in some of those payments and the Trump Organization as having knowledge of the arrangements. And although he never mentioned such to me, Michael said the president was fully aware and that nothing happened at the Trump Organization that Trump was not fully involved with.

In my experience that was true and not true. Trump was not aware of everything that transpired. Michael and others were always looking for deals, screening offers, doing the advance work, scrutinizing and even negotiating agreements before and after they came to Trump's attention. But it is also true that there were no deals signed that Donald Trump didn't know about and no signature that mattered other than his. But that is what you expect from the head of the company. This is what I do with my and my company's deals.

Similarly, Michael also implicated Trump's children, Don Jr. and Ivanka in particular, with knowledge of negotiations for a Trump Tower in Moscow. Again, based on my experience in negotiating for Trump Towers in Georgia and Kazakhstan, Donald always wanted to find ways to involve his children and keep them in the loop, but they were always his deals, not theirs. Now, whether this information contradicts what Don Jr. in particular told Congress previously, I can't say.

Michael made clear that his cooperation with the Southern District of New York was ongoing. This was in many ways, I thought, a warning to Trump and his supporters not to come after Michael and his family. And it was where, perhaps, Trump had the most to lose. But if so, it was not because of collusion with Russia.

It is hard for me to say whether Michael convinced anyone of anything they didn't believe before his Congressional appearance. The Democrats have their agenda and the Republicans theirs. I did not see much to change that.

Shortly after his testimony, my wife and I were having dinner at a popular Upper East Side restaurant when in walked Laura, Michael's wife.

She's a wonderful person who didn't ask nor deserve any of what befell her family. We hugged her and offered what little support we could.

What I told her is that I had been concerned I wouldn't recognize Michael in his testimony but that who he was had come through well. She didn't say much. Shortly after, she came back to our table and showed me a text Michael had just written addressed to me: "Send my love to him and tell him I miss him." I replied that time heals everything and that we would see each other again soon.

15

How I See the World

My America

I MUST ADMIT THAT when Trump became president, I was excited. Can you blame me? I could honestly say that I personally knew the president of the United States, and that he had visited my native country with me and that I was in business with him. That is pretty incredible for any American, much less one who came to this country with fifty dollars in his pocket.

In my own personal experience, Trump was generous and kind. Although my exposure to Trump was somewhat limited, I never heard him say anything bigoted, racist, or misogynistic.

Trump himself was nothing but fair to me, a Georgian immigrant. However, Trump's tough rhetoric about immigrants is offensive to all legal immigrants like my wife and I, who are part of what makes America great.

Trump needs to be the president of all American people, not just his base. However, he will only reach out beyond his base if doing so brings him a big "win"—something unprecedented, historic, something Obama could not do—and it has to be something that doesn't alienate his base.

Which, given that he needs the Democrats and the left to get anything done, means it probably won't happen.

In my opinion, America First, Trump's policy, can be good if what it means is a successful and prosperous United States. A strong America is good for countries all over the world because they follow our lead. The president of the United States is the de facto president of the world, and there's nothing wrong with that as long as America continues to lead for good, even if America is first and the world comes second.

Similarly, Trump is not the first president to want better relations with Russia. I seem to recall Bill Clinton playing the saxophone and dancing with Boris Yeltsin.

Putin, as I've explained, is a product of Russia's fear of crime, poverty, disorder, and vanishing Russian pride, while Trump is the beneficiary of the failed political system in Washington that Trump's base believes has deprived them of achieving their American Dream. Pride in Russia and pride in America are the platforms supporting both Trump and Putin. And each nation wants to be the world's greatest superpower.

For this very reason, I strongly believe that unless the US and Russia find a way to engage and stay engaged, the world will never know peace.

Encouraging Americans to further disengage with Russia will undoubtedly help Putin and his team to cast the United States as the ultimate enemy of the Russian people. The Russians will get behind Putin in supporting confrontation with the United States and the West. If Trump trashes Putin it may make us feel better, but doing so will only perpetuate our problems with Russia, not solve them.

Way before Trump took office, media outlets were calling Putin the most powerful and sexiest politician in the world. There was even Oliver Stone's pro-Putin HBO series. Does this make Stone a Russian agent? It is true that Stone has always stirred up the pot in the United States regarding issues such as violence and prisons, and has been supportive of Castro in Cuba and Chávez in Venezuela. But, as far as I know, Stone is not a Russian agent. He is just an antiestablishment, salon Communist, Hollywood style, who is enamored with Socialist strongmen. Sound familiar?

What Trump Did for Georgia

THE APRIL 9 TRAGEDY in Tbilisi was the beginning of the end of Soviet Georgia. No one who was there and who witnessed the uncaring, murderous actions of the Soviet forces as I did would remain loyal to Russia. And as I mentioned earlier, Putin early on targeted Georgians in Russia and Georgia itself.

It is no accident that the Kremlin still keeps Russian troops on Georgian sovereign territory. Georgia, although small in size, remains a fount of resistance to a renewed Soviet or Eurasian Union.

Given all this history, it should not be hard to understand how important Trump's 2011 visit to Georgia was, not just to me personally but to all Georgians and all people living in former Soviet republics.

At some point, my business partners and I were supporting over fifty families financially. We knew then that for America to show up and rescue us was a dream. Still, even a short statement of support from Trump was a massive adrenaline injection of hope.

No other American businessmen did what Trump did: Trump stood only several miles from the Georgian-Russian conflict zone and said, "This is not right; Georgia should get its territories back." That was music to our ears. It meant so much. And one can only imagine how much it means to me now that he is the president of the United States.

Trump has continued to demonstrate strong support for Georgia. Vice President Mike Pence and National Security Advisor John Bolton have both made visits to Georgia.

Now that Trump is president, my friends like George Ramishvili and I look back on that moment and still hope that President Trump will continue to press the case of returning the Georgian territories occupied by Russia with Putin.

If I see President Trump again, this will be one of the topics I would discuss with him. I am fascinated about where he stands on the subject right now. I truly hope that in this he stands on the right side of history; with Georgia and not with Putin.

Putin's Game

As PUTIN CONSOLIDATED POWER, he took largely symbolic actions to restore Russian pride and the semblance of being a world power with authority over former allies and satellites.

Putin set about regaining Russian dominance methodically. First, he took on the Chechens who had overrun Moscow. It took a few years to loosen their control of gambling, human trafficking, and other nefarious activities.

Next, Putin took on Georgia, attacking those Georgians who were having success in Russia as well as supporting anti-Georgian ethnicities in Georgia by annexing a number of Georgia's autonomic republics.

Then Putin turned to regaining control of Ukraine. When Ukraine was overrun with political and economic instability, Putin backed Ukranian Russians and annexed Crimea in the blink of an eye.

President Obama did nothing to directly confront Putin's aggressive military move in Ukraine—but he should have pushed back. America's inaction encouraged Putin and his supporters to test America's strength or willingness to challenge Russia over its former satellites.

Putin did as he wanted because he understood there was no one to stop him. Just like the United States, Europe, too, stood on the sidelines; and the countries themselves were in no position to mount an effective defense. As for the Russian people, Putin masterfully laid out a pro-Russia strategy to the nation.

Putin told the Russian people the West was expansionist, wanting to extend NATO into Russian territories and threaten Russians with their weapons; and that the West was insulting, offending, and dismissive of Russia's role on the world stage. Putin promised that, under his leadership, Russia would roar back, reclaiming its glory, status, and influence over its satellite territories and in world affairs.

To Russian patriots, this was music to their ears. As far as they are concerned, Putin delivered, and for them, Putin's success on the world stage is tied to Russia's success.

—

AT THE SAME TIME, what most Americans don't fully realize is that Georgia, Kazakhstan, and the other former Soviet republics continue to be experiments in democracy that are not even thirty years old!

There are generations that were raised under Communist and Soviet regimes and there is a new generation born into chaos and independence, for whom capitalism is something they must adapt to and learn how to navigate not only for their businesses but for every aspect of their lives, including education, social welfare, health, and old-age benefits. And no one really knows what the right answers or solutions are or will be. They want to be Westerners, but they are still figuring out exactly what that means.

We need to remember that these nascent independent nations continue to deal with today's Russia—a Russia that hasn't changed that much since the Soviet Era but does not admit to any difference.

Russia is still determined to remain father and mother to these nations, controlling their purse strings and the lives of their citizens instead of being a friendly, economically and socially supportive larger neighbor. Russia strives to be a world power, but in order to get there, it believes that it must weaken its adversaries, especially a superpower like the United States.

Russia's agenda may be to convince the world that it is just like us, but it is completely different.

Russia believes that it is superior to other nations. And I get it, the country has a right to claim greatness when it is known for some of the world's greatest scientists, thinkers, writers, artists, and composers. Let's not forget, Russian culture produced Pushkin, Tchaikovsky, Rachmaninov, Andrey Rublov, Dostoevsky, Chekhov, Tolstoy, and many other geniuses. But that was a long time ago. Today, Russia is mostly known for its vodka, caviar, oil money, filthy rich oligarchs (while 99 percent of the nation is starving), and superior spy network. Sadly, since the 1917 October Revolution, Bolshevik Russia has been a self-destructive, dark, and dangerous force.

Some of the greatest minds fled their beloved Russia for that reason and were forced to reinvent themselves in the West.

Can Russia be great again? I think this is the most consequential question of the twenty-first century.

What does greatness mean to Russia? Is it inclusive of other nationalities and neighboring countries or is greatness just total dominance—as was the case during Stalin's regime?

In Russia, Stalin is still considered the most successful Russian leader ever. In Georgia, where Stalin was born, he is admired for becoming a leader of Russia but reviled for the murders and imprisonment of so many Georgian intellectuals and patriots. So, again, what is greatness?

It remains to be seen if post-Putin Russia will find a way to reverse its course and reemerge as a power for good and as the cradle of great art, music, theater, dance, and film.

The real Russia is far greater than Putin's Russia. The challenge Putin poses is for us to reengage with the Russian people and show them that no Georgian, Ukrainian, or Kazakh is the enemy of the Russian people. Quite the contrary, we need to express our love for Russia—just a different Russia: the Russia of great ideas, ideals, music, culture, sports, passion, and compassion. I have experienced that Russia and I miss it. The world needs to see, hear, and experience that Russia too. And I sure hope it will soon.

The question remains: What does Putin think of his Russia? Does he truly believe that he's done the most for his motherland or is it that he got the most out of Russia?

Putin is all about Russia's glory and pride. He has been unwilling to renounce the failures of the Soviet State and the years of darkness caused by Lenin and Stalin. It is still not clear whether Putin sees himself as Stalin or Peter the Great.

The Russia of the twenty-first century deserves to be better than the Russia of the twentieth century. I understand Putin's desire for a resurgent Russian Federation, but he must know that Georgia and its Russian-occupied territories will come together again at some point, with or without him. He still has a chance to be a peacemaker and secure a place for himself and for Russia in world history.

Putin is very strategic. He understands that the United States is so dominant that there are many countries that resent America's power and are hungry for an alternative or just someone to stand up to them. Putin exploits that.

Putin saw an opening after the Iraq War, when the United States's global image was badly damaged. He was quick to act to create a global news network called RTV (Russia Today). You would not be wrong to call it a propaganda TV station posing as a real news organization, but for people desperate to hear something other than the Western perspective, RTV has become a trusted alternative.

We can complain all we want about FOX, MSNBC, or CNN, but the worst you can say about them is that they are biased to one side or one party. RTV is a worldview directed by Putin to accomplish his agenda. Putin is smart and he will use anyone, including Western journalists such as Larry King, to carry his water.

My friends look at RTV and think it's too obvious and that it will never work. But it has already worked.

America isn't perfect, but America thrives to be as good as it can be. America's ideology promotes capitalism, commerce, and free markets, all in fierce competition with no restrictions on personal freedom, individuality, ethnic identity, or religious belief. America sets no limits on how much you can achieve in life.

Today's Russia, by contrast, is willing to guarantee stability and order in return for allegiance. Russia will allow you to become rich, in some cases richer than your wildest dreams, as long as you remain loyal to Putin and to Russia. Russia has no problems with America unless America becomes too powerful in ways that reduce Russia's importance and self-image and encroach on its being a world power. To prevent that, Russia will do all in its power to exploit any divisions or weakness in the US, even if that means hacking America's cyber zone and directly into your electronic devises, your personal computer, and your smartphone.

To me, the one good thing that has come out of the Mueller investigation is that America now realizes the challenge Russia poses. Unless Trump and Putin prove the critics wrong and embrace the Reagan-Gorbachev political style of bringing the world together, we are heading toward a twenty-first-century-style divide of cyber warfare—the consequences of which are simply unknown.

Russia is not the only or even the most dangerous threat to the US and its democracy.

The Chinese government has been successful at having most of its citizens adopt its information technology by making it very convenient. In China, almost everyone uses one app through which they communicate and by which they pay for everything—and as a result, their entire life is subject to government monitoring twenty-four seven. And China now wants to bring that app to the US.

You don't need to be paranoid to see the danger in letting China control 5G, why the US is concerned about Huawei phones, and why some US government agencies advise its employees against using Lenovo computers (made in China), which even the Chinese admit have a back door implanted in them. Or why we should be suspicious of Russian government-approved software such as Kaspersky antivirus protection. If this last election and the Mueller investigation have taught us anything, it is that unfriendly foreign powers are already in your home, in your living room, and they're trying to influence you however they can.

That being said, I feel we are wasting time and energy investigating each other, and certainly that investigation of me was a waste of time. In creating a society where anybody can be a suspect, we are being distracted from our true enemies while, at the same time, our enemies seek strength in a weakened and divided United States. To combat our enemies, we are better advised to pull together than let ourselves be torn apart.

I can only hope that, in the end, the greatest achievement of the Mueller investigation will be to make Americans realize that foreign threats are real and imminent and that it is worth the expense of devoting the resources necessary to fight back against foreign bad actors.

Google, Facebook, and Instagram are all preparing for this coming war. If this means the beginning of the end of foreign interference in our social media, corporate secrets, patents, copyrights, and cybersecurity, then it will all have been worthwhile.

16

Telling My Truth

Why I Wrote This Book

IN DECIDING TO WRITE this book, I want to be clear that I did not do so for financial gain, for fame, or to portray myself as a helpless victim. As you can see from my account, I am the prime actor in my story. My dealings with Donald Trump and Michael Cohen were all at my instigation.

No one is perfect. None of us are without sin, vanity, selfishness, or pride. And there are no exceptions, including the presidents of the United States, past and present.

I can't say what, if anything, ever transpired between Donald Trump and Vladimir Putin. Or why Donald Trump behaved in certain ways toward Vladimir Putin or Kim Jong-un. About this we may never know the full truth. But the truth is that Donald Trump is the president of the United States, and every president has the right to act according to his own best judgment and to follow his own strategy and tactics. Time, only time, can tell if Trump is right or wrong, or as he often says, if his gut feeling guided him to modern American victories or failures.

All I can write about is what I know from my own personal experience. I know what I saw, and I know what my instincts tell me.

Where reports are false, I can say so and tell the truth of what I know to have happened.

I wrote this book because I was tired of hearing lies and reading false statements about me and my partners. I sat down and started to make notes and write down what I've been forced to experience since being subpoenaed before the Mueller grand jury.

Once I started to write, I began to expand my personal notes and realized that I had a unique story to tell. I wanted to do so in order to take back control of my narrative. To tell the truth, my truth, what I know to be true, and what happened to me as a result of what I did and what I knew. I can speak to the media sinkhole my partners and I fell into, and the damage done by innuendo and false reporting.

When all is said and done, I wrote this book because I want my children to know the truth, my truth, and not what they find by Googling my name, which will now call up many false accusations and inaccurate stories about me.

I hope that this book will be an eye-opener for Americans about a major distinction between being Russian and Georgian. How devastating it can be when they conveniently misidentify you as Russian in the Russia Probe when you in fact aren't. Like I've said before, there's nothing wrong with being Russian. Russia is a great culture with many great people. I am just not Russian.

And be warned, if it can happen to me, it can happen to you too…

No Collusion

THIS BOOK IS NOT about being pro-Trump or anti-Trump. I am not a Democrat nor a Republican, but I am pro-America for many reasons. I was born in Soviet Georgia, and my family and I were lucky to survive the Communism and Socialism and then the post-Soviet black hole; and trust me, that is something I never want to go back to, nor would any American if they really understood what living under a Communist or Socialist regime was like. As bad as things may get in the United States, we are a million times better than we would be under Communist rule. Socialism sounds nice in principle but it is a harsh reality to live under.

It is painful to see America divided, but this may be the best opportunity in decades for us to come together again. It is evident that the time has come to have a tough, honest, and sometimes downright nasty argument about what we believe in and what we stand for. The ability to have these sorts of debates remains the best indicator of an open society and true democracy.

Being able to speak your mind is a great blessing of our democracy, particularly when you consider that my Uncle Victor spent fifteen years in a Soviet prison for speaking his truth and criticizing the government.

As Americans, we need to make life better for everyone: those in Trump's base and those Trump speaks against. That means those who lived in the United States for many generations as well as recent emigrants.

Whether Trump acknowledges it or not, we are all emigrants (including Trump, whose grandfather came from Germany). I would hate to see my grandson speaking out against emigrants. Every time I think about what it would take for America to be less divided and more united, unfortunately the first thing that comes to mind is crises. It sure seems like unity in America comes roaring back when we are facing some sort of crisis. The strongest memory I have of that happening was the era immediately following 9/11.

Trump and Putin

IN THE LAST TWO years, I've been asked the awkward question of whether Trump and Putin are working together as a team over and over again. My answer, from the first, has been that I don't believe Trump needed to collude with anyone to win the presidency. In fact, I believe crediting Russia for Trump's presidency is an insult to our very democracy. Over sixty-two million Trump supporters are Americans too, not Russians.

Nothing I've seen or learned in the last twenty-four months changes my opinion about that. I predicted that Trump would win from the moment he declared his candidacy. The reasons were plain and simple:

1. Trump's absolute name recognition

2. His genius salesman skills

3. His extreme media savvy.

Add to that the mood of the country, which after eight years of Obama was ripe for change: the economy was stagnant; the country was racially divided with the rise of the Black Lives Matter movement that pitted police against black communities; Syria's alliance with Iran; Putin's expansion in Ukraine; and the general feeling in Israel and among hardline Israel supporters in the US that Obama was not doing enough for Israel—not to mention the all-time-low ratings of Washington politicians. The stage was set for someone blunt, tough, and unapologetic who was not a politician and was recognized as a business mogul who got things done.

Donald Trump was the right candidate at the right moment in time. He may have been lucky—but he could not have been so lucky as to have the FSB or GRU manipulate an election on his behalf. That makes no sense.

Do I believe that Trump would seize any opportunity to defeat his challengers and that he is always determined to win at all costs? Yes.

Do I believe Trump's associates would do anything and meet with anyone if they thought it would help Trump defeat his competition and win the election? Yes.

Do I believe that Putin leads Russia with an iron fist and would do anything to downgrade the fundamental core institutions of the United States? Yes.

Russia remains involved in an ideological battle with the United States where there are really no rules. But do I believe Putin and Trump colluded to get him elected? No way.

To me, the question is not whether Trump colluded with Russia. From everything I know of Trump, for better or worse, only Trump can influence Trump.

But whether Trump can have any influence on Putin is much more consequential for world peace and prosperity.

You may think it's a long shot, but Trump being Trump, long shots do sometimes come true. Trump is, after all, president. And still president despite all the attacks on him. So if you are betting on long shots, you would be smart not to bet against Trump.

As much as the idea of collusion between these two titans makes for a great story and is the excuse for countless articles and stories and fills out hours of TV discussion, to me it is a smoke screen to distract us all from our most serious problems.

As for the Mueller investigation, even as someone who was questioned by his team, I always felt that it was important to have affirmed that this is a country of laws, and that no person, even the president, is above the law.

The Mueller investigation will in time, I hope, lead to America being stronger in standing up to individual bad actors as well as countries like Russia, China, and Iran who are waging cyber war against the United States.

Will Putin go down in history as a peacemaker or a leader who left behind a legacy of conflict among a people who enjoyed eight thousand years of friendship, culture, and hospitality? Time will tell, and as they say in Georgia, "Leaders rule only for a time while time is the ruler of us all."

It's Not Over until It's Over. And, Even Then, It's Not Over.

ON THURSDAY, MARCH 22, 2019, there was an announcement that Robert Mueller had completed his investigation and submitted his report to the attorney general. In the hours and days that followed, despite intense media coverage and popular interest, there was very little information available other than Attorney General William Barr's four-page summary that announced that Mueller had found no collusion with Russia, and that he was not charging President Trump with obstruction of justice, although the report did not exonerate him of such.

After two years, it was anticlimactic. No collusion. No charges. Mueller had been true to his mandate and done his job soberly and thoroughly, with no attention to politics, only to truth, fact, and what he found by law.

This was vindication for the president who had repeatedly insisted there was no collusion.

Clearly, for Trump's enemies, this was a tremendous letdown. They had pinned all their hopes on Mueller and he left them with nothing. I suppose their attention shifts now to the Southern District of New York, but the SDNY probably wouldn't attempt to indict a sitting president. They will have to wait until 2020. Or 2024, as the case may be.

Afterward, Trump and his supporters have felt vindicated, emboldened even.

As for myself, I felt as others did, that two years had been wasted— that all that time, money, and manpower could certainly have been put to better use. I, and many others, had labored for more than a year under a cloud. To what end?

—

IN THE AFTERMATH OF the Mueller Report, there was one particular response that I'd like to point out that readers of this book will find very interesting.

Dmitry Peskov, Putin's spokesperson, was asked to comment on the Mueller Report findings. Here's what he said:

"It is hard to find a black cat in a dark room." That is EXACTLY what I said earlier in this book (and I promise you I wrote it before Peskov said it).

For Peskov to be quoting Lavrentiy Beria, the founder of the KGB, is just amazing. It is almost too much.

So, what does it mean? As in the best KGB speak, it means two different things at the same time. On the one hand, it means that nothing was there. On the other, it means the cat was there, just that it was hard to catch it.

I think that it was a very provocative comment for Peskov to make when talking about Russian collusion. Did Peskov do this to perpetuate the intrigue or to divide us more? Either way, the lesson is that we as Americans would be wise to unite against attempts to create division among us.

Although Trump, the Trump Organization, and the Trump campaign did not collude with Russia, it doesn't mean that Russia will ever stop its efforts to weaken the United States' role in global geopolitics. It should come as no surprise, given that the Kremlin and the White House have been adversaries for decades now, that Russia is all for continuing the tradition.

We can demonize Russia as much as we want, but Russia sees the above as its mission, a strategy for geopolitical gains or, ultimately global dominance. They say the best defense is an aggressive offense. The Mueller Report finding of no collusion is a win for Russia, which said all along that it never colluded with Trump. That Russia, like China, has launched cyberattacks on our country, possibly trying to influence our elections, is a great concern, but we should already be well aware of that by now.

—

My fondest wish is that the United States and Russia realize that working together to solve the world's problems will yield better results than continued spending on an unnecessary arms race and cyber and social media warfare. Maybe, just maybe, we can coexist in cyberspace and, instead of beating the drum of the cyber war, find a consensus of cyber peace more useful for all of us to the future of the entire human race. I know it may sound boring, but it sure beats a three-year investigation into possible Russian cyber influence.

My greatest dream is that we will one day soon see American and Russian leaders (maybe even Trump and Putin) sitting together at the majestic Tsinandali wine estate in Georgia, and that as they enjoy a legendary Georgian feast, with Georgian songs and dance and plenty of glorious Georgian wine, they will agree publicly to end the divide in the name of the human race and embark on a journey toward peace and prosperity for everyone, regardless of nationality, race, religious beliefs, or sexual orientation. Just imagine that, and even better, just imagine being there. Can you? I certainly can, like I once imagined the fall of the USSR…

May it be so and come to pass!

Not Just a Footnote

ON THURSDAY, APRIL 18, 2019, the redacted Mueller Report was released. It seemed like the whole country spent the day reading, digesting, and talking about its almost 450 pages, collected in two volumes. It seemed as if no one was talking about anything else other than the Mueller Report on TV, radio, and the Internet, in a constant loop of commentary to an insatiable worldwide audience.

Never in my wildest dreams could I have imagined that the emails and texts I exchanged with Michael Cohen over the years would become part of what NBC News called "the most anticipated document in a generation."

Yes, I am in the report—two whole pages are devoted to my private interactions with Michael regarding the possible Trump Tower in Moscow. I am also mentioned in a footnote in the Mueller Report (part 2, page 25, footnote 112).

I am relieved to let you know that I was found to have done no wrong and was witness to no collusion with Russia. Contrary to what various media outlets predicted, the Mueller investigation had little interest and nothing of substance to report about me and my partners' attempts to build Trump Towers in Georgia and Kazakhstan.

Given all this, there is no reason I should have received any attention for appearing in the Mueller Report. To the contrary, I should have been redacted from it. Instead, the Mueller Report chose to publish my private emails and text messages and single me out in an unnecessary footnote to the report—falsely and inaccurately. Doing so led to my being maligned once again in the mainstream media and virally on the Internet, as they must have known I would be. I can't tell you how many disparaging and toxic links have been sent my way.

Once again, I found myself in the middle of a media maelstrom.

For reasons that I still struggle to understand, the Mueller Report published false, insulting, and damaging information about me, glaring inaccuracies and misrepresentations that give a false and frankly perverted account of my actions and portray me in the worst light possible.

Let me set the record straight here so that I can begin to restore my good name. If it is at all possible.

The footnote concerns Comey briefing Trump about the infamous Steele dossier with its claim of a compromising video of Trump in Moscow—i.e., the much-sought-after kompromat. The footnote goes on to say that Trump may have already known about the alleged compromising video from Michael Cohen.

"On October 30, 2016," the footnote states, "Michael Cohen received a text from Russian businessman Giorgi Rtskhiladze that said, "Stopped flow of tapes from Russia but not sure if there's anything else. Just so u know," and it cites "a 10/30/16 Text Message from Rtskhiladze to Cohen." This text exchange has already appeared in this book more than once.

I have explained its every word and intention. And although Mueller's team had the complete texts, in the footnote they chose to edit them— leaving out certain words (i.e., "some" before "tapes") and leaving out the rest of the conversation—in a manner that insinuates that I knew about the tapes and likely suppressed them.

The footnote goes on to say that "Rtskhiladze said 'tapes' referred to compromising tapes of Trump rumored to be held by persons associated with the Russian real estate conglomerate Crocus Group, which had helped host the 2013 Miss Universe Pageant in Russia."

This too is false. Although Melanie and I gossiped and joked that if there were a tape it was most likely from Trump's time in Moscow for the 2013 Miss Universe Pageant hosted by the Agalarovs and the Crocus Group, I certainly never said Crocus had or held any such tapes, or tapes of any kind. I never said that. I never knew Crocus to make such tapes and certainly did not say the rumor was that such tapes were held by Crocus.

I may have had business differences with them, but the Agalarovs are decent people and Crocus is a reputable and very successful Russian company. The founder of Crocus, Aras Agalarov, hosted me at his apartment in Moscow where his mother cooked an incredible meal for us. I'll never forget that generosity from Aras.

—

FINALLY, THIS GRATUITOUS AND derogatory footnote of impossible length concludes with, "Rtskhiladze said he was told the tapes were fake, but he did not communicate that to Cohen."

Although media outlets and social media enthusiasts have shared this assertion as mine all over the known universe, it's simply false. I never used the word "fake" and thus certainly couldn't tell Michael Cohen that these tapes, which you may recall I had never seen and did not believe existed, were fake. There's a difference between saying a tape exists but is fake and believing that it doesn't even exist.

If, as CNN claimed, Cohen shared any information from me concerning these supposed tapes with then candidate Trump, it was that, at best, the tapes were only a rumor.

But I wouldn't know because I never discussed it with Cohen ever again. The implication by Mueller's Report that I knew tapes existed and knew that they were fake and, knowing that, that I didn't tell Cohen, is inaccurate on so many different levels. It makes me out to have knowledge of something that, in fact, I didn't have; and also to be the sort of disreputable businessman who would hide the truth from his associate and the entire American public.

None of us ever imagined in October 2016 that the Trump-Russia probe would become the biggest story of the Trump presidency. At that time, we didn't even know if Trump would win the 2016 election.

I was truthful and honest with the Mueller team. I explained myself and my heritage, even made it very clear that I was not Russian. I spoke at length about my dealings with Michael Cohen, the Trump Organization, and Donald Trump, and the truth, the whole truth, behind my October 30, 2016, text message to Cohen.

This is why I am so deeply disappointed by what I found in Mueller's Report. There is almost no doubt in my mind that these were calculated falsehoods meant to insult and discredit me only to show the collusion between Russians and Trump's inner circle, like Michael Cohen.

Despite all of Prosecutor Rhee's attempts to make much of my supposed deep connections to Russia, they found no impropriety in my actions and no improper links between Donald Trump, Michael Cohen, me, and Russia.

Mr. Mueller and Mrs. Rhee, falsely identifying an innocent American citizen of Georgian heritage (or any other heritage) as Russian in the Russian Probe, while knowing this would cause irreparable damage to that person's reputation, was immoral. For you not to know the difference between Georgia and Russia is hard to believe, especially when I was very clear about this during my interview and grand jury testimony. You can prove me wrong just by releasing the transcripts.

Mr. Mueller, if you ever read this book, I have difficult questions for you concerning why my life (and that of my family) needed to be turned upside down, my business reputation damaged, and why your final report needed not just mention me but do so inaccurately and falsely—omitting words from my texts and labeling me as Russian when I am an American who was born in Georgia.

Those are answers that I am still waiting for.

However, Mueller did appear recently before the House Committee on Intelligence. And for me, it was electrifying to watch as Congressman Devin Nunes of California asked Mueller the following pointed question: "An American citizen from the Republic of Georgia who your report misidentifies as a Russian claims that your report omitted parts of a text message he had with Michael Cohen about stopping the flow of compromising tapes of Donald Trump. In the omitted portions he says he didn't know what the tapes actually showed. Was that portion of the exchange left out of the report for a reason?"

My heart stopped as I waited for Mueller's response. Here's what he said (verbatim):

"No. We got an awful lot in the report but we didn't get every intersection, or conversation, and like, so, I am not familiar with that particular episode you're talking about."

Pretty stunning, isn't it? My life gets turned upside down for two years. I need to cull and review thousands of pages of emails, texts, and other matters, prepare for and be questioned for hours by Mueller's team, and then am disparaged in a footnote in the Mueller Report, that Mueller says he is "not familiar with."

So he didn't prepare the report? He didn't read it, and ask about those matters he wasn't familiar with? Was he lying? Obfuscating? Going senile before our eyes?

And again I ask, after spending something like $45 million of taxpayer money on his staff investigation and producing his report, what was accomplished?

Any way you look at it, it is troubling and raises more questions than it answers about why I needed to be dragged into the Mueller investigation and mentioned in the Mueller Report.

—

FOR MUELLER, THIS CASE is now closed, while for me, the false accusation made in the report will stay with me and my family throughout my life. As an American citizen and frankly as a human being, I deserve answers from Mueller and his entire team, including Mrs. Rhee.

Mr. Mueller and Mrs. Rhee, I urge you to show your good faith just like I did when I fully cooperated with your investigation. I urge you to ask Attorney General William Barr to issue a retraction to the inaccurate footnote you created (and as my attorney A. Scott Bolden of Reed Smith has asked, in writing, the attorney general to do). That would be the ethical thing to do. That would be the right thing to do.

I am still waiting for their response.

Giorgi Rtskhiladze
New York, NY
August 1, 2019

Appendix A: Letter to Attorney General William Barr

ReedSmith

A. Scott Bolden
Direct Phone: +1 202 414 9266
Email: abolden@reedsmith.com

1301 K Street, N.W.
Suite 1000 - East Tower
Washington, D.C. 20005-3373
+1 202 414 9200
Fax +1 202 414 9299
reedsmith.com

April 22, 2019

By Hand Delivery

The Honorable William P. Barr
Attorney General
U.S. Department of Justice
950 Pennsylvania Avenue, NW
Washington, DC 20530-0001

In re: Giorgi Rtskhiladze/The Mueller Investigation and Report

Dear Mr. Attorney General:

This firm represents Giorgi Rtskhiladze ("Mr. Rtskhiladze") in connection with the above-referenced matter. Please direct all further communications regarding his case to the undersigned.

In this regard, I write to address certain glaring inaccuracies and misrepresentations concerning Mr. Rtskhiladze set forth in the Report on the Investigation into Russian Interference in the 2016 Presidential Election, submitted by Special Counsel Robert S. Mueller, III pursuant to 28 C.F.R. § 600.8(c) (hereinafter, "Mueller Report") on March 22, 2019. I refer specifically to the wholly misleading and salacious account of communications between Messrs. Michael Cohen and Rtskhiladze about alleged "compromising" tapes of President Donald J. Trump when he was a private citizen, described in footnote 112 on pages 27 and 28 of the Volume II of the Mueller Report (hereinafter, "Footnote 112").

On behalf of Mr. Rtskhiladze, we strongly demand that a full and immediate retraction of these falsehoods should be issued forthwith to restore his good name. In the alternative, we would strongly urge your office to include this letter and exhibits contained herein, to the Mueller file and/or any appendixes to the Mueller Report.

Accordingly, we submit the following objections to Footnote 112:

I. **Allegation**

Mr. Rtskhiladze is a "Russian businessman."

Rebuttal

Mr. Rtskhiladze was born in the former Soviet Republic of Georgia. Since 1991, Georgia as an independent country and an important U.S. ally in the region has had a strained relationship with Russia due to the latter's military invasion in 2008 and unlawful occupation of 20% of Georgian territory. The mere suggestion that Mr. Rtskhiladze is cavorting with Russian associates belittles his personal identity and integrity, tarnishes his reputation and impedes his ability to do business in his native country.

ABU DHABI • ATHENS • AUSTIN • BEIJING • CENTURY CITY • CHICAGO • DUBAI • FRANKFURT • HONG KONG • HOUSTON • KAZAKHSTAN • LONDON • LOS ANGELES • MIAMI • MUNICH
NEW YORK • PARIS • PHILADELPHIA • PITTSBURGH • PRINCETON • RICHMOND • SAN FRANCISCO • SHANGHAI • SILICON VALLEY • SINGAPORE • TYSONS • WASHINGTON, D.C. • WILMINGTON

US_ACTIVE-145440257.2-ASBOLDEN 04/22/2019 2:46 PM

Moreover, Mr. Rtskhiladze has been an upstanding American citizen since 2017 and a permanent resident for 23 years. He fully cooperated with the Mueller probe—meeting with prosecutors on two separate occasions and appearing before the Special Prosecutor's grand jury. He dedicated considerable time and financial resources ensuring that his testimony was complete and truthful. Casting him as a "Russian businessman" implies that he participated in a conspiracy to collude or interfere with the 2016 U.S. presidential elections—which is patently false. The transcript of grand jury testimony will clearly show that my client made it abundantly clear and went to great lengths to clearly explain his Georgina and American allegiances when the prosecuting attorney attempted to paint him as "Russian businessman". The fact that after Mr. Rtskhiladze's extensive clarifying testimony the Special Counsel nevertheless decided to describe my client as same in the final Report released to the public is just incredulous.

II. <u>**Allegation**</u>

"On October 30, 2016, Michael Cohen received a text from Russian businessman Giorgi Rtskhiladze that said, 'Stopped flow of tapes from Russia but not sure if there's anything else. Just so you know....'"

<u>**Rebuttal**</u>

Mr. Rtskhiladze is a successful businessman who takes pride in his heritage by supporting the economic stability and prosperity of his native country of Georgia and invests a great deal of time and resources in strengthening the US - Georgian relationships. It is in this context that he met Mr. Cohen in 2011, when the Trump Organization expressed interest in building a residential Trump Towers in Batumi, Georgia. This relationship continued in 2015, when the failed Trump Towers Moscow development was first proposed.

After negotiating these transactions, Messrs. Cohen and Rtskhiladze developed a rapport. The excerpts of texts cited in Footnote 112 do not convey the banter between friendly business colleagues. In stark black and white, the isolated texts are suggestive of nefarious undertakings and, as such, defame Mr. Rtskhiladze's character. Viewing the texts in their entirety against the backdrop of Messrs. Cohen and Rtskhiladze's close relationship places them in their proper context.

Also, "Stopping the flow" gives the impression that you are referencing the alleged salacious content of the alleged acts viewed on the tape. To the contrary, this was colloquialism by Mr. Rtskhiladze indicating that there was nothing to the rumors of the tape, and that he did not believe there were any tapes, not had he seen what was on the tapes, even if they existed. Although this may have been a poor choice of words, he was trying to convey the same to Mr. Cohen.

Furthermore, the word "some" has been intentionally removed from the Footnote; the original text message reads "some tapes" and the word "some" is crucial as it establishes the fact that Mr. Rtskhiladze had no knowledge of the tapes' content. The footnote also omits the dialogue that follows, which is key to understanding Mr. Rtskhiladze's intentions. See Attachment 1.

Rtskhiladze: Stopped flow of **some** tapes from Russia but not sure if there's anything else. Just so u know.

Cohen: Tapes of what?

Rtskhiladze: Not sure of the content but person in Moscow was bragging [that he] had tapes from Russia trip. Will try to dial you tomorrow but wanted to be aware. I'm sure it's not a big deal but there are lots of stupid people.

Cohen: You have no idea.

Rtskhiladze: I do trust me.[1]

Both the Federal Bureau of Investigations and attorneys that authored the Mueller Report are in possession of the entire series of texts between Messrs. Cohen and Rtskhiladze, but they spliced the dialogue to produce the ugly insinuations and allegations of Footnote 112 to attract publicity—all the while impugning Mr. Rtskhiladze's character. They are also aware of what "Stop the flow…" meant coming from my client to Mr. Cohen, but have failed to explain this in the subject Report. This must be corrected immediately before any further reprehensible damage to my client's character and reputation can occur.

III.   Allegation

"Rtskhiladze said 'tapes' referred to compromising tapes of Trump rumored to be held by persons associated with the Russian real estate conglomerate Crocus Group, which had helped host the 2013 Miss Universe Pageant in Russia."

Rebuttal

The texts that were excised from the Mueller Report clearly indicate that Mr. Rtskhiladze does not have direct knowledge of what was said at the party in Moscow, which he did not attend. Mr. Rtskhiladze also does not know and cannot identify who allegedly made the statements about the tape. Furthermore, Mr. Rtskhiladze has never seen the tape and cannot opine on whether it actually exists. All of the above was communicated to Muller investigative team on multiple accessions by Mr. Rtskhiladze.

In a similar vein, Mr. Rtskhiladze has not had contact or dealings with the Crocus Group in 15 years, although he considers Crocus a reputable and successful business group. It is inaccurately stated that Mr. Rtskhiladze never had a licensing deal with the Crocus Group.

---

[1] *See* attached Exhibit A.

IV. Allegation

"Rtskhiladze said he was told the tapes were fake, but he did not communicate that to Cohen."

Rebuttal

The suggestion that Mr. Rtskhiladze tried to curry favor with Mr. Cohen, the Trump Organization and possibly President Trump himself by allegedly texting that he had "stopped the flow of tapes from Russia"—knowing all the while that the tapes did not exist—is an outrageous and sensational distortion of the communications between Messrs. Cohen and Rtskhiladze.

Footnote 112 of the Mueller Report would have the world believe that Mr. Rtskhiladze is at best a caricature of an idle gossip or, worse, an opportunist with deep ties to the Russian business community[2] and privy to untoward conduct by President Trump that Mr. Rtskhiladze and others intended to use to embarrass then Candidate Trump, derail his campaign and/or manipulate him after assuming the elected office. There is not a scintilla of evidence to support these inferences and to suggest otherwise is defamatory.

Despite having committed no wrongdoing, Mr. Rtskhiladze has been forced to defend himself against whispers and innuendo smearing him as a traitor and a liar on the global stage. Indeed, since the Mueller Report has been published, these false claims and interpretations have spread on social media inspiring further attacks on Mr. Rtskhiladze and his family. If one were to calculate each falsehood and each attack based on clicks and comments, his damages would be in the millions.

To be sure, Mr. Rtskhiladze, his family and his associates have suffered irreparable harm to their personal and professional reputations. They may never be exonerated in the court of public opinion, and the current inflammatory mischaracterizations in Footnote 112, if they remain part of the Mueller Report, will seal their fate. Mr. Rtskhiladze is entitled to have his good name cleared. In addition, the integrity of the Mueller Report itself mandates that these important changes be made and published by your Office.

Lastly, it is unfathomable how you personally, as Attorney General who specifically stated ahead of time that one of the main reasons for redacting certain information in the Mueller Report as follows could ever have allowed my client's name to have appeared in the Report released to the public in the first place. It would seem that this stated reasoning was designed to protect this exact situation from occurring, and by not redacting my client's name, you erred in a most egregious manner:

"4. Material that the Justice Department believes would unfairly infringe on the privacy and damage the reputations of "peripheral third parties.""

---

[2] *See* Mueller Rep., Vol. 1 at 70 & nn. 311, 315 & 317.

We close by again demanding a full and immediate retraction of these gross misstatements and that you include this letter and exhibits contained herein, to the file and/or any appendices to the Mueller Report.

Thank you in advance for your anticipated cooperation in this matter,

Sincerely, I am,

A. Scott Bolden
Reed Smith LLP

Appendix B: Letter from House Committee on Intelligence

ADAM B. SCHIFF, CALIFORNIA
Chairman
—————
Timothy Bergreen, Staff Director
(202) 225-7690
www.intelligence.house.gov

ONE HUNDRED SIXTEENTH CONGRESS

DEVIN NUNES, CALIFORNIA
Ranking Member
—————
Scott Glabe, Minority Staff Director

Permanent Select Committee
on Intelligence
U.S. House of Representatives

March 19, 2019

VIA U.S. AND ELECTRONIC MAIL

Giorgi Rtskhiladze
c/o The Toroil Group
Green Wind Energy Group
555 Madison Avenue, 5th Floor
New York, NY 10012
Email: giorgirt@icloud.com

Dear Mr. Rtskhiladze:

As part of its investigation of foreign influence in the U.S. political process during and since the 2016 U.S. election, the House Permanent Select Committee on Intelligence ("Committee") respectfully requests that you preserve and produce certain documents and material relevant to the Committee's investigation announced on February 6, 2019 (attached hereto), and participate in a voluntary, transcribed interview before the Committee.

We appreciate your cooperation with the Committee and ask that you provide the requested materials no later than **Friday, March 29, 2019**.

Please contact Shannon Green with the Committee's Majority Staff at 202-225-7690 if you have any questions regarding your document production as well as potential dates for testimony before the Committee.

Thank you for your prompt attention to this matter.

Sincerely,

Adam B. Schiff
Chairman

Committee Record February 6, 2019

Chairman Schiff Statement on House Intelligence Committee Investigation

WASHINGTON, DC—TODAY, REP. ADAM Schiff (D-CA), the Chairman of the House Permanent Select Committee on Intelligence, released the following statement following the Committee's organizational meeting:

"Consistent with its jurisdiction, investigative responsibilities, and building on substantial work undertaken during the last Congress, the House Permanent Select Committee on Intelligence ("Committee") will conduct a rigorous investigation into efforts by Russia and other foreign entities to influence the US political process during and since the 2016 US election. In addition, the Committee will investigate the counterintelligence threat arising from any links or

coordination between US persons and the Russian government and/or other foreign entities,

including any financial or other leverage such foreign actors may possess.

"In the more than two years since the Intelligence Community released its assessment of Russia's malign influence operation targeting the 2016 US elections, much has been learned about the scope and scale of Russia's attack on our democracy, including how covert and overt

Russian activities intersected with individuals associated with Donald Trump's presidential campaign, transition, administration, and business interests, including the Trump Organization. It is now known that, from late 2015 through early 2017, individuals close to Donald Trump engaged in a significant number of contacts with an array of individuals connected to, or working on behalf of, the Russian government, and that several of these contacts involved efforts to acquire and disseminate damaging information about Hillary Clinton and her campaign, or related to Russia's desired relief from US sanctions.

"While Special Counsel Robert Mueller continues his investigation into whether there were 'any links and/or coordination between the Russian government and individuals associated with the [Trump] campaign,' and whether any crimes were committed in connection with, or arising from, that investigation, the Committee must fulfill its responsibility to provide the American people with a comprehensive accounting of what happened, and what the United States must do to protect itself from future interference and malign influence operations.

"During the prior Congress, the Committee began to pursue credible reports of money laundering and financial compromise related to the business interests of President Trump, his family, and his associates. The President's actions and posture towards Russia during the campaign, transition, and administration have only heightened fears of foreign financial or other leverage over President Trump and underscore the need to determine whether he or those in his Administration have acted in service of foreign interests since taking office.

"Unfortunately, these and numerous other avenues of inquiry were not completed during the last Congress. Now, in the 116th Congress, the Committee's investigation will focus principally on five interconnected lines of inquiry, beginning with these incomplete or unexamined investigative threads:

(1) The scope and scale of the Russian government's operations to influence the US.

political process, and the US government's response, during and since the 2016 election;

(2) The extent of any links and/or coordination between the Russian government, or related foreign actors, and individuals associated with Donald Trump's campaign, transition, administration, or business interests, in furtherance of the Russian government's interests;

(3) Whether any foreign actor has sought to compromise or holds leverage, financial or otherwise, over Donald Trump, his family, his business, or his associates;

(4) Whether President Trump, his family, or his associates are or were at any time at heightened risk of, or vulnerable to, foreign exploitation, inducement, manipulation, pressure, or coercion, or have sought to influence US government policy in service of foreign interests; and

(5) Whether any actors—foreign or domestic—sought or are seeking to impede, obstruct, and/or mislead authorized investigations into these matters, including those in the Congress.

"The Committee may pursue additional lines of inquiry regarding matters that arise from the investigation, and it intends to cooperate with other congressional committees, as needed, on

matters of overlapping interest. The Committee also plans to develop legislation and policy reforms to ensure the US government is better positioned to counter future efforts to undermine

our political process and national security.

"As its first act, the Committee has voted to release to the Department of Justice and its components, including the Special Counsel's Office, transcripts of testimony taken before the Committee during the 115th Congress, with no restrictions on their use.

"The Committee also plans to release to the public all investigation transcripts, as it is committed to providing the American public with greater transparency and insight into Russia's operations and the US government's response. To protect ongoing investigative interests and information that remains classified, the Committee will release transcripts in a manner and according to a timetable that allows continued pursuit of important leads and testimony, while ensuring that the American people have faith in the process and can assess for themselves the evidence that has been uncovered, while legitimate national security interests continue to be protected.

"As Chairman of the Committee, I am committed to leading a thorough and impartial investigation that will follow the facts, and I hope that our Minority counterparts will join us in that effort. Congress has a duty to expose foreign interference, hold Russia to account, ensure that US officials including the President—are serving the national interest and, if not, are held accountable."

Addenda

A letter from my wife

THE EVENTS DESCRIBED HEREIN were difficult, but I could endure it because of the love of Ayanat, my wife. Going through these events would not have been possible without her. As difficult as this has been for me, it was more difficult because I knew Ayanat also had to live through it. My pain was inseparable from the pain of my spouse. But my love is hers; and her love is mine.

After I finished this book, I asked Ayanat to share something of her experience. At first she said, "No, it's your book, it's your story, I was just there supporting you just like any other wife would've done," but later that night she handed her personal letter to me. It took me a while to convince her, but I am grateful that she agreed to share her letter with all of you. Here's what she wrote:

—

BEFORE WE MET I always thought that the saying "You don't know what you've got till it's gone" was very powerful, but I didn't really know its true meaning.

I had led a fairy-tale existence: at thirteen, a famous film director discovered me on the streets of my hometown in Kazakhstan, Almaty, and cast me in a lead role in one of the biggest films my country ever made. That launched my career. I worked with some of Hollywood's greatest directors, costume designers, and filmmakers.

When fate brought us together in New York in 2007, I knew then that we would be together forever. I was prepared for challenges in the name of our happiness. In your eyes, I could already see our as-of-yet-unborn children—as you did in mine.

When you said that with me you'd be unstoppable, I was on board. We both gave our all to our love and marriage. Being with you surpassed every dream I ever had about meeting someone special.

We were free, in love, and bold. New York was our home and our fate. I couldn't have asked for more. But we got more than we bargained for. More, whether we wanted it or not.

Right before our marriage, your cancer reoccurred. A tumor needed to be removed and the doctors told us that after the operation we would never have children. The night before the operation you and I sat all night at our favorite New York restaurant.

That was the night I learned the meaning of "you don't know what you've got till it's gone." I had to face the possibility of losing the children we never had. But you, like me, were not going to live in a future where we didn't have children. So, that night, you and I made the decision that you would not have the operation. You would instead trust in God and find another way.

The next morning, the entire East Coat was hit by the worst winter storm in its history. The power went out in the hospital in Danbury where your operation was scheduled—you couldn't have had the operation then even if you had wanted to. We took that as a sign.

Soon after, miraculously, your tumor subsided and our first child, Sandro—our miracle boy—was born. As happy as I was, life continued to be bittersweet: as Sandro was born, I lost my father, who was still a young man, to a heart attack. A life was lost and a life gained.

Four years later, we had a baby girl, Ariadna—soon after I lost my grandfather (a life lost and a life gained once again).

You were on a roll with deal after deal, and I was launching my new fashion line. We were happy again! But, once again, fate intervened.

On that April evening when the FBI agents knocked on the door of our house and walked into our lives, I knew why they were there: I was there with you when you first met Michael Cohen at Trump Tower in 2010. I was there with you when you shook hands with Mr. Trump. And when Michael Cohen was raided, I knew it was just a matter of time before they came for you.

Once again, all our joy and potential happiness was put on hold. Your future, personally and in terms of your business, was suddenly uncertain. Once again, that old saying about not knowing what you have until it's gone came right back into our lives.

We lost our peace of mind, and you lost your reputation, business, and a great deal of money.

However, despite all that, one thing that never was lost throughout this ordeal, one thing that remained powerful, honest, pure, and constant is our great love.

Our love is the bedrock of everything we have and no one, and I mean no one, and no problems—including the Russia Probe—can undermine that. I love you the way you are, and the way we are, and no matter what, we remain truly and madly in love with each other and with our miracle children.

—

I am a lucky man.

Chronology of Important Dates

1918–1921	Georgian Independence
1922	Georgia becomes part of the Soviet Republic (USSR)
1922	Georgian-born Josef Stalin becomes General Secretary of the Communist Part of the Soviet Union
1932, 33, & 34	Gulo Rtskhiladze (my grandfather) becomes Gymnastics Champion of the USSR
1937	My grandfather Gulo leads Soviet team at European Champions
1938	Georgian-born Lavrentiy Beria becomes head of NKVD (the then name of the KGB)
1961	My parents, Vasili and Giuli, marry
1967	I'm born, named Giorgi after my grandfather
1984	I trained at the Gessin Music Academy in Moscow
1987	I am drafted into Military Service and serve in the Red Army in the Internal Security Forces
1989	Berlin Wall falls. Soviet republics begin to agitate for independence

1989	The Tbilisi Tragedy
1991	I leave Georgia, arrive in New York
1991	Georgia gains independence. First president.
1992	Attempted coup in Georgia, second president
1993	Michael Danieli dies; I receive my cancer diagnosis
2001	I open office in Tribeca on August 11, a month before 9/11
2004	Mikhail Saakashvili becomes president.
2009	Trip to Georgia with Ivana Trump
2010	Trip with Michael Cohen to Georgia
2011	Press conference at Trump Tower with Donald Trump
2011	Trip with Michael Cohen to Kazakhstan
2012	Trump travels to Georgia, holds press conference in Batumi
2015	Trump announces candidacy for president
2015	Michael Cohen pursues Moscow Tower deal
2016	Trump wins election as forty-fifth president
2016	Trump cancels Batumi Tower deal
2016	I text Michael Cohen rumor about tapes
2017	Michael Cohen's offices raided by FBI
2018	I appear before Mueller grand jury
2019	Mueller Report is released
2019	I testify before House and Senate Committees
2019	Mueller testifies before House and Senate Committees

Acknowledgments

THERE ARE MANY PEOPLE to thank for my writing this book. I could not have written this without the support of my amazing wife and the love of my life, Ayanat, and without the love of my children, Sandro and Ariadna. My father, Dato, my sister, Lilly, and my niece, Natasha. While I am crazy about my children, they sometimes make it impossible for me and my wife to work, so I can't thank my mother-in-law enough, Aliya Ksenbai, who left behind everything in Kazakhstan, including her successful banking career, to help us raise our children. I must thank my friend and publisher Tyson Cornell of Rare Bird Books, as well as my other friends at Rare Bird including Guy Intoci and Julia Callahan, who make the impossible possible. Tom Teicholz, who introduced me to Tyson and Rare Bird, provided expert guidance at each step. Melanie Bonvicino has steered me through the dark waters of publicity for more than twenty years, for which I am eternally grateful. My friends in New York, like Camilla Olsson, who seems to be connecting the whole world; in Connecticut, like Michale Daniele and Michael Chen; and in Los Angeles, like my close friend and advisor, Fred Goldring, who has been there for me for over twenty years and shared both my pain and happiness. Also my friend Yerkin Tatishev, a visionary I want to thank with all my heart for introducing me to my wife, helping me create the biggest and dearest thing to me in my life, my incredible family. These friends and others continue to show me the best of America, especially my good friend and in many ways mentor, an iconic American General, Wesley Clark, who I always thought could lead this country of ours to even bigger greatness. My homeland of Georgia, its current Prime Minister Mamuka Bakhtadze, a young leader who can change the political landscape in the region for better, and my friends in Tbilisi, especially the brother I never had, George Ramishvili, for his vision of Georgia and for standing strong for our native country when it matters most. They are the reason I spend every day trying to bring the United States and Georgia closer and have more people know the wonders of Georgian culture, history, food, wine, and hospitality. At the end, I want to thank President Donald J. Trump in advance for uniting our divided country even though it has not happened yet. I have no doubt that the man who against all odds and singlehandedly won the presidency of the United States of America is capable of uniting the country he is leading—if he only desires to do so.